New in this Edition

This edition has been updated to cover Flare Versions 5 and 6. We've also enhanced the book with new sections and expanded content based on your comments.

Here's a summary of what's new in this edition:

New content	In this book
WebHelp Mobile (Version 6). Create XHTML output for mobile devices.	Step 5B: Create Online Output
Link Viewer (Version 6). See what a topic or file is linked to. You can check links such as topics, TOCs, targets, snippets, skins, and variable sets.	Step 3: Develop Content
File and Project Templates (Version 6). Create and manage file and project templates using an improved process.	Step 1: Get Started
Multiple HTML File Import and Conversion (Version 6). Import multiple HTML files into your project and automatically convert them to XHTML.	Appendix B: Importing Content
DITA Import and Export (Version 5). Import DITA content and export DITA output. As of Version 6, you cannot create DITA content in Flare.	Appendix G
Text redaction (Version 5). Conceal confidential or sensitive information in printed output.	Step 3: Develop Content
Image Thumbnails (Version 5). Display images as thumbnails in online output or in the XML Editor window.	Step 3: Develop Content
Index Formatting Options and instructions for formatting a print index.	Step 4: Create Navigation Aids

New content	In this book
Styles. Concepts for using cascading stylesheets and style classes, including procedures for: • Resizing images with styles • Applying a style to selected text • Customizing styles with Flare's Stylesheet Editor in Simplified and Advanced Views • Adding a style class	Step 3: Develop Content

For a full list of features in various versions of Flare, see "What's New in This Version" in Flare's Help.

What readers are saying

"*Five Steps to MadCap Flare* is a must-have for any serious Flare user. If you're just starting out, *Five Steps* will give you the confidence and direction you need to get going. Even expert users will find useful tips and tricks in these pages. Whether used as a reference or training book, *Five Steps* has the essential information you need to make using Flare easier."

> — *Paul Pehrson, MadCap Flare Certified Instructor,*
> *DocGuy Training*

"This book provides a guided, controlled introduction that will help new authors get out of the starting blocks and quickly become productive. An excellent addition to an online developer's library."

> — *Neil Perlin, Madcap Flare Certified Instructor,*
> *Hyper/Word Services*

"This book focuses more deeply than any other resource on the importance of understanding a project as the foundation of success with Flare. Written in plain, conversational language, the book helps readers determine project needs by asking questions—plus it supports Flare's own increased emphasis on templates and how you can use them at many levels."

> — *Eddie VanArsdall, MadCap Flare Certified Instructor,*
> *VanArsdall InfoDesign, Alexandria, VA*

"The hardest part about learning Flare is figuring out where to start. It's overwhelming! This book is a wonderful guide through the maze of Flare features."

> — *Cheryl Landes, Tabby Cat Communications, Seattle WA*

"Typically, I've only focused on one type of output from Flare—help systems. Using this book, however, I would be well equipped to try other output formats since the detail given in the book leaves no room for guesswork or error. When you are under pressure of deadlines, this book is the helping hand you need!"

> — *Brian Laing, Documentation and Training Analyst,*
> *Xerox Corporation*

"The 'learn and do' approach significantly cuts the learning curve. The roadmap and project forms alone are worth the cost of the book!"

> — *Susan Huckle, Freelance Technical Writer, Irving, Texas*

"This book provides a real jump-start on the Flare learning curve, and the step-by-step tutorial for creating print output is worth the price of the entire book."

> — *Ginny Reynolds, Bridge-Tek Services*

"I wish I could have tapped into the advice on multi-level numbered lists when I began using Flare—plus the appendix on building context-sensitive help is terrific. This information would have saved me hours."

> — *Doug Eaton, Technical Publications Lead, Sensis Corporation*

"This book is exactly what I need to get jump-started using Flare!"

> — *Jeff O'Gorman, Specifications Writer, InterSpec*

"This book is incredible! It's designed for new users in a way to help them get a handle on how to use Flare and does so quickly with just enough detail. If you're new to Flare, you'll want to read this book. If you've used Flare for a long time, keep this book on your bookshelf as a quick reference."

> — *Deb McNally, Technical Communications Specialist*
> *Dover, NH*

Five Steps to

 madcap
software

FLARE

Use it to learn
—keep it for reference!

Lorraine Kupka and Joy Underhill

fiddlehead publications

a division of
NorthCoast Writers, Inc.
Fairport, New York
USA

Foreword

By Anthony Olivier, CEO of MadCap Software

We developed MadCap Flare in part because we believe that good documentation shouldn't be hard—and it all begins with content management. To that end, Flare uses a native XML architecture that enables you to reuse content and publish in online, desktop and print formats.

Five Steps to MadCap Flare is a great resource, especially if you're new to Flare and topic-based authoring. It uses a step-by-step approach to unravel the complexities—and flexibility—of the user interface so that you can determine how best to use the product in your environment.

At MadCap Software™, we liken learning Flare to "peeling back the layers of an onion." This book helps you take the first step and realize success with an initial project so that you're ready to take on more. Best of all, it describes the concepts behind the procedures and many of the interdependencies that are not always obvious to new users.

Acknowledgements

Assistance with DITA import and export: Brian Laing, Creative and Technical Communications, Xerox Corporation.

Indexing assistance: Cheryl Landes, Tabby Cat Communications, (www.tabbycatco.com)

Cover design and business graphics: Cindy Harris, Harris Studios, Inc. (www.HarrisStudios.com).

We are especially grateful to our families for their encouragement and patience as we spent many evenings and weekends writing this book or getting caught up on other work projects that couldn't slide.

Contents

Step 2: Learn the XML Editor.. 71

Step 3: Develop Content 97

Step 4: Create Navigation Aids 159

Introduction

In this chapter ...
- ➤ Why we wrote this book
- ➤ Who this book is for
- ➤ What this book discusses
- ➤ What this book does not discuss
- ➤ How this book is organized
- ➤ A step-by-step approach
- ➤ A strategy for learning Flare
- ➤ Got feedback?

WHY WE WROTE THIS BOOK

We wrote this book because we needed it when we were learning Flare!

We have found Flare to be a progressive and powerful authoring tool, but one with a steep learning curve. Although the Flare Help system is extensive, we wanted a book that would tell us how to get started so that we would be comfortable exploring more on our own.

But when we looked in bookstores, there was no such book. So we wrote one!

WHO THIS BOOK IS FOR

This book is intended for new and experienced Flare users. If you've never used Flare, this book will get you through the basics. If you're an experienced Flare user, this book will help expand your knowledge of Flare and refresh your memory when needed. Our best practices are helpful for both new and seasoned users.

Our hope is that by stepping through this book, you'll be able to successfully plan for and create a Flare project. It won't have all the bells and whistles that you can create with Flare, but it will produce clean online, print, or DITA output.

Once you've mastered the Flare user interface—and have a good idea of how to build a project using Flare—you'll be able to learn more as you use Flare to create more complex projects.

Flare is like an onion. You learn it by peeling back layers one a time as you gain experience. Our goal is to help you peel back that first layer—without any tears!

WHAT THIS BOOK DISCUSSES

Five Steps to MadCap Flare describes how to get started using Flare. You will learn how to:

- Plan for a Flare project

- Create projects and topics

- Develop content

- Format content with styles

- Use features for navigating in output (Table of Contents, links, cross-references, indexes)

- Create context-sensitive help

- Use Flare features for reusing content (condition tags, snippets, variables)

- Create targets for online, print, and DITA output

- Build and distribute your output

This book also provides details about many useful features, such as importing content and troubleshooting your project.

WHAT THIS BOOK DOES NOT DISCUSS

This book does not contain comprehensive information about Flare. The extensive documentation provided by the Flare Help system provides a wealth of information, and we encourage you to use it frequently. (Throughout this book, we tell you where to find specific topics in Flare's Help.)

Our intent is to give you enough information to familiarize you with Flare concepts and procedures, become comfortable using the user interface, and create a basic project.

HOW THIS BOOK IS ORGANIZED

This book contains the following chapters:

- **Document Basics** — Provides an overview of topic-based authoring and the types of documents Flare can be used to create.

- **A Quick Tour** — Explains the primary components of the Flare user interface.

- **Step 1: Get Started** — Details how to plan a Flare project and complete the plan using a task roadmap. This chapter also explains common tasks you'll do for Flare projects.

- **Step 2: Learn the XML Editor** — Provides a step-by-step tutorial for using common features of the XML Editor and includes supplemental information.

- **Step 3: Develop Content** — Outlines how to create lists and tables, insert images, symbols, and special characters into your content—plus how to use image thumbnails, mark text for redaction, create and change styles, and format your content with and without styles.

- **Step 4: Create Navigation Aids** — Describes how to include features, such as links, Tables of Contents, indexes, and cross-references, that let users navigate in output.

- **Step 5A: Create Print Output** — Details how to create simple print output and provides a tutorial for creating more complex print output. This chapter also describes how to build and distribute print output and use page layouts.

- **Step 5B: Create Online Output** — Describes how to create and distribute online output (Help systems and knowledge bases).

- **Appendix A: Planning Worksheets** — Provides worksheets for planning your project and tracking multiple targets.

- **Appendix B: Import Content** — Explains how to import content from Microsoft® Office Word, Adobe® FrameMaker®, and HTML files.

- **Appendix C: XML Editor Reference** — Provides supplemental reference information about the XML Editor.

- **Appendix D: Context-Sensitive Help** — Describes how to create context-sensitive help.

- **Appendix E: Troubleshoot** — Details how to troubleshoot your project and use the internal analyzer provided with Flare.

- **Appendix F: Single-Sourcing** — Explains Flare's features for reusing content from a single source, including how to use condition tags to create customized output, and how to create and insert snippets and variables.

- **Appendix G: DITA Import and Export** — Explains how to import DITA content into Flare and export DITA code from Flare.

- **Appendix H: The Next Step** — Lists some of the Flare features you might explore on your own after completing your first project.

This book also contains an index.

A STEP-BY-STEP APPROACH

This book is organized sequentially, meaning you should start at the beginning and proceed forward. Once you are more familiar with Flare, you can use the Table of Contents and index to jog your memory about certain features.

How you will use this book depends on your experience. We recommend that:

- **If you haven't used a topic-based authoring tool**, read the Document Basics chapter first, followed by the Quick Tour and each of the five steps.

- **If you're familiar with topic-based authoring tools**, scan the Document Basics chapter to learn basic Flare terminology. Then begin with the Quick Tour, followed by each of the five steps.

> **Note** — Depending on whether you're creating online, print or DITA output, you will use Step 5A: Create Print Output, Step 5B: Create Online Output, *or* Appendix G: DITA Import and Export. However, if you want to produce *all* types of output from a single project, you will use all of these steps.

A STRATEGY FOR LEARNING FLARE

For your first Flare project, consider creating a small "throwaway" project. You can make mistakes without worrying how it will affect your real work.

Use this project to develop the styles you'll use later. If your throwaway project is bloated with local formatting, it won't hurt anything. By the time you're ready to work on a real project, you'll be more comfortable using styles and your XML code will be much cleaner.

FIRST, LEARN THE BASIC FLARE WORKFLOW

- Create a new project and add 5 or 6 topics.

- Copy and paste text into each topic so you have some content to work with. You can use content from a Word document, a FrameMaker document, or even a text file.

- Create two lists and insert a table.

- Create a TOC. Drag a few topics from the Content Explorer into the TOC to add them. Then add one or two topics to your project and TOC simultaneously.

- Set up WebHelp and PDF targets (without any page layouts).

- Build and view output.

- Save your project.

NEXT, EXPAND YOUR KNOWLEDGE

- Learn to use the XML Editor. Enter and change text in a topic or two.

- Check spelling. Create a spelling error in a topic and learn to spell-check a topic and your entire project.

- Insert an image.

- Create a few text hyperlinks that are linked to other topics in your project.

- Create a few index entries.

- Apply a condition tag. Mark some text with the default condition tag "PrintOnly" and set up the WebHelp target to exclude the PrintOnly condition tag. Then build and view the output to see that the marked text is excluded.

- Add your own condition tag and apply it to text.

- Insert a variable. Use one of the default variables (CompanyName or PhoneNumber).

- Add your own variable and insert it into a topic.

- Build and view WebHelp output. Click an index entry after clicking the Index bar, and click a hyperlink or two. Make sure the index entry and hyperlinks open the correct topics.

THEN TRY FORMATTING

- Learn to use local formatting. It's not bad to use local formatting in a few isolated places; but as a best practice, we suggest you use styles instead.

> **Note** — To see what local formatting does to your XML code, open a topic in Flare's text editor and click in the XML Editor's top toolbar. Switch to the XML Editor by clicking . Then apply some local paragraph formatting and save the topic. Look again at the topic's XML code to see the extra code that local formatting adds.

- Learn to use styles. Apply styles from the default stylesheet (Styles.css).

- Change styles. Use the Stylesheet Editor in Simplified View to change the formatting applied to the "p" and "h1" styles.

- Add your own styles. Add a class of the "p" style and change its formatting. Apply the class you created to text in a topic.

FINALLY, USE MORE ADVANCED FEATURES

What you do next depends on what you want to create.

To ...	Do this ...
Create context-sensitive Help	Read Appendix D.
Create print output	Learn about cross-references (Step 4). Complete the tutorial in Step 5A.
Import Word, FrameMaker, or HTML files	Read Appendix B.
Import or export DITA content	Read Appendix G.

GOT FEEDBACK?

We love to hear from our readers!

Your comments and suggestions are welcome. Please contact us at:

info@NorthCoastWriters.com

Document Basics

In this chapter ...
➤ About topic-based authoring
➤ Terms to understand
➤ About print documents
➤ About online documents
➤ About DITA documents

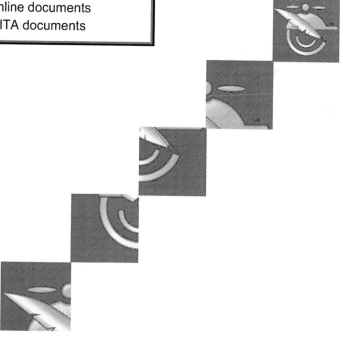

OVERVIEW

This chapter provides an overview of topic-based authoring and how Flare is used to create documents that are topic-based. It also describes terminology and capabilities that will familiarize you with some of the language and concepts used in the remainder of this book.

WHAT IS TOPIC-BASED AUTHORING?

According to a recent Wikipedia post, topic-based authoring is:

... a modular content creation approach (popular in the technical publications and documentation arenas) that supports XML content reuse, content management, and makes the dynamic assembly of personalized information possible.

Let's clarify that.

- **Modular content creation** — As simple as it sounds, the heart of topic-based authoring is creating topics. Modular simply means that content exists in units—called topics.

- **XML content reuse, content management** — Topics are discrete units of information, which makes them easy to reuse and maintain.

- **Dynamic assembly of personalized information** — Because topics are discrete units of information, they can be combined in various ways for customized results.

HOW TRADITIONAL AND TOPIC-BASED DOCUMENTS DIFFER

When you write a *traditional*, print-based document, you organize information—**content**—in a linear fashion, usually to be read front to back. With larger documents, you use various **navigational aids** to help readers find information quickly, such as a Table of Contents, index, and cross-references.

When you write a *topic-based* document, rather than concern yourself with the order of content, you typically develop content—divided into several **topics**—in a way that you can easily rearrange to produce output tailored to different needs.

With *online topic-based* documents, readers point-and-click to obtain information when they need it instead of reading in a linear fashion. With *print topic-based* documents, readers might still choose to read in a linear fashion, but more likely, they'll read only the topics of interest and they'll find those topics by using navigational tools, such as a Table of Contents, index, and cross-references.

WHAT FLARE DOES FOR YOU

Here's a brief sampling of what Flare lets you decide:

- Which topics to include in a document

- How topics will be assembled and organized

- The navigational tools used to help readers find the topics they need

- How content will be reused in the print and online worlds

- What content will be included in various topics (Flare lets you exclude content from a topic as well as exclude topics from output.)

The important thing to take away is that when you create documents with Flare, they will be topic-based, not linear. With Flare projects, you'll be able to reuse content and maintain it much more easily.

TERMS TO UNDERSTAND

Topic-based authoring and Flare itself both have unique terminology that you'll see throughout this book. Take a moment to review this list so you won't be caught off-guard when you see these terms.

- **Output** — What is created after you build a Flare target. This will be a print document (e.g., Word, FrameMaker, PDF file), an online document (Help system or knowledge base), or DITA code. Output consists of one or more files and folders, depending on the type of output you build.

> **Note** — Although a PDF file is delivered online, it is considered a print document.

- **Target** — A Flare file you create that defines settings used to build output. When you build your output, you select the target to build it from. Typically, a project has many targets. For example, you might have two WebHelp targets for two different levels of software, such as a regular and light. One target is designated as "primary." (For more information, see "Primary targets" on page 256.)

> **Best Practice** — Create one target for each different deliverable output.

- **Build** — The process of creating output for the selected target using Flare project files.

- **Distribute** — Giving Flare output to others. The output type determines the files you need to send. You might distribute Flare output to colleagues, users, software developers, or your IT staff for further usage.

- **Publish** — Copying online output to a location such as a website, a network, or a hard drive. Publishing does not create the output; it simply transfers it. However, for new users, we discourage this practice until you're more familiar with Flare.

BUILD, GENERATE, COMPILE: WHAT'S THE DIFFERENCE?

You're likely to see several terms that mean the same thing when you use the Flare Help system. We've tried to remain consistent in this book. This formula might help:

Generate = Compile = **Build** (our term)

Just remember: **build** is the process of creating your **output**, based on the **target** you select.

ABOUT PRINT DOCUMENTS

You can create these types of print documents with Flare:

- Microsoft Word

- Adobe FrameMaker

- Adobe PDF

- Microsoft XPS

- XHTML

Step 5A: Create Print Output, describes in detail these types of print documents and what you need to do to create them. Step 5A also contains instructions for creating a simple print document and a tutorial for creating a more complex print document that includes a Table of Contents and alternating headers and footers.

ABOUT ONLINE DOCUMENTS

Online documents typically refer to Help systems and knowledge bases. You can create both types of online documents with Flare.

For detailed information about creating online documents after you have finished developing your content, see Step 5B: Create Online Output.

HELP SYSTEMS

A Help system is a method of delivering topic-based information to users from within a software application. When a user clicks the application's Help menu, the Help system opens.

A Help system includes a Table of Contents, an index, and the ability to search for words in help topics. Help systems created with Flare can also allow users to rate the usefulness of help topics.

Context-sensitive help

A context-sensitive help system is one in which topic-based information is accessed from buttons placed on dialogs and windows in a software application. In such systems, a software developer places a button on a window or dialog for which a writer has written a help topic. When a user clicks the button, it opens a help topic that provides information about the window or dialog.

Flare includes context-sensitive help on some of its dialogs as shown next.

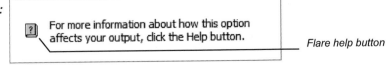

For more information about how this option affects your output, click the Help button.

Flare help button

KNOWLEDGE BASES

Knowledge bases are collections of information, often used to share knowledge in an organization or to supplement a Help system. The contents of a knowledge base are documents, such as frequently asked questions, user documentation, and articles.

The primary differences between a knowledge base and a Help system are:

- A knowledge base is not opened from within a software application.

- A knowledge base cannot contain context-sensitive help topics.

Knowledge bases are stored online and are searchable much like Help systems. Users may also browse through topics to find what they need.

ONLINE DOCUMENT FORMATS

Flare can create online documents in any of the following formats:

- DotNet Help

- Microsoft HTML Help

- WebHelp

- WebHelp Plus

- WebHelp AIR

- WebHelp Mobile

Each of these formats is described in Table 5B-1 on page 249.

Choosing the right format

Your work environment may only support certain online document formats. It's a good idea to contact technical personnel in your organization to understand which format they expect you to create.

The following table briefly outlines when to choose each online document format. The Flare Help system contains additional information about these formats.

Table DB-1: Choosing online document formats

Choose this format ...	When ...
DotNet Help	▪ You need to support Microsoft .NET® applications. ▪ Your HTML Help is inadequate for various reasons. ▪ You want users to be able to choose to view the output in English, French, German or Japanese (via MadCap Help Viewer). ▪ You want users to be able to search by using wildcards.
HTML Help	▪ You need to support 32-bit Microsoft Windows® applications. ▪ Users will be using Internet Explorer®. (Users must use Internet Explorer Version 4.0 or later running on Windows 95 or later.) ▪ Users are not connected to a network. ▪ You want a single file for your output.
WebHelp	▪ You need to distribute output to the Internet or an Intranet. ▪ You want to create output in various languages (by using language skins). ▪ You want to include online documentation in a desktop application. ▪ Users are using different Internet browsers or platforms.

Table DB-1: (Cont.)	Choose this format ...	When ...

	WebHelp Plus	▪ You need to support Windows XP or Windows Server® 2003.
		▪ You want all of the WebHelp features plus:
		  - Quicker user searches
		  - The ability to perform searches for non-XHTML files, such as PDFs or Excel files, that may or may not be part of your project
		  - The ability to merge Flare output so it appears as a single Help system

	WebHelp AIR	▪ You want all of the WebHelp features plus:
		  - You want a single file for your output.
		  - Your users will store and open your output locally (not from a server or website).
		To create online documents in WebHelp AIR:
		▪ You and users must install Abobe® AIR™ (go to http://get.adobe.com/air/ for a free download).
		▪ You must install Java Runtime Environment (go to http://java.sun.com/javase/downloads/index.jsp for a free download).

	WebHelp Mobile	▪ Your users need to access web-based XHTML documentation from various mobile platforms such as iPhone, Windows Mobile, and Blackberry. ▪ You want to create an output interface in various languages.

HOW ONLINE OUTPUT LOOKS (SKINS)

The appearance of online output is controlled by a **skin**. A skin is a file that stores settings that determine how your online output looks (size, position), including its features (Table of Contents, index, glossary, search) and buttons.

Flare comes packaged with a default skin, which is automatically added to each new project you create. The default skin is located in the Skins folder of the Project Organizer.

> **Note** — Flare includes three WebHelp Mobile skins. You'll need to add a mobile skin to your project to build WebHelp Mobile output.

Figure DB-2:
Skins folder
of the
Project
Organizer

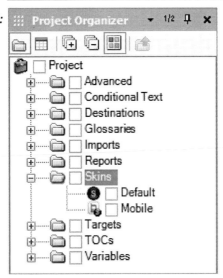

A Flare project can have multiple skins. For example, you might have different skins for different types of online output.

You can change the appearance of online output by editing the skin. See "Adding and editing skin" on page 255.

ABOUT DITA DOCUMENTS

Flare Version 5 introduced the ability to import DITA documents and to export DITA from a Flare project. DITA output is code output—XML tags encode text and external file links. You can create print or online output from your DITA output by using any application that can publish DITA content.

WHAT IS DITA?

DITA—Darwin Information Typing Architecture—is an XML-based technical documentation standard developed by the Organization for the Advancement of Structured Information Standards (OASIS) to support content sharing and reuse by using standard types of topics (such as concept, task, and reference topics).

DITA documents include multiple files (one per topic) and a DITAMAP file (like a table of contents) that contains links to topics.

For more information about the DITA standard see: http://xml.coverpages.org/dita.html.

Refer to Appendix G to learn how to import or export DITA content using Flare.

WHAT'S NEXT?

Before you tackle your first Flare project, take a look at the next chapter, "A Quick Tour." It will help you become more familiar with the Flare user interface before you begin using the product.

Then proceed to Step 1: Get Started, where you'll start planning and creating your first Flare project.

A Quick Tour

In this chapter …
- ➤ About the Flare workspace
- ➤ Left pane
- ➤ Middle pane
- ➤ Right pane
- ➤ Toolbars
- ➤ Status bar

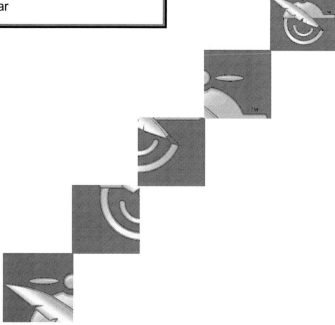

OVERVIEW

Flare is a powerful tool for developing topic-based documents. However, its flexible user interface can be a challenge for new users.

This chapter describes the basic elements of the Flare user interface. Our examples, (shown in Windows Vista®), will give you an idea of what to expect when you start using Flare for yourself. When you become more comfortable using Flare, you'll probably want to adjust the user interface as you prefer.

THE FLARE WORKSPACE

When you first open Flare, you'll see a Getting Started Wizard as shown in Figure QT-1. After you use or close the wizard, you'll see the Flare **workspace** as shown in Figure QT-2. Notice that the Flare workspace contains a left, middle, and right pane, each of which is discussed next.

ABOUT ACTIVE PANES AND WINDOWS

In the Flare workspace, toolbars and menu options will change, depending on which part of the workspace is **active**. This concept applies to tabs in the middle pane as well.

To make a pane or tab active, simply click in the desired part of the workspace. Unavailable options are dimmed.

Figure QT-1:
*Getting
Started
Wizard*

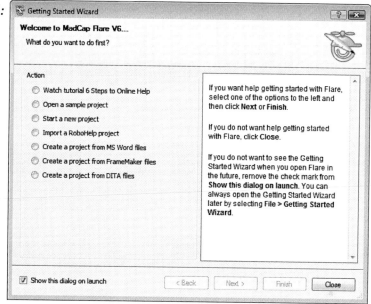

Figure QT-2:
*Flare
workspace*

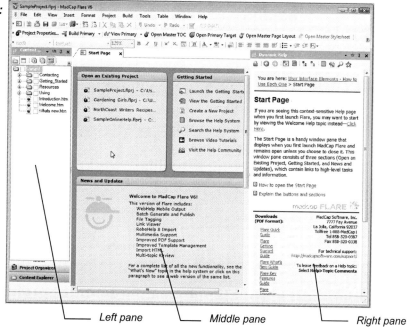

Left pane   Middle pane   Right pane

LEFT PANE

The left pane of the Flare workspace helps you organize and move among the parts of your Flare project.

ACCORDION BARS

In the left pane, you'll notice **accordion bars** as shown in Figure QT-3. (Accordion bars apply to the right pane also.)

Accordion bars indicate which window is active in the pane. You can easily switch from one window to another by clicking its accordion bar, which brings the window to the front and makes it active.

Figure QT-3:
Left pane

Accordion bars

When you begin using Flare, the **Project Organizer** and **Content Explorer** open in the left pane, both of which you'll use often.

> **Note** — If there isn't enough room to show accordion bars for all of the open windows, you'll see icons directly below the accordion bars as shown in Figure QT-4. Click an icon to open the window and make it active

Figure QT-4:
Icon for
additional
windows

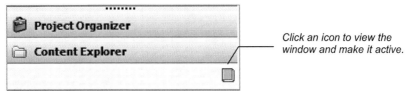

Click an icon to view the
window and make it active.

PROJECT ORGANIZER

The Project Organizer is used to view project files and open them in
the middle pane. Figure QT-5 shows how the Project Organizer
looks when fully expanded after creating some targets.

Click **Expand All** to view all files
in the Project Organizer.

Figure QT-5:
Expanded
Project
Organizer

Click this button to show or
hide the condition tag
boxes for project files.

You don't need to understand all of the folders and files in the Project Organizer right now, but you will use them frequently as you create your projects.

> **Note** — Double-clicking a file in the Project Organizer opens it in the middle pane.

CONTENT EXPLORER

You'll use the Content Explorer to open and move among topics in your Flare project. **Topics** can contain text, images, audio files, movie files, and other items.

Figure QT-6 shows how the Content Explorer looks after you create a few topics. Notice that it contains several folders in addition to topic files (HTM files) and resource files.

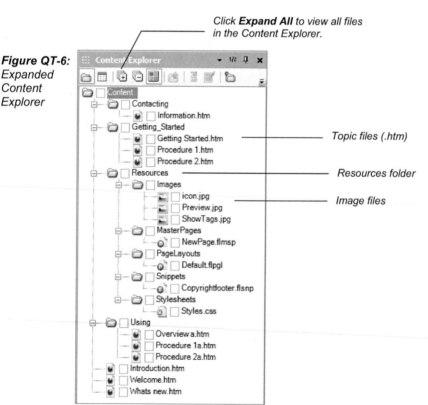

Click **Expand All** to view all files in the Content Explorer.

Figure QT-6:
Expanded
Content
Explorer

Topic files (.htm)

Resources folder

Image files

As shown in the previous figure, every new Flare project contains a **Resources** folder that holds parts of your project that are not topics, such as images, master pages and page layouts. You'll learn more about these items later.

MIDDLE PANE

When you first launch Flare, the middle pane shows the Start Page (Figure QT-2), a handy place to open a project, view news from MadCap, or submit feature requests and bug reports.

Most of the time, the middle pane shows one of Flare's numerous editors. Figure QT-7 shows the middle pane with three editors open: the XML Editor (active), the TOC Editor and the Target Editor.

In some editors, it's common to have several items of the same type open. For example, you can have several topics open at the same time, each in their own instance of the XML Editor.

> *Tip* — As you work with Flare, you're bound to lose track of what's open in the middle pane. When this happens, first save all open documents by clicking **Save All** 🖫 on the Standard toolbar, and then click **Window → Close All Documents** or **Close All Documents Except This One** (meaning the active document). You can also close a single document by clicking **x** on its tab.

Editor name ——— Active editor ——— Editor tabs show file names.

Figure QT-7:
Open editors in the middle pane

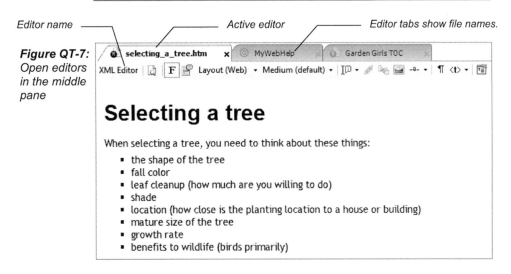

In some editors, you may also see tabs along left edge as shown in Figure QT-8. In such instances, the highlighted tab is the open one.

Figure QT-8: Tabs along the left edge of an editor

Tabs ⟋

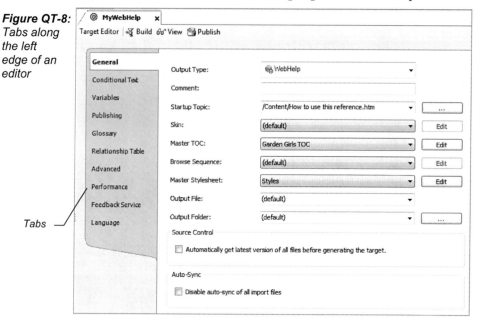

Now let's look at a few commonly used editors.

XML EDITOR

The XML Editor, shown in Figure QT-9, is used to create and edit topics. You'll use this editor to:

- Enter, edit, and format text

- Insert images, symbols, links, and cross-references

- Create and format tables and lists

Despite this editor's name, you don't need to be an XML expert in order to use it.

Figure QT-9:
XML Editor

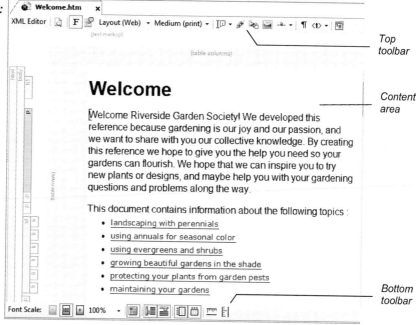

Top toolbar

Content area

Bottom toolbar

With the XML Editor, you can view content in two modes:

- **Web Layout mode** — To see how a topic would look as online output (Help systems and knowledge bases).

- **Print Layout mode** — To see how a topic would look as print output (such as Word or PDF files).

Regardless of the mode, the XML Editor has three main parts:

- **Top toolbar** — To switch viewing modes and add things such as links, cross-references and images.

- **Content area** — To enter, edit, and format content.

- **Bottom toolbar** — To magnify text and view XML Editor components, such as rulers and structure bars.

The XML Editor is more fully described in Step 2: Learn the XML Editor, and Appendix C: XML Editor Reference.

TOC EDITOR

The Table of Contents (TOC) Editor is used to create a Table of
Contents, which is used to organize and open topics.

Double-clicking a TOC in the Project Organizer opens that TOC in
the TOC Editor (Figure QT-11). You can name your TOC files as you
please.

Figure QT-10:
TOC file in
the Project
Organizer

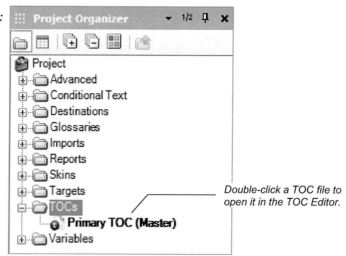

Like other editors, the TOC Editor opens in the middle pane with its
own toolbar. Figure QT-11 shows how a fully expanded TOC in the
TOC Editor looks.

You'll learn more about using the TOC Editor in Step 4: Create
Navigation Aids.

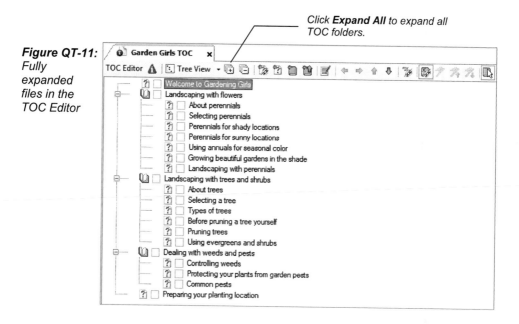

Click **Expand All** to expand all TOC folders.

Figure QT-11:
Fully expanded files in the TOC Editor

RIGHT PANE

The right pane houses a variety of windows, such as the Spell Check window and Flare's Help system. As in the left pane, each window has an accordion bar, and some also have their own toolbars.

You'll learn more about the contents of the right pane in other chapters.

TOOLBARS

As you've already learned, many editors and windows in Flare have their own toolbars, which apply only to their individual windows.

Flare also has several global toolbars that are always in view (as long as you haven't hidden them), regardless of what else is open. Let's take a quick look.

> *Tip* — Certain options on the global toolbars may be dimmed (unavailable), depending on which window is active.

STANDARD TOOLBAR

The Standard toolbar (Figure QT-12) offers many of the shortcuts
seen in other Windows applications, such as opening projects,
cutting and pasting, and saving files. It also includes Flare shortcuts,
such as **Open the Start Page** and **Source Control,** and indicates
when MadCap news is available.

Figure QT-12: Standard toolbar

PROJECT TOOLBAR

The Project toolbar (Figure QT-13) contains shortcuts for common
project tasks, such as building your output (like a Help system or
print document). You can also add topics to your project using this
toolbar.

> ***Tip*** — Drop-down arrows to the right of the Build Primary and View Primary
> buttons let you select a target other than the primary to build or view.

Figure QT-13: Project toolbar

TEXT FORMAT TOOLBAR

The Text Format toolbar (Figure QT-14) offers shortcuts for applying
styles and other formatting to text. (To conserve space, we show
some of this toolbar's buttons on a pull-down list at the far right.)

Figure QT-14: Text Format toolbar

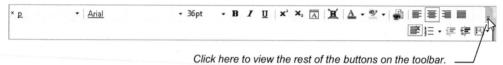

Click here to view the rest of the buttons on the toolbar.

REVIEW TOOLBAR

The Review toolbar includes shortcuts for tasks related to documentation reviews. For example, you'll find shortcuts for emailing a topic to reviewers, inserting and editing annotations (review comments), and importing a reviewed topic.

This book does not cover inserting or processing annotations or conducting documentation reviews.

STATUS BAR

The Status bar (at the bottom of the Flare workspace) shows the progress of MadCap Analyzer as it scans your project.

Flare automatically scans your project with its internal analyzer whenever you open it. (A more robust external analyzer—MadCap Analyzer™—can be purchased separately.)

This book describes how to use the internal analyzer (see Appendix E: Troubleshoot). To learn about the external analyzer, search on "About Analyzer" in the Flare Help system.

WHAT'S NEXT?

Let's get started!

Move on to Step 1: Get Started, where you'll plan your project and learn about a few common features.

Step 1:
Get Started

STEP 5: Create Output
5A: Print Output
5B: Online Output

STEP 4:
Create
Nav Aids

STEP 3:
Develop
Content

STEP 2:
Learn the
XML Editor

STEP 1:
Get Started

In this chapter ...
- ➤ Plan your Flare project
- ➤ Use our Flare roadmap
- ➤ Create a Flare project
- ➤ Opening a Flare project
- ➤ Add a topic
- ➤ Preview a topic
- ➤ Open a topic
- ➤ Check spelling
- ➤ Add a target
- ➤ Save your work
- ➤ Create and manage templates

OVERVIEW

We've found that a bit of planning is the key to satisfaction and success with Flare, including planning for maximum content reuse. If you take the time to plan out your project, the learning curve will be shorter and you'll be happier with the outcome—plus you can focus on only the Flare features you need.

To help you get started, we've created a series of planning worksheets in Appendix A: Planning Worksheets, which are intended to be used together.

In this chapter, you'll learn what you need to think about, which decisions to make up front, and where to go from here.

PLANNING YOUR FLARE PROJECT

To plan your Flare project, copy Parts 1, 2, and 3 in Appendix A: Planning Worksheets, and answer these questions.

DO YOU HAVE EXISTING SOURCE CONTENT?

If no, you'll type your content directly into Flare.

If yes, you'll also need to answer these questions using Part 1 of Appendix A:

- What form is your source content in (Word, FrameMaker, HTML, DITA, print, other)?

- Do you need to keep the source content and the Flare content in synch when the content changes? Do both need to be updated?

- Will you maintain the content by using the source application (Word, FrameMaker, etc.) or by using Flare? In other words, do you want changes to flow from content in the source application to Flare or do you want to make changes only in Flare?

WHAT KIND OF OUTPUT DO YOU WANT TO CREATE?

You can create output that will be used online or printed. You can also export DITA code (Flare Version 5 and later). Use Part 2 of Appendix A to complete this information.

Print output can be any of the following:

- Microsoft Word document

- Adobe FrameMaker document

- Adobe PDF file

- Microsoft XPS file (Flare Version 4 and later)

- XHTML (Flare Version 4 and later)

Online output can be any of the following:

- Microsoft HTML Help

- DotNet Help

- WebHelp

- WebHelp Plus

- WebHelp AIR

- WebHelp Mobile (Flare Version 6 and later)

See the Document Basics chapter for more information about the types of output you can create with Flare.

WHAT ARE THE SIMILARITIES AND DIFFERENCES BETWEEN OUTPUTS?

Plan for content reuse by identifying content that is common to multiple outputs, content that is unique, and content that is likely to change. Define variables, and condition tags upfront. Determine if you need to use the global project linking feature and store common content in a global project.

HOW WILL CONTENT BE REVIEWED?

How content gets reviewed depends on the software your reviewers have and their preferred way of working. Use Part 3 of Appendix A to identify how content will be reviewed.

WHAT'S NEXT?

Ready to press on?

Let's take a look at a "roadmap" to help you navigate from here, so you can ignore the features that don't pertain to your project.

ROADMAP FOR USING FLARE

When you begin using Flare, you may find the user interface and the huge range of options a bit overwhelming. We created a roadmap to help you determine the features you need to use for your project.

Again, follow along in Appendix A and complete the worksheets to get started.

HOW TO USE THIS ROADMAP

Start with "Basic tasks," which you'll need to complete for every Flare project.

Next, look at "What's your input?" **Input** is your source content. On the left, find the column that represents the type of input you're working with. The right column shows the tasks for each input type.

Lastly, look at "What's your output?" **Output** is what you want to create from your Flare project. On the left, find the column that represents the type of output you want to create (online, print, or DITA code). Review the decisions you need to make and complete the tasks in the right column.

BASIC TASKS

For every Flare project, do these tasks …

- Create a new Flare *project*—the structure that contains your content and the project's supporting files (page 43).

- Create a Flare TOC and add items to it. (Step 4: Create Navigation Aids)

- Add content to your project. (Step 3: Develop Content)

- Create navigation aids. (Step 4: Create Navigation Aids)

- Apply styles from a stylesheet to control the appearance of topic content. (Initially, use the default Flare stylesheet, Styles.css. (page 142).

- Build and distribute your output.

WHAT'S YOUR INPUT?

Input type	Decide …	Do these tasks …
No existing electronic source content	Which topics will you include? Which images will you include?	• Create an outline for the Table of Contents (not a Flare task). It doesn't have to be perfect since you can easily change the Flare TOC at any time. • Create content with Flare's XML Editor. Type text, create lists and tables, insert images, add other optional elements (such as snippets and variables) to topics (Step 2: Learn the XML Editor, Step 3: Develop Content, Step 4: Create Navigation Aids, and Appendix F: Single-Sourcing).

Input type	Decide …	Do these tasks …
Word or FrameMaker files	Which application will you use to maintain the content—Flare or the source application?	▪ Prepare your Word or FrameMaker document for importing (page 281). ▪ Set up the import details (how to handle styles, where to split content into topics, whether to link source files to Flare, whether to use Easy Sync for automatic importing of changed source files, etc.; page 281). ▪ Import the content (pages 287 for Word and 296 for FrameMaker).
HTML files	Do you want to keep source content styles or use a Flare stylesheet?	▪ Import the content (page 306).
DITA files	Which application will you use to maintain the content—Flare or the source application?	▪ Set up the import details: how to handle styles, whether to link source files to Flare, whether to use Easy Sync for automatic importing of changed source files, etc. (page 370). ▪ Import the content (page 373). For more information, see Appendix G and search for "DITA" in the Flare Help system.
X-Edit (Full or Contribute)		▪ Receive topics via email from an X-Edit author. ▪ Incorporate topics into your project. *Note*— You can also receive stylesheets and page layout files from X-Edit Full or Contribute.

WHAT'S YOUR OUTPUT?

Output type	Decide ...	Do these tasks ...
Online output	Which type of online output do you need (WebHelp, HTML Help, WebHelp Mobile, etc.)? How will you structure topics in the TOC? How will your final output look (fonts, colors, spacing)? Will you use the default skin or a custom skin? (Custom skins are not covered in this book.)	■ Create online navigation aids (TOC, index entries, links). See Step 4: Create Navigation Aids, on page 159. ■ *(If you want headers, footers, or mini-tocs)* Create a master page and set up headers and footers. See procedure beginning on page 253. ■ *(If you want to change the appearance of the skin)* Edit the default skin (or one of your own). See page 255. ■ Set up the target with the output file name, TOC name, condition tags to include or exclude, and master page (if using one). See page 237. ■ Build the online output. See Step 5B: Create Online Output, on page 259. ■ Test the online output. See page 261. ■ Deliver the online output. All of these are described in Step 4: Create Navigation Aids, and Step 5B: Create Online Output.

Output type	Decide …	Do these tasks …
Print output	Which type of print output do you want to create? (PDF, Word, FrameMaker, XPS, XHTML)	■ Add optional elements (images, cross-references, snippets, variables).
	What will the print output contain (Table of Contents, index, glossary)?	■ (*Depending on your decisions*) Create topics for front and back matter elements, such as a print TOC and print index. See page 215.
	Do you need a simple layout or a more complex layout with different headers, footers, or page-number formats for front matter, chapters, and back matter?	■ Create a topic outline (a Flare TOC) that indicates the topics to be included in the print output. See page 218.
	What should headers and footers contain?	■ (*Depending on your decisions*) Set up and customize page layouts (headers and footers). See procedure beginning on page 221.
		■ (*If you set up page layouts*) Set chapter breaks by linking page layouts to topics in the topic outline (Flare TOC). See procedure beginning on page 233.
		■ Set up the target with the output file name, outline TOC name, page layout names, and condition tags or exclude. See page 237.
		■ Build the print output. See page 238.
		All of these are described in the chapters for Step 3: Develop Content, Step 4: Create Navigation Aids, and Step 5A: Create Print Output.

Output type	Decide …	Do these tasks …
DITA code	Which topics will you include? How will you structure topics in the TOC?	▪ Create a TOC. See page 160. ▪ Set up the target. See Appendix G. ▪ Build, test, and deliver the exported DITA files. See Appendix G. For more information, search for "DITA" in the Flare Help system.

COMMON TASKS

There are certain tasks that you'll do over and over again in Flare, so we've grouped them here. They consist of:

- Creating a new Flare project

- Opening an existing Flare project

- Adding a topic

- Previewing a topic

- Checking spelling

- Adding a target

- Saving your work

Always consult the roadmap beginning on page 37 if you're uncertain where to begin.

CREATING A FLARE PROJECT

Regardless of what you're creating and where the content comes from, you always need to create a Flare **project** to hold your content. Let's get to it!

A project is like a container that holds related information (topics, TOCs, image files, dictionary, stylesheet) in a single unit.

Flare simplifies the process of creating a project by providing a wizard that walks you through the choices you need to make. The wizard creates the project framework, to which you'll add topics, a TOC, and possibly an index.

Before using the Start New Project Wizard next, use Part 4 of Appendix A to decide:

- Where you will store your project if not in the default folder

- If a source control application will be used (optional)

Using the Start New Project Wizard

Use this procedure to create a new project.

When you launch Flare, the Getting Started Wizard opens first, as you read about in the Quick Tour chapter. If you select **Start a new project**, Flare opens the Start New Project Wizard.

The **Start New Project Wizard** asks you to make choices about your project. Click **Next** to move from one screen to the next. As you move through the screens, you can accept the default settings for all remaining choices by clicking **Finish** instead of **Next**. This closes the wizard and skips additional choices.

> **An exception** — If you create the project and import the content simultaneously, you don't have to use the wizard. However, for simplicity, we don't cover that feature in this guide. To learn more about this option, open the Flare Help system and search on "Creating a project by importing."

To keep things simple, we'll take you through the steps for creating a new project that is *not* bound to a source control application. If you want your Flare project to be bound to a source control application (such as Microsoft Visual Source Safe®), see "Binding your project to a source control application" on page 46.

To create a project:

1. Select **File → New Project**. The Start New Project Wizard opens.

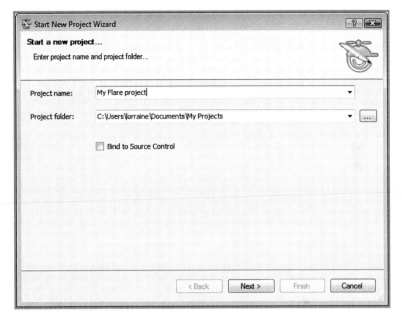

2. Type a unique project name.

3. (*Optional*) To save your project in a folder other than the default folder, click 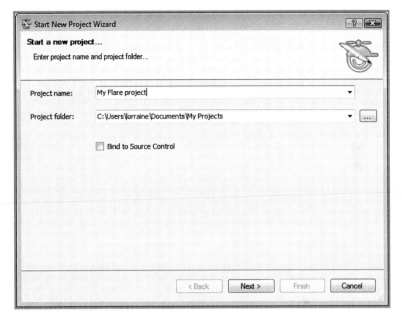 and select a different folder.

4. (*Optional*) To use a source control application with your Flare project, see "Binding your project to a source control application," next.

5. Select the language you want Flare to use when spell-checking your topics.

6. Select **Empty** from the Source section.

> **Note** — As you gain experience, you might want to use one of your own templates ("My Templates") for new projects instead of using factory templates. To learn how to create a project template, see "Creating a project template" on page 66.
>
> Flare contains several sample templates that contain starter topics and files. This is an alternative to starting from scratch.

7. From the list of Available Targets, select the type of output you want to create.

8.   Click **Finish**.

The project is created and the Content Explorer (left pane) lists your first topic, "Topic.htm."

> **Best Practice** — Store a backup copy of your entire project on a server or secondary storage device, and back up often! A quick way to back up your project is the select **File → Zip → Zip Project**.

Binding your project to a source control application

Binding your project to a source control application is optional. Source control applications can help you manage your Flare content by allowing you to coordinate and control changes to it. This is especially helpful when:

- Multiple authors need access to content.

- Authors need to store backup versions of files as they change.

Binding (linking) your Flare project to a source control application lets you take advantage of your source control application's version control and change control features.

When you create a Flare project, you can indicate which source control application you are using and where to store Flare project files within it. The source control application manages versions of project files as they change and prevents multiple users from accessing the same file simultaneously.

Flare provides *programmatic support* for Microsoft Visual Source Safe (VSS) and Microsoft Team Foundation Server (TFS). This means that tasks such as checking in and checking out files, and adding files to source control *can* be done from within Flare.

Because Flare files are stored in XML format, Flare is *compatible* with all source control applications on the market. This means that you can add your project files to any source control application to use that application's source control features. However, for applications other than VSS and TFS, source control tasks, such as checking in or checking out files, *cannot* be done automatically from within Flare.

> **Note** — To use a source control application other than VSS and TFS directly from Flare, see "Using an API to Integrate Source Control" in the Flare Help system. You can also search on "source control" in the Flare Help system for detailed information about using Flare with a source control application.

The source control application must already be installed on your computer before you can bind a new project to it.

To create a project that is integrated with source control:

1. Complete Steps 1 – 3 of the procedure for creating a new project (page 44).

2. Click **Bind to Source Control**, then **Next**.

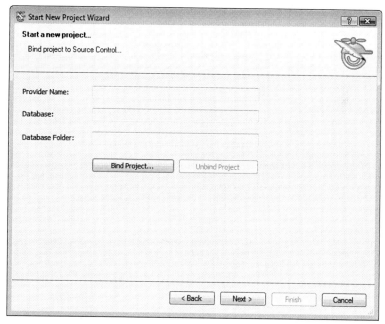

3. Click **Bind Project**.

4. Complete the fields *in one section* of this dialog:

   If you have Visual Source Safe (VSS),

   a. Select **Visual Source Safe**.

   b. Click **Browse** to select the INI file for the VSS database.

   c. Click **Browse** to select the VSS database folder in which to store your Flare project files. (You might need to log on to Visual Source Safe to do this.)

   If you have Team Foundation Server (TFS),

   a. Select **Team Foundation Server**.

   b. In the Server field, type the URL for the server.

   c. Click **Browse** to select the Team Foundation project to bind your Flare project to. (You might need to enter a user name and password to log in to the Team Foundation Server.)

If you are using a different source control application,

a. Select **Source Code Control Plug-in**.

b. Select your source control program from the Provider list.

c. Click **Browse** to select the project to bind your Flare project to. (You might need to enter a user name and password to log in.)

5. Click **OK** twice after making your selections.

6. Continue with Step 5 of the procedure for creating a new project. (page 44).

OPENING A FLARE PROJECT

Flare lets you open and work with only one project at a time. If you open an existing project, the current project closes automatically. If you have unsaved changes, you'll be prompted to save them.

To open an existing Flare project:

1. Select **File → Open**.

2. Navigate to the folder that holds the project you want to open (Documents\My Projects\<project name>, by default).

3. Double-click the project file (For example, MyProjectName.flprj).

> *Tip* — The Start Page shows projects you've recently opened. You can open a project listed on the Start Page by clicking its project name; or, you can select **File → Recent Projects** and open if from the recent projects list.

ADDING A TOPIC

Throughout this book, you'll see the words **topic**, **content**, and **project** used often. Let's take a moment to review what these terms mean:

- A **topic** is the "box" in which content is stored. Each topic is a file (with an .htm extension) that conforms to the XML specification.

- **Content** is various types of information contained in a topic, such as text, tables, lists, and images.

- A **project** is simply a collection of topics and related files, which are stored in project folders.

To create a new project, you'll create Flare topics and add content to them. Your content can be new or imported (see Appendix B: Import Content, for more about importing content).

Methods used to add a topic

You can add topics from the TOC, from the Content Explorer, or by using the Project menu. Which method should you use? Read on …

Table 1-1:
Methods
used to
add a
topic

To …	Do this …
Create a topic *and* add it to a TOC (and save time)	Add a topic from the TOC. This method adds a topic to your project and to your TOC simultaneously—plus it automatically links the topic to the TOC entry it creates. (A TOC entry must link to a topic in order to open that topic in the output.)
Quickly add a topic that doesn't need to link to a TOC	Add a topic using the Content Explorer or Project menu. This method adds a topic without linking it to a TOC entry. This option is a good choice when you're creating websites and short documents that don't need a TOC.

> **Note** — If you decide to add a TOC later, you can do so easily. See "Creating a Table of Contents" on page 160.

To add a topic:

1. Make sure that the Flare project to which you want to add topics is open.

2. If you need a TOC, take these steps. Otherwise, skip to Step 3, next.

   a. Select the Project Organizer.

   b. Expand the TOCs folder.

    c. Double-click the TOC you want to open. The TOC Editor opens in the middle pane.

    d. On the TOC Editor's toolbar, click **Create a new topic and link to it** .

    e. Skip to Step 4 below.

3. If you don't need a TOC, do one of the following:

    ▪ Select **Project → Add Topic**.

    or

    ▪ On the Content Explorer toolbar, click **Create a new Topic file** .

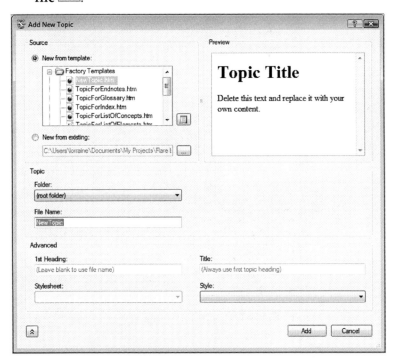

4. Fill in the fields on the Add New Topic dialog.

Option	Description
New from template	(Recommended) **Factory Templates** provided with Flare.

Option	Description
New from existing	Used to choose one of your own project or topic templates. To learn more about creating your own templates, see "Working with templates" on page 64.
Preview	A preview of the selected template.
Folder	(*Optional*) The sub-folders contained in the Content Explorer's Content folder. Select the sub-folder to store the topic in.
File Name	The file name for the topic. **Best Practice** — Avoid spaces between words. This causes problems on UNIX servers. Use underscores instead.
1st Heading	The text of the first heading.
Title	The topic title. Leave this field blank if you want the first heading in your topic to be used as a topic title (recommended). **Note** — A topic's title is shown in the TOC when you link to or insert that topic.
Style	The style for the first heading in your topic. Leave blank to use Flare's h1 style (recommended).
Stylesheet	This field is unavailable if you've specified a stylesheet for the project or primary target; otherwise, you can select a stylesheet to attach to the topic.

5.   Click **Add**, then **OK** to copy the new topic to your project.

The new topic opens in the XML Editor and is added to the list of topics in the Content Explorer. If you added the topic from a TOC, the new topic is also added to the TOC.

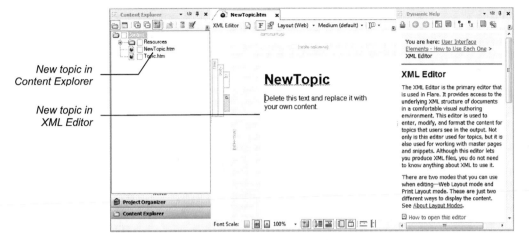

New topic in Content Explorer

New topic in XML Editor

Now you can add content to your topic in the form of text, lists, tables, audio files, movies, and images.

PREVIEWING A TOPIC

Previewing a topic lets you:

- See what the topic will look like when it is built.

- Test the topic's links before you build the output.

You can preview the topic that is active in the XML Editor. When you preview the topic, you can include or exclude text that is tagged with a condition tag.

The primary target's type determines the format Flare uses for the preview.

Table 1-2:
Formats used to show topic previews

If the primary target type is …	Flare uses this format for preview …
Online	DotNet Help
PDF	Adobe PDF
XPS	Microsoft XPS
XHTML	Print Layout mode
Word or FrameMaker	*Preview is not available for these targets.*

> **Note** — To designate a target as primary, right-click the target in the Project Organizer and select **Make Primary** from the menu.

To preview a topic:

1. Click **Preview compiled topic** 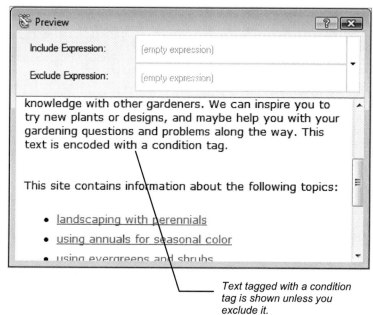 on the XML Editor's toolbar.

Text tagged with a condition tag is shown unless you exclude it.

2. If you want to exclude text that has been tagged with a condition tag, click the arrow to the right of the Include and Exclude Expression fields. A list of condition tags opens.

> **Note** — By default all text is included, even if tagged with a condition tag.

3. Check the **Exclude** box for each style to be excluded, then click **OK**. The Preview window is re-displayed without the excluded text.

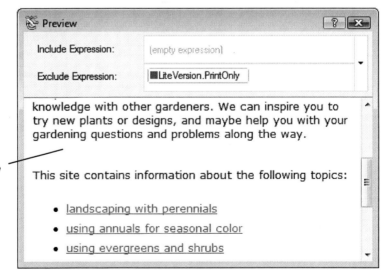

The tagged text is not shown in the Preview window because it was excluded.

4. Close the Preview window.

OPENING A TOPIC

You can have several topics open at once, each in its own XML
Editor page. Each topic has a tab. The **white tab** indicates which
topic is active and visible in the XML Editor window.

Figure 1-1:
An active
topic in the
XML Editor
window

To open a topic:

1. Make sure that the Flare project is open and that the Content
    Explorer is in view.

2. Do one of the following:

    ▪ Double-click the topic in the Content Explorer. (If you've
      created sub-folders in the Content Explorer, you might have
      to expand a sub-folder to find the topic.)

    ▪ If the project's TOC is open and in view in the middle pane,
      right-click the topic in the TOC and select **Open Link** from
      the menu.

    > **Note** — You can also open a topic from the TOC, if the ⬚ **Toggle the
    > double-click behavior: open topic or display properties** button on the
    > XML Editor toolbar is set to open topics, not topic properties. We
    > recommend that you leave it set to open topics.

The topic opens in its own XML Editor page in the middle pane.

CHECKING SPELLING

You have these options for spell-checking your project's topics:

- Flare can check spelling automatically as you type, or

- You can check spelling manually.

Checking spelling as you type

Flare can check spelling as you type in the topic (or snippet) currently in view. With this option turned on, Flare highlights possible spelling errors with a red zigzag underline.

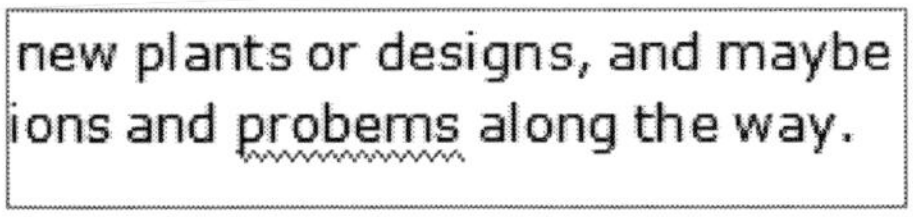

Figure 1-2:
A spelling error

```
new plants or designs, and maybe
ions and probems along the way.
```

You can turn this option on or off for individual topics. You might have two topics open and have Spell Check While Typing turned on for one topic and off for the other. If your spelling errors aren't being highlighted in the active topic, you probably have this option turned off for that topic.

To turn on spell-checking while typing:

- Select **Tools → Spell Check While Typing**.

To resolve a potential spelling error:

1. Right-click the word that Flare highlighted. A menu appears listing possible spellings of the word.

```
flourish  We hope that we can inspire you to t
design:      problems                        arde
probem       probes
             proems
This sit     problem                         llov
    •   la   poems
    •   u:   probe
    •   u:   proem
    •   g|   robes
    •   p|   ─────────────────────            sts
             Ignore All
    •   m    Add To Dictionary
```

2.   Do one of the following:

To ...	Do this ...
Replace the misspelled word with a suggested word	Select the correct word from the list.
Keep the highlighted word spelled as it is and ignore other instances of this word in this topic file	Select **Ignore All**. This option does not affect other topics. Flare will still flag this word as a possible spelling error in other topics if spell-checking is turned on for those topics.
Keep the highlighted word spelled as it is and add the highlighted word to the dictionary	Select **Add To Dictionary**. If you add the word to the dictionary, Flare will not flag this spelling as questionable in other topics or snippets.

Checking spelling manually

You can have the spell-checker check one or more topics for possible spelling errors in:

▪   The active topic (the one that is currently visible)

▪   All open topics

▪   All topics in the same folder as the active topic

- All topics (even if not open) in the project

To check spelling in one or more topics:

1. Select **Tools → Spell Check Window**. The Spell Check window opens in the right pane, and the first misspelled word in the active topic is highlighted.

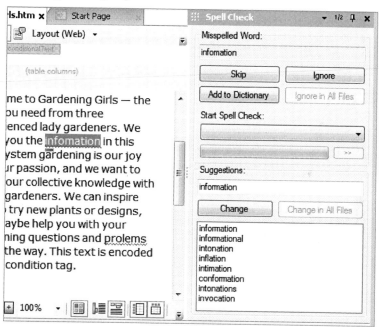

2. To check spelling in the active topic only (the default), skip to Step 4, below.

3. To check spelling in more than one topic, select these options from the Start Spell Check field:

To check spelling in ...	Do this ...
All topics in the open project	Select **whole project**. Flare opens topics that have questionable spellings one at a time in the order in which they are listed in the Content Explorer.
All open topics	Select **all open documents**.

To check spelling in ...	Do this ...
All topics in the same folder as the active topic	Select **documents in same folder**. Flare opens topics with questionable spellings one at a time in the same order in which they are listed in the folder.

4. Do one of the following:

To ...	Do this ...
Change the spelling to a suggested word	Select a suggested word and select **Change**.
Keep the word as it is and move to the next misspelled word	Select **Skip**.
Keep the word as it is, move to the next misspelled word, and ignore other occurrences of this word in this *topic*	Select **Ignore**.
Keep the word as it is, move to the next misspelled word, and ignore all other occurrences of this word in this *project*	Select **Ignore in All Files**.
Keep the word as it is, add the word to the dictionary, and move to the next misspelled word	Select **Add to Dictionary**.

5. When the spell-check is complete, click **OK**.

6. (*Optional*) Close the Spell Check window.

7. Click **Save All** to save all spelling corrections and terms you added to the dictionary.

8. (*Optional*) Close the topics that Flare opened due to questionable spellings.

Adding terms to the dictionary

Use this procedure to add new terms to an existing dictionary. (If the dictionary doesn't exist, you can create it by adding a word to it when you check spelling.)

To add terms to a dictionary:

1. If the dictionary already exists in the Project Organizer, expand the **Advanced** folder, then double-click the dictionary. The Dictionary Editor opens in the middle pane, showing current entries.

2. Click **New item** in the Dictionary Editor's toolbar. A new blank line appears.

3. Type the term to be added in the Word column. You can also type a Comment if desired.

4. Click **Save** to save the dictionary file.

ADDING A TARGET

Use the following procedure to add a target to your project.

To add a target to your project:

1. In the Project Organizer, right-click **Targets** and select **Add Target** from the menu. The Add Target dialog opens.

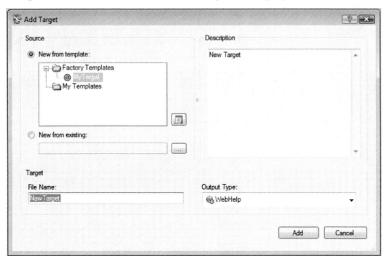

2. In the File Name field, type a name for the new target.

3. Select the Output Type from the list.

4. Click **Add**, then **OK** to add the new target.

   The new target is listed in the Targets folder and opens in the Target Editor.

5. Set up the target for the type of output you want to create.

   - **To set up a target for print output**, see "Task 8: Set up the print target" on page 237.

   - **To set up a target for online output**, see "Setting up an online target" on page 256.

SAVING YOUR WORK

It's a good idea to save your work periodically instead of waiting until you're ready to exit Flare. There are two ways to save your work:

- **Save only the item currently in view.** You might be viewing a topic, a TOC, a list of styles in a stylesheet, a variable list, a list of condition tags, or any other content related to your project.

- **Save your entire project.**

As shown in Figure 1-3, Flare lets you know if you have any unsaved work by placing an asterisk (*) to the right of the file name on the tab for any item (topic, TOC, index, stylesheet, import file, etc.) that has changed.

Figure 1-3:
An unsaved topic

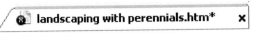

> **Note** — The active topic is the one currently visible in the middle pane of the XML Editor.

As shown in Figure 1-4, there are no unsaved changes in the active topic ("Selecting a tree"), but there are unsaved changes in another open topic ("landscaping with perennials").

Active topic

Figure 1-4:
Unsaved changes in an inactive topic

> **Best Practice** — Use **Save All** routinely to save the changes in all open topics.

To save the active file:

Do one of the following:

- Click **Save File** 💾.
- Select **File → Save**.
- Type **CTRL + S**.

Flare saves the active file (the file shown in the middle pane).

To save your entire project:

Do one of the following:

- Click **Save All** 📑.
- Select **File → Save All**.
- Type **CTRL + SHIFT + S**.

Flare saves all project files.

> **Tip** — As you work with Flare, you're bound to lose track of what's open in the middle pane. When this happens, first save all the open documents, and then click **Window → Close All Documents** or **Close All Documents Except This One** (meaning the active document). You can also close a single document by clicking **x** on its tab.

WORKING WITH TEMPLATES

You can save a lot of time by creating templates. Templates allow you to create topics that are consistent in appearance, without creating and reformatting elements you use frequently. You can also create templates for project files, such as TOCS, targets, and page layouts. You can even create a template of an entire project.

When you add a new topic from your own topic template, you'll replace any placeholder text with new content just as you would do with any MadCap-supplied template.

> **Important** — If you create a template from a file that contains links to other files, those links remain in place. Copy the linked files into your project and store them in the same location relative to the files they link to.

OUR RECOMMENDATIONS

- Create more than one topic template to use with different types of topics. For example, you might have one template for overviews, another for step-by-step procedures, and a third for frequently asked questions.

- Include an empty formatted table in your topic templates. (You can delete it from topics later if you don't need it.) See "Adding a table" on page 113 for details.

BEFORE CREATING YOUR FIRST TEMPLATE

Use the Template Manager to assign a folder, either on your local computer or on a network drive, for storing your templates.

> **Tip** —Selecting a network folder to hold your templates allows you to share template files with other Flare users.

When you use the Template Manager to assign a folder, Flare creates sub-folders for each different template type—content (topics), TOCs, page layouts, skins, and projects, for example. When you create templates, Flare automatically places your template files in the appropriate sub-folders.

To assign a template folder, see "Using the Template Manager" on page 68.

CREATING A TEMPLATE FOR A FLARE TOPIC OR PROJECT FILE

This procedure describes how to create a template for any Flare file—TOCs, topics, skins, targets—except for a Flare project. To create a template for a project, see "Creating a project template" on page 66.

To create a template for a Flare topic or project file:

1. Open the Flare file you want to use as a template.

2. *For topic templates,* add items you'll use often, such as paragraphs, headings, tables, and lists, and format them as you want future elements to look. Add any boilerplate text required (see Step 2: Learn the XML Editor).

   For other types of templates, set up the file as desired. For example, for a page layout template, set up headers and footers.

3. Select **File → Save As Template** from the File menu.

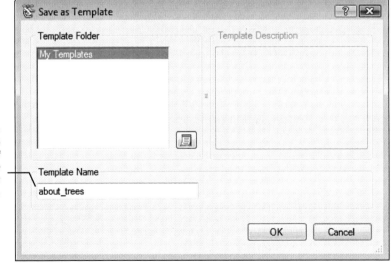

The template name defaults to the file name of the topic you are saving as a template.

4. Under Template Folder, select the folder in which to save the template.

5. Type a Template Name and click **OK**.

6. A confirmation box opens, showing the template name and path. Click **OK**.

   When you add a new topic or other project file, the new template will be listed in the folder you selected in Step 4.

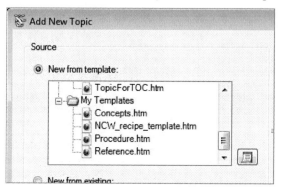

CREATING A PROJECT TEMPLATE

This procedure describes how to create a template for a Flare project. When you create a project template, you can choose which files to include in the template.

To create a project template:

1. Open the Flare project you want to use as a template.

2. Select **Project → Save Project As Template**. The Project Template Wizard opens.

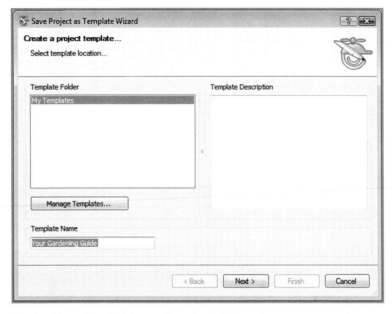

3. Under Template Folder, select the folder where your template will be saved.

4. In the Template Name field, type a name for the template.

5. Click **Next**. The wizard displays folders and files from the (Content Explorer's) Content folder that can be included in the template. By default all content files are checked (included).

Tip — Fully expand folders to view their contents.

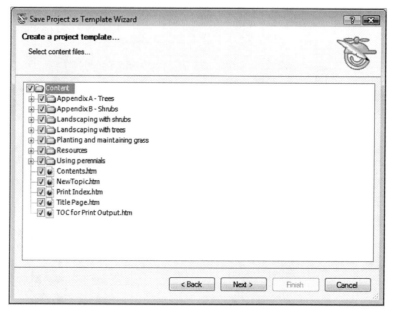

6. Deselect the content files you want excluded from the template and click **Next**. The wizard displays folders and files from the (Project Organizer's) Project folder that can be included in the template.

7. Deselect the project files you want excluded from the template and click **Finish**. The project's files are copied and a confirmation box opens showing the template name and path.

8. Click **OK**.

   When you add a new project, the new template will be listed on the "Select a project template" dialog of the Start a New Project Wizard.

USING THE TEMPLATE MANAGER

The Template Manager makes it easy to work with templates. You can perform tasks such as:

▪ Adding template files

▪ Creating template folders

- Opening templates for editing

- Deleting template folders and files

- Editing template descriptions

To use the Template Manager:

1. Select **Tools → Manage Templates**.

> **Note** — You can also open the Template Manager by clicking 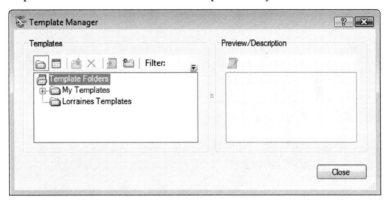 (on the Save as Template dialog) or Manage Templates... (on the Save Project as Template Wizard) when you create templates.

2. Expand the folders to view the templates they contain.

3. Use these options as desired:

To ...	Do this ...
Browse for and add a new template folder to the list	Click **New Template Folder** .
Create a new folder that you can add as a template folder	Click . In the Browse For Folder dialog, click Make New Folder .
See a preview of the template	Click the template.
Open the selected template for editing	Double-click the template.

To ...	Do this ...
Edit the template description (does not apply to topic templates)	Click the template and click **Edit Template Description** . In the Edit Template Description dialog, change the description and click **OK**.
Rename the selected template	Press **F2**.
Copy, paste, or cut the selected template	Use standard editing commands (**CTRL + C, CTRL + V**, and **CTRL + X**).
Delete the selected template	Click **Delete** .
Browse for and add an existing template from the Windows Explorer Open dialog	Click **Add Template File** .

4. When finished, close the Template Manager.

WHAT'S NEXT?

If you've created a project, added a topic to it, and you're not sure what to do next:

- Look at the roadmap beginning on page 37.

- Find the rows that match your scenario.

- Follow the list of tasks in each part of the roadmap.

You might even place a bookmark (the old-fashioned kind) at page 37, because you'll want to come back to the roadmap as you work through your first Flare project. Good luck to you, and enjoy!

OUR RECOMMENDATION

At this point, we strongly recommend that you complete the next chapter, Step 2: Learn the XML Editor. It will give you a solid background in using the XML Editor to add text to a topic as you try out additional features in the remainder of this book.

Step 2:
Learn the
XML Editor

STEP 5: Create Output
5A: Print Output
5B: Online Output

STEP 4:
Create
Nav Aids

STEP 3:
Develop
Content

STEP 2:
Learn the
XML Editor

STEP 1:
Get Started

In this chapter ...
- ➤ De-clutter your workspace
- ➤ Enter text
- ➤ View tags
- ➤ View cursors and text blocks
- ➤ Manipulate text
- ➤ Format text
- ➤ View layout modes
- ➤ Create a new topic
- ➤ Save a project

OVERVIEW

This chapter contains a tutorial and supplemental information about using the Flare XML Editor. With the tutorial, you'll learn how to:

- Add topics and enter text into them

- Reveal the tags associated with text

- Change the appearance of text by applying styles and local formatting

- Save your work

You'll also learn about certain elements in the XML Editor that you'll see commonly, such as tags, structure bars, and various types of cursors.

WHAT IS XML?

XML (Extensible Markup Language) is a World Wide Web Consortium (W3C) specification that defines markup languages used to support document sharing.

Content is marked with **tags** that describe the content according to XML rules. In essence, this lets you separate the content from its formatting, making content easy to reuse in other applications or on different computers.

You can even edit XML files in a different XML editor without losing data or formatting. Hence, you are not locked into using the Flare XML Editor if you prefer to use a different one.

TUTORIAL SETUP

Before you begin this tutorial, make sure you have completed these tasks in Step 1: Get Started, using the default values that appear:

- Create a project (page 43)

- Add your first topic (page 49)

Be sure to **set aside 45 minutes** to complete this tutorial chapter. It's better to complete all of the tasks in succession.

TASK 1: DE-CLUTTERING YOUR WORKSPACE

As you learned in Step 1: Get Started, when you create or open a topic, the XML Editor opens in the middle pane. To make viewing cleaner, we recommend de-cluttering your workspace by closing a couple elements you won't be using routinely.

Start page tab

Dynamic Help window

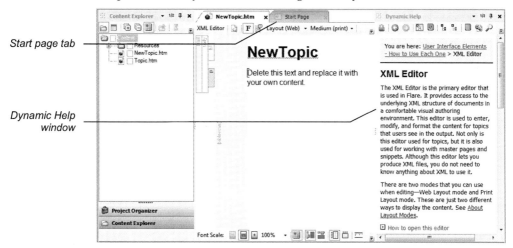

1. Close the Dynamic Help window.

2. Close the Start Page (click the **x** on its tab). (This maximizes the space available for the XML Editor.)

The workspace should now look like this:

TASK 2: ENTERING TEXT

To get started, you'll type a heading and few paragraphs of text, which you'll use to learn more about the XML Editor in the rest of this chapter.

1. Highlight **New Topic** in the XML Editor and type **Welcome**.

    Notice that what you typed replaces the existing placeholder text. You'll also see that the cursor changes shape, which you'll learn about later.

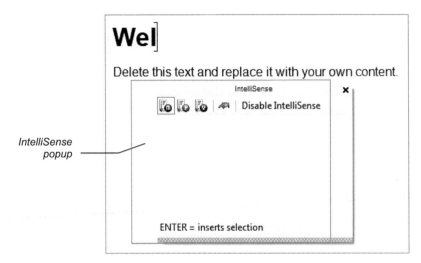

IntelliSense popup

As you type, you'll probably see the IntelliSense popup as shown above. **IntelliSense** anticipates what you're typing and offers suggestions for automatically completing a word.

If you just keep typing, the IntelliSense popup will disappear. But while learning the XML Editor, we recommend that you disable it. If you want to turn it back on later, see "Disabling and enabling IntelliSense" on page 322.

2. To disable IntelliSense, click **Disable IntelliSense** on the IntelliSense popup the next time it appears. Then click **Yes** on the confirmation box.

3. Highlight **Delete this text and replace it with your own content** and type:

   Welcome to Gardening Girls, the help you need from three experienced lady gardeners. We created this website because gardening is our joy and passion, and we want to share our knowledge with other gardeners.

As you can see, entering text in the XML Editor is very much like using a word processor, but there are important differences, as you'll learn in a bit. Let's type more text.

4. Press **ENTER** to begin a new paragraph, just as you would with a word processor. Don't worry about the spacing between paragraphs. You'll fix that later.

5. Now enter the following paragraphs:

    What we offer

    This site contains information about the following topics:

    Landscaping with perennials

    Using annuals for seasonal color

    Growing beautiful gardens in the shade

    When you're finished, the XML Editor should look like this:

Tag bars

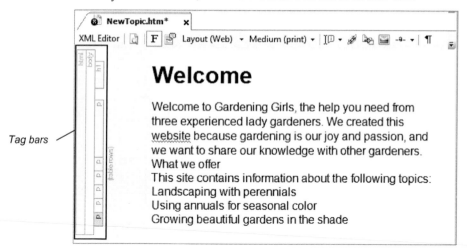

Notice the tag bars at the left of your content. Tag bars tell you important information about how your document is constructed. You'll learn more about tag bars shortly.

That's enough typing for now. Let's see how you can view the structure of the text.

TASK 3: VIEWING TAGS

Let's see what tags look like.

1. Click **Toggle show tags** ⟨t⟩ ▾ in the top toolbar.

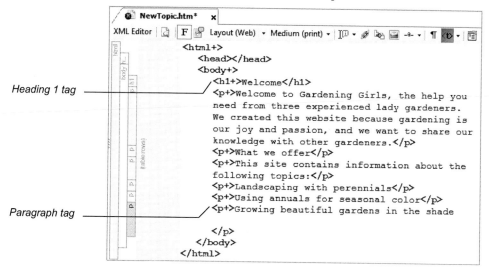

Heading 1 tag ⎯⎯⎯⎯⎯⎯⎯⎯⎯

Paragraph tag ⎯⎯⎯⎯⎯⎯⎯⎯⎯

Notice what just happened. Flare now shows you the **tags** it automatically assigned to the text you entered ("body," "h1" and "p").

Flare also decided where your tags should begin and end, based on when you pressed **ENTER**. The beginning of a tag is followed by a plus sign (as in <h1+> and <p+>) and the end is preceded by a slash (as in </h1> and </p>).

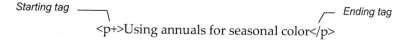

Starting tag ⎯⎯⎯⎯⎯   ⎯⎯ Ending tag

<p+>Using annuals for seasonal color</p>

So why does this matter? Because although you probably won't work with tags in your XML code when you're new to Flare, eventually you probably will. It's good to know what lies underneath the text you see in the XML Editor.

> **Note** — You can edit topic tags and content with Flare's text editor. Click **Send this file to the text editor** 📇 in the top toolbar.

Now let's hide the tags to make for easier viewing.

2. Click **Toggle show tags** ⟨t⟩ ▾ in the top toolbar again. (This button toggles the tag view on and off.)

   Although tags sound complicated if you're not familiar with them, the good news is that Flare manages XML rules for you so you can't create an XML document that is not well-formed.

   With more complex topics, you'll see several additional tags. Here are some of the more common Flare tags, shown in the tag bar you'll see to the left of your content.

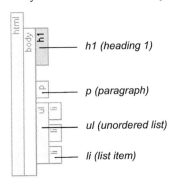

h1 (heading 1)

p (paragraph)

ul (unordered list)

li (list item)

TASK 4: VIEWING CURSORS AND TEXT BLOCKS

Most people use the word **paragraph** to describe a unit of text in a document. Flare uses the term **block** to describe any major unit of content that is within a starting and ending tag.

This is done to avoid confusing the concept of paragraphs with paragraph tags (<p>). In this book, when we talk about units of text, we use the term **text block**.

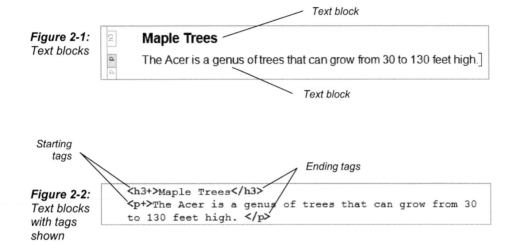

Figure 2-1:
Text blocks

Figure 2-2:
Text blocks
with tags
shown

> **Note** — When using the XML Editor, you cannot type more than one consecutive space unless they are non-breaking spaces.

Flare also gives you clues about how tags are related to your content by changing the shape of the cursor. Let's see how this works.

1. Click after the word "Welcome." Notice how the cursor changes to a right bracket (]).

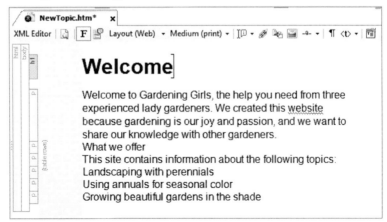

A right bracket indicates that whatever you type will have the characteristics of the text to the left of the cursor. The tag bar is also highlighted (in this case, h1).

2. Type **Gardeners!** See how the text takes on the characteristics of the text in first text block?

Asterisk indicates unsaved changes in this topic

2. Now click before the "W" in "What we offer." The cursor changes to a left bracket ([), indicating that what you type will have the same formatting as the text to the right. Notice that the tag bar now shows p as the current tag.

Tag bar

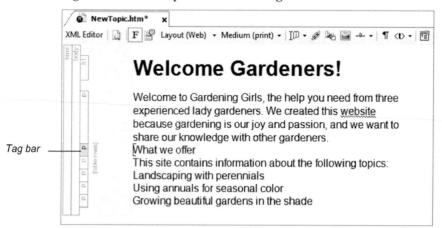

3. Click anywhere in the first paragraph to see how the cursor changes again.

This is the traditional "insert" cursor you're probably used to from word processing.

There are lots of cursors in Flare as described in "Cursor types" on page 314. For now, just make sure you understand how the bracketed cursors work.

TASK 5: MANIPULATING TEXT

The XML Editor works very much like a word processor when it comes to manipulating text.

1. Move your cursor to a new location and click it once, then again and again until you've clicked it a few times in succession. See how Flare progressively selects more and more text as you continue to click?

This is a great shortcut when you want to select words and text blocks for editing. Try it out a few times, and notice how the tag bars change to indicate what is highlighted.

You can copy (**CTRL + C**) and paste (**CTRL + V**) text in Flare just as you would in most word processors. (You can copy and paste within a topic, from one topic to another, or from an external source—such as a Microsoft Word document.)

> ***Note*** — A complete list of common editing functions, plus navigation commands such as **PAGE UP** and **HOME**, are listed in "Shortcuts when working with text" on page 317 and "Navigational shortcuts" on page 319 for your reference.

You can also right-click to view a menu that contains options like copy, paste, and delete.

> ***Note*** — Right-click a tag bar for options that affect the entire text block. Right-click selected text for options that affect only the selected text.

Let's see how this works by deleting a text block. When you delete an entire text block you'll need to delete the tags associated with it.

2. First, click in the word **shade**.

3. Now hover your cursor over the block's tag bar (p). When the cursor changes to a hand 🖑, right-click and press **Delete**.

The entire text block is deleted, including the starting and ending tags.

Now let's see how to copy selected text.

4. Double-click to select the word **perennials**.

5. Right-click the word **perennials** (not the tag bar) and select **Copy** from the resulting menu.

6. Click before the word **for** and press **CTRL + V** to paste in the text.

7. Correct the wording by typing a space after perennials and by typing the word **and** between annuals and perennials.

TASK 6: FORMATTING TEXT

When using Flare, it's important to understand the difference between local formatting and formatting with styles.

- **Local "inline" formatting** — Used to format characters, such as making certain words bold, underlined, or italicized in a paragraph. With this method, formatting is applied only to the selected text.

- **Styles** — Used to control formatting that you set up ahead of time in a **stylesheet**, which is simply a collection of styles. When you change a style, it changes in every place where the style was applied.

Whether you choose to use local formatting or styles to control the look of your content depends on several factors, as discussed in "Local formatting vs. styles: which to use" on page 138.

> ***Best Practice*** — Use styles instead of local formatting. Local formatting increases the size of the XML code, which means your browser may take longer to display the content.

In this tutorial you'll practice both applying styles and adding local formatting.

1. Click **Open the Text Format Toolbar** $\boxed{F}$ in the XML Editor's toolbar. This is where local formatting is typically done.

> **Note** — You can also use the Format menu to do local formatting.

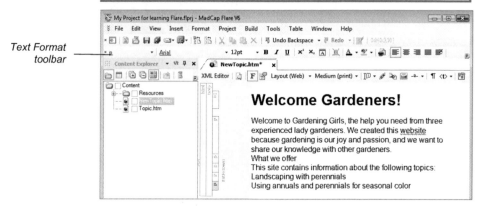

Text Format toolbar

2. Highlight **joy**.

3. Click $\boxed{B}$ and then $\boxed{I}$ make the selected text bold and italicized.

4. Highlight **passion**.

5. Click $\boxed{B}$ and then $\boxed{I}$ make the selected text bold and italicized.

6. Click anywhere in the text you formatted.

Span bars

Notice that a new type of structure bar, called span bars, has appeared along the top of the content area. **Span bars** indicate how formatting is applied where the cursor is located.

> **Note** — If you don't see span bars, click **Toggle show spans** ▦ at the bottom of the screen.

Now you'll see how styles are used. Unless you specify otherwise, Flare attaches its default stylesheet, called **Style.css**, to your topic.

You can attach a different stylesheet if you create one, but since you don't have any, you'll use Flare's default stylesheet.

7. Highlight **Gardening Girls**.

8. Click (text) ▾ on the Text Format toolbar to open a list of styles that apply to selected text.

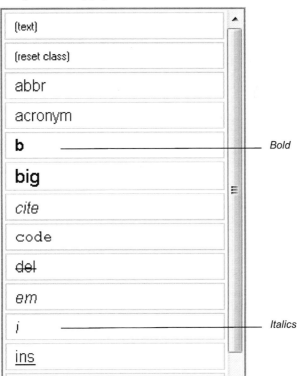

9.   Select **b** (bold). The bold style is applied to the selected text.

Next, you'll see how to apply a style to a text block.

10. Click in **What we offer**.

> **Note** — When applying styles to a text block, click anywhere in the text block where the style will be applied. You can click anywhere in a text block and select **Format → Font** (or another option) to apply local formatting.

11. Click [p ▾] on the Text Format toolbar to open a list of styles applicable to text blocks.

> (reset class)
>
> *address*
>
> div
>
> fieldset
>
> # h1
>
> ## h2
>
> ### h3
>
> #### h4
>
> ##### h5
>
> ###### h6
>
> p
>
> pre

Notice that the style button on the Text Format toolbar now shows a "p" like this: [p ▾] instead of "text" like this: [(text) ▾].

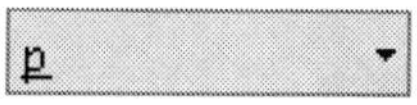

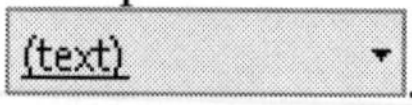

Notice also that the list of styles for text blocks is different than the list of styles for selected text. Flare shows you only those styles that apply *either* to selected text *or* to a text block.

12. Select **h2** (heading level 2). Voila! The h2 style is applied to the entire text block as shown next.

Tag bar for h2 style

Notice that Flare shows a tag bar for the h2 style you just applied. You can always look at the tag bar to see which style is applied to a text block.

Next, you'll take a look at various layout modes in Flare.

TASK 7: VIEWING LAYOUT MODES

As you will learn in Step 5A: Create Print Output, and Step 5B: Create Online Output, you can create content specifically designed to be used online or in print. To help you see how your content will look, the XML Editor can display your content in two modes:

- **Web Layout mode** — To see how your content will look as online output (websites, Help systems, etc.) Headers and footers *are not* shown in this mode.

- **Print Layout mode** — To see how your content will look as print output (Word, PDF, FrameMaker files, etc.) Headers and footers *are* shown in this mode if you created a page layout and selected it when you set up the target currently designated as "primary."

> **Note** — To designate a target as primary, right-click the target in the Project Organizer and select **Make Primary** from the menu.

When you're writing content for each type of output, it's helpful to see the components that make up that output—right in the editor you're working in. That's where Flare's layout modes can help. Let's see how this works.

1. Click Layout (Web) ▾ in the toolbar above your topic. Notice that the button indicates the current mode (Web Layout).

   A message appears stating that the medium will change (to "default" for Web layout mode, and "print" for Print Layout mode). You'll learn a bit about mediums in a moment.

2. Click **OK**. The XML Editor re-displays your topic in Print Layout mode.

Print Layout mode

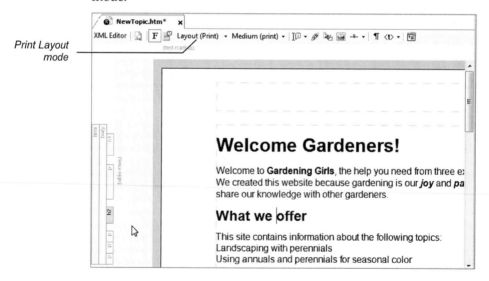

WHAT ARE MEDIUMS?

Mediums let you customize styles for a particular output. For example, you might want the "p" style for online output to use a sans serif font (like Verdana), which is easy to read onscreen. But for print output, you might want the "p" style to use a serif font (like Times New Roman), which is easier to see when reading printed documents.

If you want to use a medium, you must set up the medium's styles in the Stylesheet Editor and then select the applicable medium when you set up a target. The medium you select will be used for that target's output.

For now, you only need to remember that Flare automatically changes the medium when you change the layout mode.

TASK 8: CREATING ANOTHER TOPIC

As you use Flare, you'll probably have more than one topic open at once, each with its own tab in the XML Editor. But only one topic— the **active topic**—is visible at a time. To switch to a different open topic (and make it active), just click its tab.

Now you'll create a new topic (without creating its corresponding TOC entry) to see how the topic tabs work.

1. Select **Project → Add Topic**. The Add New Topic dialog opens.

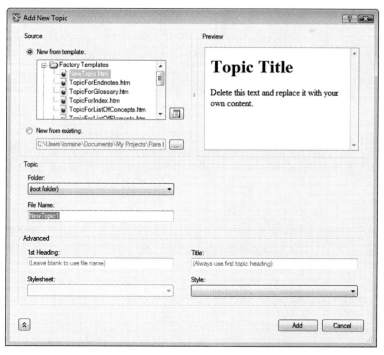

2. Fill in the fields as described in the procedure for adding a topic on page 50.

3. Click **Add**, then **OK** to confirm where the file will be copied.

The new topic opens in its own tab and is listed in the Content Explorer to the left of the XML Editor.

Topic tabs

4. To switch between topics and make a topic active, click its tab. Try switching between topics a couple times to see how this works.

> **Best Practice** — Don't have more than three or four topics open at one time. Most people find it difficult to keep track of several topics at once.

TASK 9: SAVING A PROJECT

Enough practice for now. It's time to save your work.

Flare allows you to save the active topic or your entire project. You'll save your project.

1. Click **Save All**  in the Standard (top) toolbar. Notice that the topic tabs do not show asterisks, meaning that all changed content has been saved.

2. Close Flare if you're not ready to move on to Step 3: Develop Content, in this book.

> **Best Practice** — Use **Save All** rather than **Save File**. That way, you'll be sure to save all your work before exiting.

LEARN MORE

This section provides more detail about some of the features you used during this tutorial. Appendix C: XML Editor Reference, has even more information about other XML features you might find useful, plus shortcuts and charts for quick reference when working with the XML Editor.

USING XML EDITOR TOOLBARS

The XML Editor has two local toolbars:

-   **Top toolbar** — To switch view modes and add links, cross-references, and images.

Figure 2-3:
Top toolbar

- **Bottom toolbar** — To change the magnification of the text in Web Layout mode, to page through a document in Print Layout mode, and to view structure bars.

Figure 2-4:
Bottom toolbar in
Web Layout mode

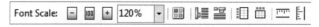

Figure 2-5
Bottom toolbar in
Page Layout mode

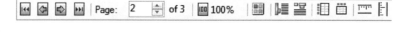

See Appendix C: XML Editor Reference, for complete list of toolbar buttons.

USING STRUCTURE BARS

Structure bars—visual cues that show the structure of a topic's tags—provide a quick and convenient way to access XML Editor features (such as inserting rows and columns in tables). Flare contains these structure bars:

- **Tag bars** — Appear to the left of the content area and show tags for each block in your topic. (The highlighted bar shows which block your cursor is in.)

Figure 2-6:
Tag bars

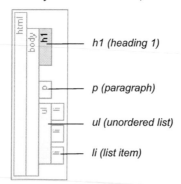

- **Span bars** — Appear at the top of the content area and show span tags—formatting such as bold, italics, and conditional text applied directly to characters.

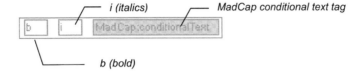

Figure 2-7:
Span bars

Note — Figure 2-11 shows both tag and span bars in the XML Editor window.

- **Table Row bars** — Show structure bars for rows in the table in which your cursor is positioned. There is one numbered bar for each header row and one numbered bar for each body row. (The following figure has one header row and four body rows.)

Figure 2-8:
Table row
bars

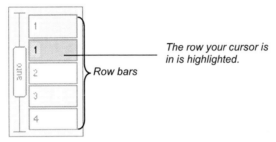

- **Table Column Bars** — Show structure bars for columns in the table in which your cursor is positioned. There is one bar for each column.

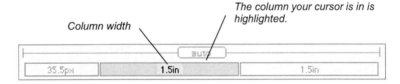

Figure 2-9:
Table column
bars

Structure bar menus

Besides providing visual cues, structure bars provide menus for
working with the text in your topics. Right-clicking a structure bar
causes its menu to appear. Left-clicking selects the block or table.

Figure 2-10:
Menu for
a tag
structure
bar

TOGGLING TAG AND SPAN BARS ON AND OFF

To view more of a topic, you may want to toggle tag and span bars
off in the XML Editor tab for that topic. If you use them frequently,
you may want to toggle them on.

> **Note** — Structure bars can be turned on for one topic and off for another.

Figure 2-11:
*XML Editor
tag and
span bars*

Span bar

Tag bars

To ...	Click ...
Toggle the tag bars on or off	
Tag bars appear on the left and show tags that surround text blocks.	
Toggle the span bars on or off	
Span bars appear at the top and show character formatting, such as bold, italics, and condition tags.	

VIEWING MARKERS

Markers are used to flag certain elements (such as index entries, bookmarks, and variables) that you've inserted into a topic or snippet. You can view or hide them by selecting **Show Markers** from the list on the **Toggle show tags** button of the XML Top toolbar.

Marker

Figure 2-12:
*Bookmark
marker in
view*

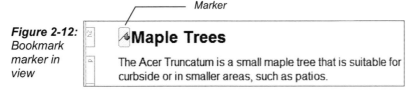

You'll learn more about markers later when we discuss creating an index in Step 4: Create Navigation Aids. See "Creating index entries" on page 186.

WHAT'S NEXT?

Ready to learn more about Flare?

The next chapter, Step 3: Develop Content, describes how to develop content after you have entered or imported it. Specifically, you'll explore how to work with lists, tables, images, styles, special symbols and characters, image thumbnails, and text redaction.

Step 3:
Develop Content

STEP 5: Create Output
5A: Print Output
5B: Online Output

STEP 4:
Create
Nav Aids

STEP 3:
Develop
Content

STEP 2:
Learn the
XML Editor

STEP 1:
Get Started

In this chapter ...
➤ Copy text into a topic
➤ Delete a topic
➤ Check for links to files
➤ Work with lists
➤ Work with tables
➤ Work with images
➤ Show image thumbnails
➤ Add symbols and
   special characters
➤ Format your content
➤ Customize styles
➤ Mark text for redaction

OVERVIEW

Throughout this book, you'll see **content** and **topic** used often. Let's take a moment to review what these terms mean:

- A **topic** is a standalone unit of content. Each topic is a file (with an .htm extension) that conforms to the XML specification.

- **Content** is various types of information contained in a topic, such as text, tables, lists, images, links, and multimedia.

A Flare **project** is simply a collection of topics and related files, which are stored in **project folders**.

In this chapter, you'll learn how to:

- Copy and paste content into a topic (without importing it)

- Delete a topic

- See what a file links to

- Add lists, tables, images, and special characters to topics

- Format your content

- Customize styles

- Mark sensitive text to be concealed (text redaction)

Your content can be new or imported (see Appendix B: Import Content, for more about importing content). This chapter does *not* describe how to create navigational aids (links, TOCs, indexes) that point to topics. We'll cover those in Step 4: Create Navigation Aids.

Let's begin by learning how to copy text into a topic.

> **Note** — To learn how to create new topics, see "Adding a topic" on page 49.

COPYING AND PASTING TEXT INTO A TOPIC

There may be times when you have small pieces of text you want to insert into topics. Copying and pasting is the fastest and easiest way to do it. This method works well for small blocks of text that will not become standalone topics.

Flare's paste feature is smart! It lets you decide which format to use when pasting the text.

To copy and paste text into a topic:

1. Open the Flare topic you want to paste the text into.

2. Select the source text and press **CTRL + C** to copy it (from Word, FrameMaker, another Flare topic, or any other word processing application).

3. Place your cursor where you want to insert the text and press **CTRL + V**. If you're pasting content from another application, the Paste Text dialog opens and shows a preview of the text you are pasting; otherwise, the content is pasted immediately.

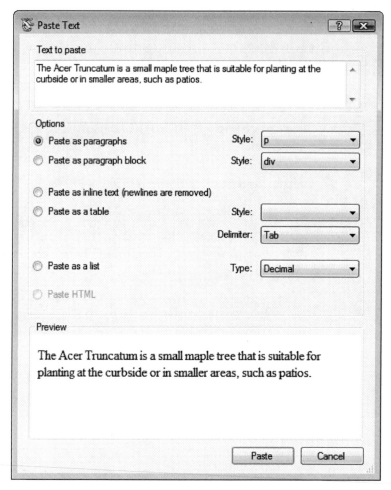

4. In the Options section, choose how you want the text pasted (as paragraphs, paragraph block, list, table, etc.). To the right of your choice, select the style to apply to the text (if applicable).

5. Click **Paste** to paste the text.

DELETING A TOPIC

You can delete a topic from your project, but use caution when doing so, as other topics or project files might link to that topic. When you delete a topic, its index markers are also deleted.

> **Best Practice** — Before deleting a topic, save a backup copy of your project. Then check for and remove links to that topic. See "Checking for links to a topic" on page 102.

Use the following procedure to delete a topic from your project.

To delete a topic:

1. Make sure that the Flare project is open and the Content Explorer is in view.

2. Do one of the following:

   - Select the topic in the Content Explorer and select **Edit → Delete**.

   - Right-click the topic and select **Delete** from the menu.

3. Click **OK** to confirm the deletion.

   If the topic has links to other files, such as links to other topics or a TOC, the Link Update dialog opens.

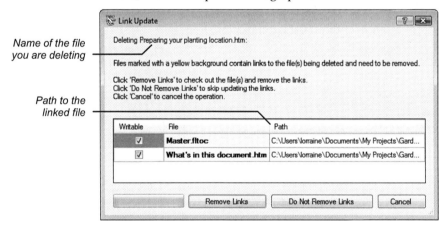

Name of the file you are deleting

Path to the linked file

4. Do one of the following:

To ...	Do this ...
Delete the topic and remove all links to it	Click **Remove Links**. > **Note** — *Removing* the link to a TOC creates an unlinked TOC item. *Removing* the link to another topic leaves the unlinked text of the link in the other topic.

To ...	Do this ...
Delete the topic without removing links to it	Click **Do Not Remove Links**.
	Note — *Leaving* the link to a TOC or other topic creates a broken link in the TOC or topic.
Cancel without deleting this topic	Click **Cancel**.

If you selected **Remove Links** or **Do Not Remove Links**, the topic is deleted from your project.

5. Click **Save All** [icon] to save your work.

CHECKING FOR LINKS TO A TOPIC

The Link Viewer window lets you see what a topic or file is linked to. You can check links to and from any project file, such as topics, TOCs, targets, snippets, skins, even variable sets. For example, you might want to see if a topic is included in a TOC before you delete that topic.

Use the following procedure to check for links to and from a topic or project file.

To check for links:

1. From the Content Explorer or Project Organizer, open the topic or project file you want to check links for.

> **Tip** — To open the Link Viewer window without first opening the topic right-click the topic or project file and select **View Links** from the menu.

2. Select **View → Link Viewer**. The Link Viewer window opens in the right pane (by default).

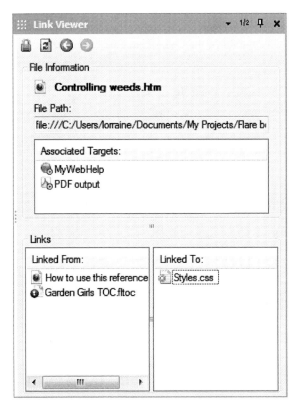

Broken links are identified in the Link Viewer window with a red icon [image].

3. (*Optional*) Complete the following tasks as needed.

To ...	Do this ...
Open a linked file	Double-click the file name in the Link Viewer. (You can then change or remove the link, if you wish.)
View links for a different topic or file	▪ Click the file's tab (if the file is open in the middle pane). ▪ Open the file. (It becomes the active topic or file.) ▪ Right-click the file in the Content Explorer or Project Organizer and select View Links.

To ...	Do this ...
Refresh the Link Viewer window (Helpful if you make changes to links.)	Click **Refresh** 🔳 in the Link Viewer toolbar.
Toggle between locking and unlocking what's currently shown in the Link Viewer window (Locking lets you activate other topics and files without changing the display.)	Click **Lock the Link Viewer** 🔒 in the Link Viewer toolbar.
View the previous set of links you've already viewed	Click **Show links for previous file** 🔵 in the Link Viewer toolbar.
View the next set of links you've already viewed	Click **Show links for next file** 🔵 in the Link Viewer toolbar.

4. Close the Link Viewer window.

WORKING WITH LISTS

As with most word processing programs, Flare lets you add various types of lists to your content, including:

- Single-level lists

- Multi-level lists

- Numbered lists, sequenced by numbers or letters

- Bulleted lists

You can also add items to lists, rearrange and sort them, and merge lists.

CREATING A LIST

Before you create a list, you should know your options.

DECISION TIME!

✓ Do you want to create a bulleted list or a numbered list?

✓ If you want a bulleted list, what type of bullets do you want (black circle, empty circle, or square)?

✓ If you want a numbered list, what type of numbers do you want (Arabic, lower-case alphabetic, upper-case alphabetic, lower-case roman numerals, or upper-case roman numerals)?

Note — In the XML world, bulleted lists are also called **unordered lists** because the order of the items *is insignificant*. Numbered lists, such as step-by-step procedures, are called **ordered lists** because the order of list items *is* important.

Creating a single-level list

Use this procedure to create single-level bulleted or numbered lists.

To create a single-level list:

1. In the desired topic, place your cursor where you want the list to start.

2. If the Text Format toolbar is not in view, click **Open the Text Format Toolbar** F in the XML Editor's toolbar.

3. Click the list button's right arrow.

   Note — The appearance of the list button changes to reflect the type of list you last chose. For example here are just a few possibilities for the appearance of the list button: ▤ ▾ ▤ ▾ ▤ ▾

   If the list type you want is the one last used, you can click the button instead of the right arrow and skip Step 4, next.

▤	Bullet List ————————————	black circular bullet
▤	Circle Bullet List ————————	empty circular bullet
▤	Square Bullet List ———————	square bullet
▤	Numbered List	
▤	Lower-alpha Numbered List	
▤	Upper-alpha Numbered List	
▤	Lower-roman Numbered List	
▤	Upper-roman Numbered List	

4. Select the type of list you want to create.

5. Type the text of the list item.

6. At the end of the line for the first list item, press **ENTER** (only once). A second list item is created.

> *Tip* — If you press **ENTER** more than once, Flare thinks that you're done creating the list. Instead of giving you more list items, it gives you paragraphs in which to type text. If this happens, simply place your cursor at the end of the last list item you typed, and press **ENTER**. Your list will continue where you left off.

7. Continue adding items if desired (Steps 5 and 6 above).

> *Note* — You can also create a list by a) typing the text first, selecting it, and then selecting the type of list to apply to the text or b) placing your cursor where you want to start the list, selecting **Format → List**, and selecting the type of list.

Creating a multi-level list

You've just seen how to create a simple one-level numbered or bulleted list. But not all lists are simple. For example, if you're writing step-by-step instructions, you might need to break out one step into a series of smaller tasks—each one a step.

Example of a multi-level list

1. First numbered item
   a. First second-level item
   b. Second second-level item
2. Second numbered item
3. Third numbered item

Use the following procedure to create a multi-level list with Flare's indenting feature.

> **Note** — To learn how to create a multi-level list by using styles, search on "creating multi-level lists" in the Flare Help system.

To create a multi-level list:

1. Create a single-level list that contains all of the items.

2. Indent the desired items by clicking **Indent Items**.

3. Apply the desired list type to the indented items. (Click the list button's right arrow and select the list type.)

> **Note** — You can also place your cursor where you want to start the list and select **Format → List**. Then select the type of list.

CHANGING LISTS

Flare includes many options for changing lists, such as:

- Rearranging items

- Sorting items

- Assigning a different number to an item

- Merging two or more lists into one

The **Drop down menu of assorted list actions** button shows what you can do with lists. Next, you'll read about some of the more frequently used options.

Figure 3-1:
Menu of
assorted list
actions

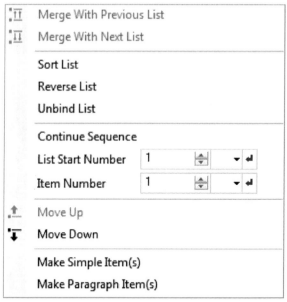

Rearranging lists

You can easily rearrange the items in a list by moving them up or down.

 To rearrange a list:

1. Place your cursor within the list item to be moved.

2. Click **Drop down menu of assorted list actions** .

   > **Note** — You can also place your cursor on any item in the list and select **Format → List → List Actions**.

3. Select **Move Up** or **Move Down**.

4. Continue moving items until the list is arranged to your liking.

Sorting a list

List items can be sorted in ascending order based on the text contained in each list item. For example, suppose you have the following list items:

1. AAA
2. SSS
3. MM
4. MMMMM
5. BB
6. FFF

A sorted list would look like this.

1. AAA
2. BB
3. FFF
4. MM
5. MMMMM
6. SSS

Notice that the sequence numbers don't stay with the text. In this case, the list started with number 1 and it still does, even after being sorted.

To sort a list:

1. Place your cursor anywhere in the list.

2. Click **Drop down menu of assorted list actions**.

> **Note** — You can also place your cursor on any item in the list and select **Format → List → List Actions.**

3. Select **Sort List**.

   The list items are sorted in ascending alphabetical order.

> **Note** — To switch the order from ascending to descending or vice versa, select **Reverse List** from the List Actions menu.

Re-numbering a list

Flare lets you assign a starting sequence number to any item in an ordered list. Items that follow that item will automatically be re-numbered (unless you have set their starting sequence number.)

You can also reset the sequence number of an item. Resetting assigns the next number in the sequence (based on the previous list item).

The **Drop down menu of assorted list actions** 🔲▾ contains three options for setting and resetting sequence numbers in ordered lists.

Figure 3-2:
Options for setting and resetting sequence numbers

Continue Sequence	
List Start Number	1
Item Number	1

We'll talk about these options next.

🎁 To assign a sequence number to the first item in a list:

1. Place your cursor on any item in the list.

2. Click **Drop down menu of assorted list actions** 🔲▾.

    > **Note** — You can also place your cursor on any item in the list and select **Format → List → List Actions**.

3. Select a starting number by clicking the up or down arrow next to **List Start Number**, then click the blue arrow on the right.

List Start Number   1 — Click to set the starting number.   Then click here.

The first item in the list is set to the starting number you selected, and the remaining list items are re-sequenced in ascending one-unit increments. For example, if you set the first item to 20, the remaining items will be numbered starting at 21.

To assign a sequence number to any item in a list:

1. Place your cursor on the list item whose number you want to set.

> **Note** — You can also place your cursor on any item in the list and select **Format → List → List Actions.**

2. Click **Drop down menu of assorted list actions** .

> **Note** — Notice that our cursor was on the list item whose number is currently "9" and "**Item Number 9**" appears in the List Actions menu. (Don't get confused between an item's sequence number and its placement in the list. Just because its sequence number is 9 does not mean that it's the ninth item in the list.)

3. Select a starting number for that item by clicking the up or down arrow next to **Item Number**, then click the blue arrow on the right.

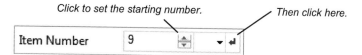

The item is set to the starting number you selected and the items that follow it are re-sequenced in ascending order.

Merging lists

If your topic has lists that need to be combined, you can easily merge them. But before merging them, the lists must be consecutive (in other words, you cannot combine lists that have non-list elements between them). Make sure you delete any non-list items before trying to merge two lists or move the second list so it immediately follows the first.

> **Tip** — To merge three lists, just merge the first two into one, and then merge that list with the next one.

Can I merge different types of lists?

Yes, you can merge two lists that are of different types. For example, you can merge a numbered list with a bulleted list. When Flare combines the lists, it applies the list type from the first list to the second list.

Suppose the first list looks like this:

1. first numbered item
2. second numbered item
3. third numbered item

And the second list looks like this:

- first bullet item
- second bullet item
- third bullet item

After you combine them, the list will look like this:

1. first numbered item
2. second numbered item
3. third numbered item
4. first bullet item
5. second bullet item
6. third bullet item

What happens to the sequence numbers when I merge lists?

As you can see from the example, if the first list is an ordered list, Flare automatically applies the next number in sequence to the first item in the second list. So the result is a seamless, perfectly sequenced group of list items.

To merge two lists:

1. In the topic that contains the two lists, verify that there are no non-list elements between the two lists.

   > **Note** — You might have to remove the text that's between the lists or copy the second list and paste it immediately after the first list. (To delete text, see "Deleting text" on page 317.)

2. Place your cursor on any item in either list.

3. Click **Drop down menu of assorted list actions** .

> **Note** — You can also place your cursor on any item in the list and select **Format → List → List Actions**.

4. Select **Merge With Next List** or **Merge With Previous List** (depending on which list—the first or second—your cursor is located in).

WORKING WITH TABLES

Tables allow you to organize information in a graphical format that is easier for most people to read than blocks of text. Tables consist of cells (the intersection of rows and columns), which can contain text, images, variables, or snippets.

ADDING A TABLE

Follow these instructions to add a table to the active topic.

To add a table:

1. Place your cursor where you want to insert the table.

2. Select **Table → Insert → Table**. The Insert Table dialog opens (page 153).

3. Fill in the fields on each tab of the Insert Table dialog. For descriptions of the fields, see Table 3-2 and Table 3-3.

> **Tip** — You can easily change a table's characteristics later by selecting **Table → Table Properties**, or by using styles.

4. When finished, click **OK**.

You now have a table that is ready for content. To type text in the table's cells, simply position your cursor in a cell and type. You can also add images and links. To format the table, see page 139.

SHOWING GRID LINES

Table gridlines help you to see where table cells are. You can easily turn gridlines on or off as needed.

Grid lines appear in the XML Editor only; they do not show up in your output. (If you want borders around cells, see "Formatting tables" on page 139.)

To show grid lines:

- Select **Table → Show Gridlines**.

USING TABLE STRUCTURE BARS

With Flare's XML Editor you can show or hide structure bars that represent your table's rows and columns.

- **Table Row Bars** — Appear to the left of your topic. There is one numbered bar for each header and body row in your table.

- **Table Column Bars** — Appear above your topic. There is one bar, labeled with the column's width, for each column in your table.

Table row and column bars make it easy to insert, delete, and resize rows and columns in your tables. You can also use Flare's **Table** menu to delete rows and columns.

To show table row and column bars:

- Click anywhere within the table and do the following:

Click ...	To show ...
	Column bars
	Row bars

Here's a table with row and column bars in view.

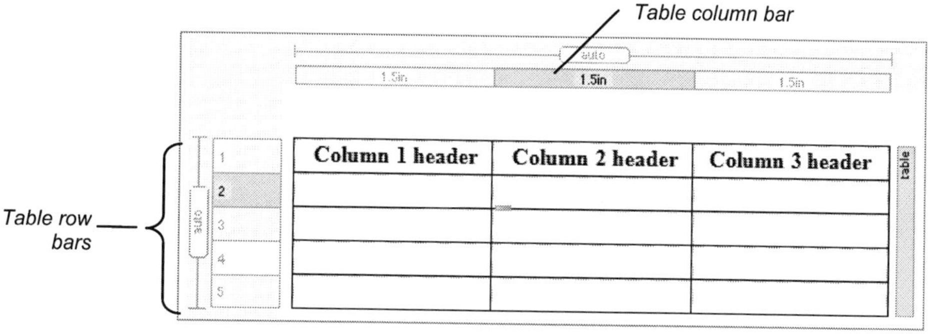

Table column bar

	Column 1 header	Column 2 header	Column 3 header
1			
2			
3			
4			
5			

Table row bars

Structure bars have menus with choices that are meaningful based on your cursor location. For more information about structure bars and their menus, see "Using structure bars" on page 92.

To select a row or column:

1. View the table row or table column bars.

2. Click the applicable row or column bar.

   Note — You can also place your cursor in the desired row or column and select **Table → Select → Column or Row**.

To select the entire table:

1. Place your cursor anywhere in the table. A table bar appears to the right of the table.

2. Click the table bar and choose **Select**.

   Note — You can also place your cursor in the table and select **Table → Select → Table**.

INSERTING ROWS AND COLUMNS

Follow these instructions to insert rows and columns in tables.

To insert a row:

1. If not in view, show table row bars (see page 114).

2. Click the bar for the row after which (or before which) you want to insert a row.

3. Right-click the table row bar and select **Insert New (Above)** or **Insert New (Below)**.

   A blank row is inserted either above or below the row whose bar you clicked.

Tips
You can also place your cursor where you want to add the row and select **Table → Rows Above** or **Rows Below**.
To insert a row at the end of the table, place your cursor at the end of the table's last cell and press **TAB**.

To insert a column:

1. If not in view, show table column bars (see page 114).

2. Click the bar for the column after which (or before which) you want to insert a column.

3. Right-click the table column bar and select **Insert New (Left)** or **Insert New (Right)**.

   A blank column is inserted to the left or right of the column whose bar you clicked.

Note — You can also place your cursor where you want to add a column and select **Table → Insert → Columns to the Left** or **Columns to the Right**.

DELETING ROWS AND COLUMNS

Follow these instructions to delete rows and columns from tables.

To delete a row or column:

1. If not in view, show the row or column structure bars (see page 114).

2. Right-click the applicable table row or column bar and select **Delete**.

> **Note** — You can also place your cursor in the row or column you want to delete and select **Table → Delete → Columns** or **Rows**.

RESIZING ROWS AND COLUMNS

Follow these instructions to resize rows and columns in tables.

To resize a row:

1. If not in view, show the row structure bars (see page 114).

2. In the row structure bars, hover your cursor between the row you want to resize and the row below it (over the row numbers) until you see a vertical double-arrow.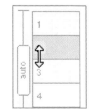

3. Drag the arrow to change the row's height.

   Flare shows the height of the row in pixels, which changes dynamically as you drag the row. When you stop dragging, the structure bar shows the new height in pixels.

> **Note** — You can also right-click the row's structure bar and use the resize arrows in the menu to set the size. (Click the blue arrow when done.)

🎓 To resize a column:

1. If not in view, show the column structure bars (see page 114).

2. In the column structure bars, hover your cursor over the line between the column you want to resize and the column to its right until you see a horizontal double-arrow.

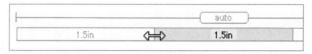

3. Drag the arrow to change the column's width.

    Flare shows the width of the column in pixels, which changes dynamically as you drag the column. When you stop dragging, the structure bar shows the new width in pixels.

> **Note** — You can also resize a column by right-clicking the column's structure bar whose menu shows the current size Use the resize arrows in the menu to set the size. (Click the blue arrow when done.)

MOVING ROWS AND COLUMNS

You can move rows and columns in your table by dragging and dropping. Here's how to do it.

🎓 To move a row:

1. If not in view, show the row structure bars (see page 114).

2. Move your cursor over the structure bar of the row to be moved. The mouse pointer turns into a hand.

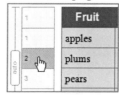

3. Drag the row and drop it when the arrow points to the place you want to move it to.

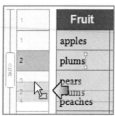

Here's the result after moving
the sample row.

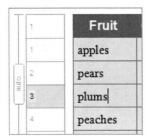

To move a column:

1. If not in view, show the column structure bars (see page 114).

2. Move your cursor over the structure bar of the column to be moved. The mouse pointer turns into a hand.

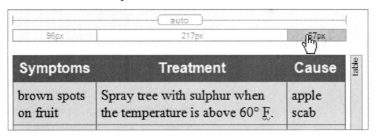

3. Drag the column and drop it when the arrow points to the place you want to move it to.

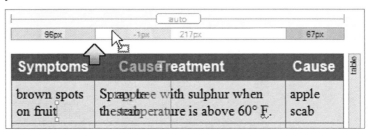

Here's the result after moving the sample column.

		auto	
96px	67px	217px	
Symptoms	**Cause**	**Treatment**	table
brown spots on fruit	apple scab	Spray tree with sulphur when the temperature is above 60° F.	

WORKING WITH IMAGES

Flare lets you add images, such as photographs, screen captures, and illustrations, to your topics.

The image can be a vector or raster file in any of these formats: BMP, EMF, EXPS, GIF, HDP, JPG, JPEG, PNG, SWF, TIF, TIFF, WDP, WMF, XAML, and XPS.

IMAGE THUMBNAILS

Starting with Flare Version 5, you can show images as thumbnails (miniature, low-resolution images) in your online output or in the XML Editor window. This gives you more room for viewing text in the XML Editor. In output, this lets users see more of a topic's text. See "Showing images as thumbnails" on page 127.

WHERE ARE IMAGES STORED?

By default, Flare stores images in the Resources\Images folder of the Content Explorer. If the image you want to add is not already in this folder, Flare puts it there when you add the image to your topic.

> **Tip** — If desired, you can copy images to the Resources\Images folder from Windows Explorer before you're ready to add them to topics.

You can add an image from the Resources\Images folder to any topic in your project. By reusing images, you'll keep your project size smaller, since Flare keeps only one copy of each image in this folder.

FLARE MANAGES IMAGE FILE CHANGES

When you add an image to a topic, Flare keeps a link to that image. If you later change its name in the Resources\Images folder—even from Windows Explorer—Flare handles the name change without any further action on your part. Your link between the file and the image in your topic will not be broken! The Content Explorer's Resources\Images folder shows the new name, and the link in the topic is also correct. How cool is that?

And here's another feature that we think is pretty neat. If you edit the image using an external application and replace it (keeping the file name the same), the image in your topic is automatically updated.

An example

Let's say that you copied a photograph called "MyPhoto.jpg" to the Resources\Images folder, inserted it into a topic, and then noticed that the photo has red-eye. To fix it, you can just open the photo in your photo editing software, remove the red-eye, and re-save the photo to the Resources\Images folder. When you view the photo in your topic you'll see that the red-eye is gone!

ADDING AN IMAGE

Follow these instructions to add an image to a topic and to the open project.

To add an image to a topic:

1. Place your cursor where you want to insert the image in the topic.

2. Select **Insert → Picture**. The Insert Picture dialog opens, showing the images in the Resources\Images folder.

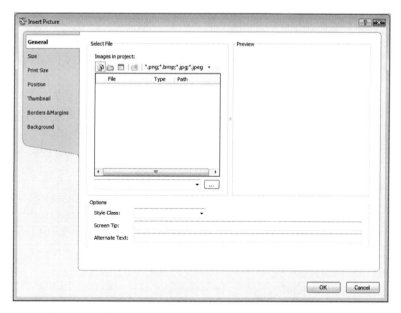

3. In the General tab, select an image to insert by doing one of the following:

   ▪ Select one of the images listed.

      – or –

   ▪ Click [...] to navigate to it.

   A preview of the image appears at the right of the dialog.

4. (*Optional*) Select a style to apply to the image. If no style is selected, the style defaults to "img."

5. (*Optional*) Type a screen tip (text that appears when you hover your cursor over the image in the built output).

6. (*Optional*) Type alternate text if you need to produce output that is compliant with Section 508 of the United States Rehabilitation Act. Alternate text could be useful for visually impaired individuals who might use screen readers. (For more information, search for "Section 508" in the Flare Help system.)

7. Click **OK**.

If the image is not already in your project, a dialog confirms that the image will be copied to your project.

8. Click **OK** to copy the image to your project.

    The picture is added to your topic and to your project's Resources\Images folder (if not already there).

9. Save your topic.

ADDING SCREEN CAPTURES FROM MADCAP CAPTURE

If you have MadCap Capture™, Flare lets you add and edit screen captures directly from Capture. Capture stores graphic elements in layers, so you can capture a screen shot and add graphic elements (like callouts) to it. To find out more, see your MadCap Capture Help system.

RESIZING AN IMAGE

After you add images to your topics, you have a few ways to resize them. You can resize an image locally or you can control an image's size with styles.

So which method is right for you? Here's what we suggest.

Do this ...	When ...
Resize images locally	You have only a few images in a project and image sizing doesn't need to be consistent, or you have one or two images that need to be sized differently from the others.
Resize images with styles	You have many images and need consistent image sizing throughout your project

Resizing and image quality

Flare supports images in vector or raster format. The type of format determines if image quality is affected when images are resized or cropped.

- **Vector images** — Can easily be resized without any loss of quality. (Vector images are composed of points connected by lines and curves that form objects that are defined mathematically.)

- **Raster (bitmap) images** — Can be resized, but when you enlarge them, the image might become blurry because the dots move farther apart. (Raster images are composed of a collection of dots, called pixels, arranged in a grid pattern called a bitmap.) You can however, crop a raster image with no loss of quality.

Digital cameras and scanners generally create files in raster formats, such as JPG, BMP, TIF, TIFF, GIF, and PNG files. Some illustration applications (such as CorelDRAW®) create files in vector format; others (such as Adobe Photoshop®) create files in raster format.

> **Best Practice** — Create your images in their final size if possible, to avoid any issues with resizing.

Resizing images locally

Here are two ways to resize images locally.

To resize an image locally by using a mouse:

1. Hover your cursor over the image to be resized. A button appears in the image's lower right corner.

2. Drag the button diagonally *toward* the center of the image (to reduce image size) or diagonally *away from* the center of the image (to enlarge the image).

To resize an image locally by using properties:

1. In the XML Editor, right-click the image to be resized.

2. Select **Edit Picture** from the menu. The Edit Picture dialog opens.

3. Click the **Size** tab.

4. On the **Size** tab, set image sizes as follows:

To ...	Do this ...
Set an exact image size	In the Size section, set the Width or Height and unit of measure. To maintain an image's aspect ratio (keep it in proportion), either set the image to the desired Width (select **Length** to do this) and select **Automatic** for the Height, or vice versa.

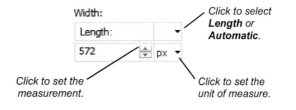

To ...	Do this ...
Set a minimum image size	In the Minimum Size section, set the minimum Length and unit of measure. To maintain an image's aspect ratio (keep it in proportion), set either the Width or the Height, but not both. **Note** — If the original image is *smaller* than the measurement you set, Flare enlarges the image. If the original image is *larger*, Flare doesn't change the image size.
Set a maximum image size	In the Maximum Size section, set the maximum Length and unit of measure. To maintain an image's aspect ratio (keep it in proportion), set either the Width or the Height, but not both. **Note** — If the original image is *larger* than the measurement you set, Flare reduces the image size. If the original image is *smaller*, Flare doesn't change the image size.

Important — If you set Size tab options only, those settings will be used for both online and print output. If you set options on the Print Size tab also, then its options will be used for print output and Size tab options will be used for online output.

5. If you want the image to be one size for online output and a different size for print output, click the **Print Size** tab to set the image size for print output only. (The **Size** tab settings will then be used for online output only.)

   Use the chart above to set the options for the **Print Size** tab.

6. Click **OK**. The image is resized according to the size(s) you entered.

Resizing images with styles

Use the "img" style or a class of the img style to control the size of images in your topics.

⚠ To resize an image with styles:

1. Open your stylesheet in Simplified View.

2. Double-click the **img** style or the style class applied to the image you want to resize.

    > **Note** — The Size tab of the Properties dialog used by the Stylesheet Editor in Simplified view is identical to the Size tab of the Properties dialog you use when formatting an image locally.

3. On the Size tab, set image sizes as described in Step 3 of the procedure for formatting an image locally by using properties (the previous procedure).

For more information about formatting with styles, see "Applying styles from a stylesheet" on page 142.

SHOWING IMAGES AS THUMBNAILS

Flare lets you show images as thumbnails (miniature, low-resolution images) in your online output or in a topic as you edit it.

WHY SHOW IMAGES AS THUMBNAILS?

Viewing images as thumbnails gives you more room for viewing text as you edit a topic in the XML Editor. In output, it lets users of your content see more of the topic's text while still giving them the option of viewing the full-size image. You can easily see the full-size image by clicking or moving the mouse over the thumbnail, depending on how you format the thumbnail image.

SHOWING IMAGES AS THUMBNAILS WHILE EDITING A TOPIC

In the XML Editor, you can easily toggle between viewing images in the active topic as thumbnails and viewing them in full size. You can set this option on a topic-by-topic basis. If you choose to view image thumbnails in the active topic, the images are reduced to a maximum size of 48 pixels high by default. (You can change the maximum size.)

> **Note** — Viewing images as thumbnails in the active topic does not affect how those images appear in the output. However, if images are formatted as thumbnails for output, those images will appear as thumbnails in the XML Editor. To view images as thumbnails in output, see "Showing images as thumbnails in online output" on page 129.

Example

Here's an example of a topic with a full-size image.

Figure 3-3:
A full-size image in a topic.

Here's an example that shows a Limelight Hydrangea when its blooms are first open. These snowball-like blooms open to a creamy white, but change to a mix of light pink and light green. Gardeners often cut the blooms just after they start to turn pink and bring them inside for dried flower arrangements.

The image takes up a good deal of space in the topic. Here's the same topic with image thumbnails turned on.

Figure 3-4:
A thumbnail image in a topic.

Here's an example that shows a Limelight Hydrangea when its blooms are first open. These snowball-like blooms open to a creamy white, but change to a mix of light pink and light green. Gardeners often cut the blooms just after they start to turn pink and bring them inside for dried flower arrangements.

To toggle between thumbnails and full-size images:

Do one of the following:

- Click the arrow to the right of **Show tags** in the XML Editor's top toolbar, and select **Show All Images As Thumbnails**.

- Select **View → Show → Show All Images As Thumbnails**.

All images in the topic are either shown as thumbnails or full size (depending on how you viewed them previously).

SHOWING IMAGES AS THUMBNAILS IN ONLINE OUTPUT

To minimize the space taken up by images in your online output, you can show images as thumbnails. Users will then see more of a topic's text. When they want to view the image, they either click the thumbnail or move the mouse over it (depending on how you set up the thumbnail). The full-size image appears in a window or popup.

An example

Here's an example that shows how your image might look if you don't use thumbnails in your output.

Figure 3-5: Online output showing a full-size image (no thumbnail image)

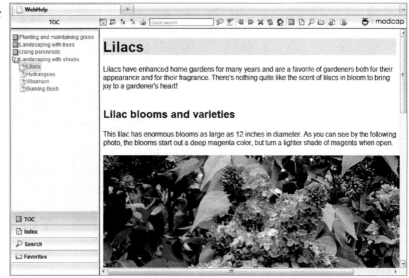

Figure 3-6 shows the same topic with images shown as thumbnails. In this example, we set up the thumbnails to show the full-size image when we move the mouse over a thumbnail.

Figure 3-6:
Online
output
showing an
image
thumbnail

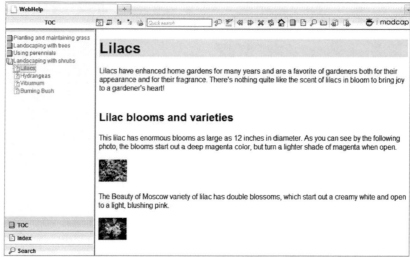

When you move the mouse over the thumbnail, the full-size image opens in a popup.

Figure 3-7:
Full-size
image that
appears
when the
mouse
hovers over
the
thumbnail

How to show thumbnails in online output

You'll show thumbnails in online output by formatting the image, either locally or with a style from a stylesheet.

> **DECISION TIME!**
>
> ✓ Do you want to apply thumbnails to only one or two images? If so, apply local formatting to images.
>
> ✓ Do you want many images in your project to appear as thumbnails in output? If so, apply styles to images.

Applying local formatting to images

When you want to format only a few images as thumbnails, local formatting is a fine choice. To format all images in your project as thumbnails, it's best to use a style. See "Applying formatting to images from styles" on page 133.

To format an image as a thumbnail with local formatting:

1. Open the topic containing the image.

2. Right-click the image.

3. Select **Edit Picture** from the menu. The Edit Picture dialog opens.

4. Click the **Thumbnail** tab.

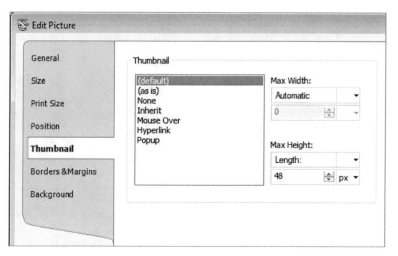

5. Select one of the following options:

Select this option ...	If you want the user to see the full-size image ...
Mouse Over	In a popup window when the mouse is over the thumbnail.
Hyperlink	In a new window after clicking the thumbnail.
Popup	In a popup window after clicking the thumbnail.

6. To set a maximum thumbnail image size, set either the Max Width or the Max Height (but not both). Select **Length**, a unit of measure, and a value for the unit of measure.

7. Click **OK**. The image is shown as a thumbnail in the XML Editor window (even if the **Show All Images As Thumbnails** option is not selected).

8. Click **Save All** 🖼 to save your work.

After building your online output, you'll see the image appear as a thumbnail as in Figure 3-6. View the full-size image by clicking it or by moving the mouse over it (depending on the choice you made in Step 5 above).

Applying formatting to images from styles

If you want to format more than one or two images as thumbnails, then styles are a better choice than local formatting.

To format images as thumbnails with styles:

1. Open the topic containing the image.

2. Right-click the image and select **Style Class → Edit Style Class** from the menus. The stylesheet opens in the Stylesheet Editor.

    If the Editor is in Simplified View, the style applied to the image is highlighted at the top of the styles list. If in Advanced View, the style is highlighted in the Styles column on the left.

    This procedure covers the Stylesheet Editor in Simplified View, which you can see in the following figure.

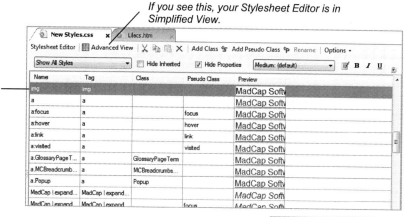

If you see this, your Stylesheet Editor is in Simplified View.

The style applied to the image we right-clicked

3. If you're in Advanced View, you'll see the Simplified View button to the right of "Stylesheet Editor." Click it to switch to Simplified View.

    > **Tip** — Create a class of the img style to use only for thumbnails and use the img style for other images that you don't want displayed as thumbnails.

4. Double-click the highlighted style. The Properties dialog opens.

5. Click the **Thumbnail** tab.

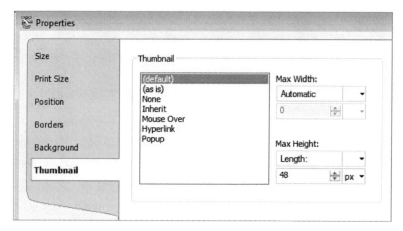

6. Select one of the following options:

Select this option ...	If you want the user to see the full-size image ...
Mouse Over	In a popup window when the mouse is over the thumbnail.
Hyperlink	In a new window after clicking the thumbnail.
Popup	In a popup window after clicking the thumbnail.

7. To set a maximum thumbnail image size, set either the Max Width or the Max Height (but not both). Select **Length**, a unit of measure, and a value for the unit of measure.

8. Click **OK** then click **Save All** to save your work.

9. Close the Stylesheet Editor.

    The image is shown as a thumbnail in the XML Editor window (even if the **Show All Images As Thumbnails** option is not selected).

After building your online output, you'll see the image as a thumbnail as in Figure 3-6. View the full-size image by clicking it or by moving the mouse over it (depending on the choice you made in Step 6 previously).

Other options

Selecting **None** causes the full-size to be displayed rather than a thumbnail. **Inherit** causes the image to use the thumbnail settings that are applied to the tag in your topic in which the image is nested.

PROBLEMS WITH THUMBNAIL SETTINGS

When viewing output, if you see a distorted image when you click or when you mouse over the thumbnail, your original image might be larger than the Maximum Width or Maximum Height you set for the "img" tag. Here are two ways to fix this:

- Select Hyperlink instead of selecting Mouse Over or Popup.

- Reduce the size of your original image so it does not exceed the maximum size set for the img style.

ADDING SYMBOLS AND SPECIAL CHARACTERS

To add symbols and special characters:

1. Place your cursor where you want to insert the special character.

2. Do one of the following:

    - To insert the default quick character, click the **Quick Character** ⊟ button.

    - To select a different character to insert, click the down arrow on the **Quick Character** ⊟ button and select the symbol or character from the list.

SETTING THE DEFAULT QUICK CHARACTER

To set the default quick character:

1. Click the down arrow on the **Quick Character** $\boxed{-\text{a}-}\boxed{\blacktriangledown}$ button and select **Select 'Quick Character'** from the list. The Quick Character dialog opens.

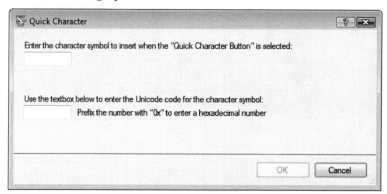

2. In the top box, type the character to be inserted *or* in the bottom box, type the Unicode code for the character or symbol you want to be the default quick character.

FORMATTING YOUR CONTENT

Formatting makes your content look better. For example, you can make your content pop by giving it a background color or changing the color of your text. Even a few changes make a big difference!

Typically, you'll want to use different font sizes for different types of headings. And for your body text, you'll likely want a font that is smaller than the font you use for headings. Actually, we can't think of a good reason *not* to format your content.

When you create topics from a Flare template, Flare's **Styles.css** stylesheet is automatically attached (more about stylesheets coming up.) Your topics will have some styles applied, as shown in Figure 3-8.

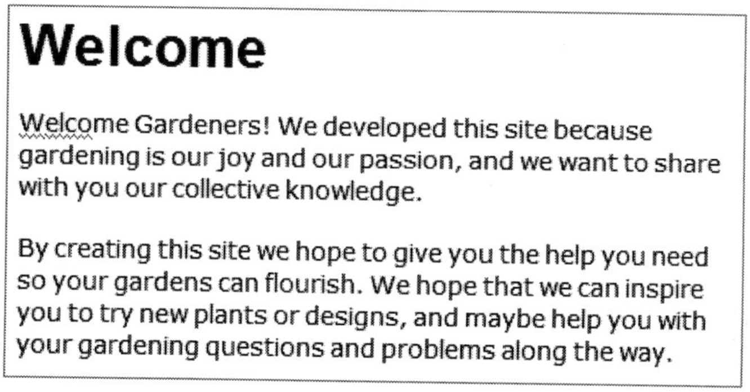

Figure 3-8:
Topic with
default
styles

Welcome

Welcome Gardeners! We developed this site because gardening is our joy and our passion, and we want to share with you our collective knowledge.

By creating this site we hope to give you the help you need so your gardens can flourish. We hope that we can inspire you to try new plants or designs, and maybe help you with your gardening questions and problems along the way.

By changing the formatting, you can add eye-catching touches such as those shown in Figure 3-9.

Figure 3-9:
Topic with
color, italics,
bold added

Welcome

Welcome Gardeners! We developed this site because gardening is our *joy* and our *passion*, and we want to share with you our collective knowledge.

By creating this site we hope to give you the help you need so your gardens can flourish. We hope that we can inspire you to try new plants or designs, and maybe help you with your gardening questions and problems along the way.

WAYS TO FORMAT CONTENT

As mentioned earlier in this book, there are two ways to apply formats to your content:

- With local formatting
- With styles from a stylesheet

We'll cover both of these methods in this section.

WHAT'S THE DIFFERENCE?

Both styles and local formatting can be applied to selected text, text blocks, and tables. The difference between them is how the formatting is applied, how it's maintained, and the amount code each add to your topic files.

Local formatting

Local (inline) formatting is applied by clicking a toolbar button (bold, italics, etc.) **or by setting properties** (bold, font, indentation, etc.) for the selected text, text block, or table. To change the format later, you must find the text that you applied it to. If you applied the same format in many places (in one or more topics), it could be a daunting task.

Formatting with styles

A style's formatting is applied by selecting a style from a stylesheet (a collection of styles). A style is a named set of characteristics (formats) that are contained in a file called a cascading stylesheet (CSS). It's called "cascading" because the styles flow down from higher-level "parent" elements (such as body tags) to lower-level "child" element (such as paragraph tags). Child elements inherit the formatting of their parent elements.

By applying styles to text throughout your project, you can give your project a consistent look that is easy to change. If you need to change the formatting, you change it in one place—in the stylesheet—and the change is propagated everywhere the style is applied.

You can apply a stylesheet to a project to target or to a topic. When applied to a project, the styles are available for all project content. When applied to a target, the styles are available for all target content.

> **Note** — If you use one master stylesheet for a project and another for a target, the stylesheet applied to the target takes precedence. The stylesheet applied to a topic takes precedence over the one applied to a target.

LOCAL FORMATTING VS. STYLES: WHICH TO USE

Both local formatting and styles are useful in different circumstances. Here's some information to help you decide which to use when.

Table 3-1: When to use local formatting vs. styles	Use this option ...	When ...
	Local formatting	▪ You want to apply the format to only one or two areas of text in one topic. (Applying lots of local formats increases the size of the underlying XML code, which means the browser might take longer to display the content for WebHelp.)
		▪ You don't need to use the same formatting in other topics or projects.
		▪ The formatting is not likely to change.
	Style from a CSS	▪ You want your topics to have a consistent appearance.
		▪ You want to use the same formatting in many places in the same or different topics.
		▪ You want to use the same formatting in different projects.
		▪ The formatting is likely to change.

FORMATTING TABLES

Besides local formatting and topic stylesheets, Flare gives you an additional option for formatting tables: table stylesheets. Table stylesheets allow you to define formatting patterns, such as shading on alternating rows or columns. Table stylesheets are an advanced topic not covered in this book.

So which option are you going to choose?

OUR RECOMMENDATION

For your "throwaway" Flare project, we recommend that you start with local formatting. Then use the styles that Flare provides. When you're ready, try changing the properties of those styles as desired.

The default topic stylesheet (Styles.css) contains styles (table, th, td, and tr) for formatting table content.

> **Note** — For more detailed information about styles, see the *MadCap Flare Styles Guide*, available by selecting **Help → Guides → Styles Guide**.

APPLYING LOCAL FORMATTING

You can apply formatting within a text block or to an entire block of text by using the Text Format toolbar or by changing the properties of the text you select or text block your cursor is in.

To apply local formatting to selected text:

1. Select the text to apply the format to.

2. Do one of the following:

    ▪ From the Text Format toolbar, select the toolbar button for the format you want (font, point size, bold, italics, color, background color).

    ▪ Change the properties of the text by selecting **Format → Font**. Then select the font, size, color, style (bold, italics), background color as desired.

To apply local formatting to a text block (paragraph):

1. Place your cursor anywhere in the text block you want to format.

2. Select **Format → Paragraph**. Then change the properties as desired on the various tabs of the Paragraph Properties dialog.

Applying local formatting to tables

If you select "default" for the table style when you insert a table in a topic, your table will be formatted like this:

Figure 3-10:
Default
table style

Most likely, you'll want to format the table for maximum readability (as well as for aesthetics). For example, you might add color to the background or to the text of your table's cells; or maybe you'd like the table header to be distinct from the table rows. You can apply formatting (color, borders, spacing) to tables by using buttons on the Text Format toolbar or by changing the properties of a table's text.

Here's an example of how you can dress up the table shown in Figure 3-10.

Figure 3-11:
Table after
formatting
with
color

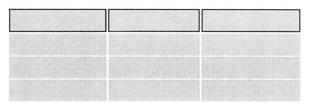

Use this procedure to format tables with local formatting.

To apply local formatting to a table:

- Set the formatting for the text in a table's cells as described in this table:

To ...	Do this ...
Apply a background color to text	Select the text to apply the color to, select **Format → Background Color**, and select a color from the color chart.
Format text in one cell	Click inside the cell you want to format, select **Format → Font**, and select the font characteristics (font, size, style, text color, background color, effects) from the Font Properties dialog. Then select **OK**.
Format text in cells	Select the text to format, select **Format → Font**, and select the font characteristics (font, size, style, text color, background color, effects) from the Font Properties dialog. Then select **OK**.
Do any of the following for one or more cells: • Align the text • Set the first line indentation • Set line spacing • Set borders • Set spacing around cell text (padding) • Set hyphenation	To format one cell, click inside the cell to be formatted. To format contiguous cells, select the cells. Then select **Format → Cell**, and select the paragraph characteristics (space before and after, borders) from the Cell Properties dialog. Then select **OK**.

APPLYING STYLES FROM A STYLESHEET

Flare projects use two types of stylesheets:

- **Topic stylesheets** — Used to format content in your topics.

- **Table stylesheets** — Used for advanced formatting options such as shading on alternating rows and columns. (Table stylesheets are not covered in this book.)

Flare comes packaged with one topic stylesheet (**Styles)** and four table stylesheets (**Basic, Columns, Inner, Rows**). A Flare project can have multiple stylesheets of each type.

In this book, we describe how to apply styles from a topic stylesheet to text in a topic (including text in tables). When you add a table, the *topic* styles "th" (table header) and "td" (table data) are automatically applied to your header and non-header rows. Changing those topic styles changes the look of your table text.

> **Note** — Topic stylesheets are stored in the Resources\Stylesheets folder of the Content Explorer. Table stylesheets are stored in the Resources\TableStyles folder of the Content Explorer.

Figure 3-12: The Styles Stylesheet in the Resources \Stylesheet folder

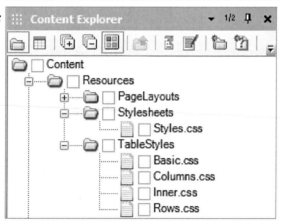

When you create a new Flare project, Flare automatically makes **Styles** the default topic stylesheet for the project. When you create a topic for that project, Flare automatically uses the project's master stylesheet for that topic. So, styles from the default Flare stylesheet are automatically available for your use.

However, Flare does *not* automatically attach table stylesheets to projects. If you want to add a table stylesheet to your project, you can do that when you create the table.

Where do styles come from?

Flare stylesheets use the standard styles (like p and h1 – h6) and properties developed by the World Wide Web Consortium, plus special styles and properties defined by MadCap to support Flare features. MadCap styles begin with "MadCap" (for example, MadCap|xref) and MadCap properties begin with "mc" (such as mc-heading-format).

These styles are automatically included in every Flare stylesheet. You cannot delete standard or MadCap styles; however, you can disable them so they don't appear in the Stylesheet Editor's styles list. We don't recommend that new users disable styles.

> **Important** — Use caution if you disable styles as they will not be available for use in Flare (unless re-enabled).

Applying styles to text

There are different ways to apply a style to text in a topic. You can use the styles list on the Text Format toolbar, the Style window, the Floating Style Picker, or tag structure bars. We'll show you how to use the Text Format toolbar to apply styles.

If the Text Format toolbar is not in view, click **Open the Text Format Toolbar** F in the XML Editor's toolbar.

> **Note** — Use the styles list on the Text Format toolbar, not its formatting buttons.

For text blocks, the tag bar is labeled with the tag, which is named for the style that is applied to the text block ("h2" as shown here).

Tag bar ——— **Growing grass**

The style list on the Text Format toolbar also shows that h2 is currently applied.

Click to show the styles list.

To apply a style to selected text:

1. Select the text to apply the format to.

2. From the styles list on the Text Format toolbar, select the text style you want to apply.

   The style you selected is applied to the text.

To apply a style to a text block:

1. Click anywhere in the text block where you want to apply a style.

2. From the styles list on the Text Format toolbar, select the style you want to apply.

   The style you selected is applied to the text block and the text block's tag is changed to reflect the new style. (Notice in our example that the tag bar now shows h1.)

CUSTOMIZING STYLES

In this section, you'll learn how to customize styles in a topic stylesheet by using Flare's Stylesheet Editor. First, we'll look at what's in a cascading stylesheet.

CASCADING STYLESHEETS

Stylesheet (CSS files) contain style rules that define how your content is formatted. Here's an example of a style rule for the "p" style:

```
p
{
    font-size: 10pt;
    font-family: verdana, sans-serif;
    margin-top: 0pt;
    margin-bottom: 0pt;
    margin-left: .5in;
}
```

Property ⎯⎯ (label pointing to left side)
Value ⎯⎯ (label pointing to right side)
Declaration block ⎯⎯ (label pointing to right side)

A style rule consists of a selector ("p" in this example) and one or more declaration blocks. A declaration block contains a property (such as "margin-bottom"), and a value ("6pt"), plus appropriate syntax (colons and semi-colon).

Style classes

If you want a custom version of a style, you'll use a style "class." A style class inherits its formatting from its parent. However, a style property assigned to a class overrides the same property if assigned to the parent. Here's an example of a class of the p style:

```
p.note
{
    font-size: 9pt;
    margin-top: 3pt;
    margin-bottom: 3pt;
    padding: 3px;
    color: #004a6f;
    border-style: solid;
    border-width: 1px;
    border-color: #0080c0;
}
```

The class name is separated from its parent class with a period. The selector is "p.note" in this example. Notice that the style rule for p.note does not contain the property font-family. It inherited that style from its parent, the p style.

> **Note** — A Pseudo class is a special type of class used to format hypertext links in different states (active, hover, visited, etc.) or to format an initial cap or drop cap.

Here's what these two styles look like in our topic:

My Topic

This text block is formatted with the "p" style.

Note: This text block is formatted with the "p.note" style class.

WAYS TO CHANGE STYLES

There are two ways to change style rules in a stylesheet:

- Use Flare's Stylesheet Editor, which writes the style rules to the CSS file for you

- Use a text editor to directly edit the style rules in a CSS file

This section discusses how to use the Stylesheet Editor. If you wish to edit style rules directly in your CSS file, you need a text editor (such as Flare's Internal Text Editor or MS Notepad) and a good CSS reference. (We like *Styling Web Pages with CSS*, by Tom Negrino and Dori Smith for an introduction to CSS, and *CSS The Definitive Guide*, by Eric A. Meyer as a reference.)

> **Note** — If you open a CSS file with a text editor, you won't see all of the styles listed in the Stylesheet Editor. You'll see only those styles whose values override default values. To override a style not shown in text editor, simply type the style rule with new values for its properties.

CHANGING STYLES WITH THE STYLESHEET EDITOR

The Stylesheet Editor has two views: Simplified and Advanced. You'll switch between them by clicking the Simplified View or Advanced View buttons. In Simplified View, you'll use dialogs to change style formatting. In Advanced view, you'll assign values to CSS style properties.

> **Note** — Both Simplified View and Advanced View list every style. However Simplified View does not show every property of every style. It lists only the most common properties. In Advanced View you can see and change all properties.

The following procedure covers both views.

To change a style with the Stylesheet Editor:

1. In the Content Explorer, expand the Resources and Stylesheets folders and double-click Styles.css (or the stylesheet you wish to change). The stylesheet opens in the Stylesheet Editor.

> **Important** — In the Stylesheet Editor, be sure to select the medium whose styles you want to change (such as "default" for online output and "print" for print output). If you don't see your style changes applied in your topic, you might have changed the styles in a different medium than the one you intended to change.

If you're in Simplified View, the **Advanced View** button is visible and you'll see this:

Before changing styles, make sure the correct medium is selected.

You can filter the list of styles with this button.

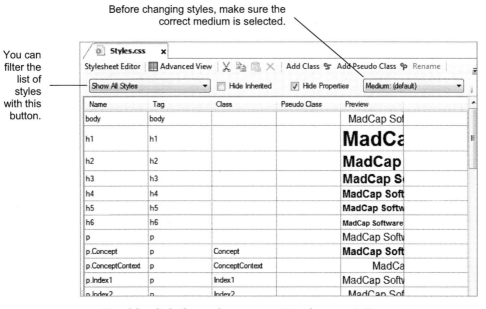

a. Double-click the style you want to change. A Properties dialog opens that contains tabs and options applicable only to the style you selected. Here is the Font tab of the Properties dialog for the p style:

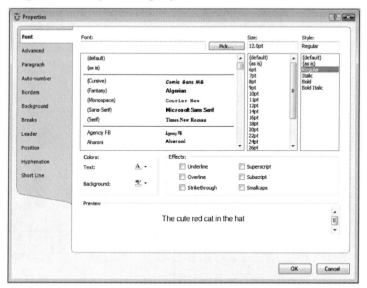

b. Change options on the Properties dialog as desired.

If you're in Advanced View, the **Simplified View** button is visible and you'll see this:

You can filter the list of styles with this button.

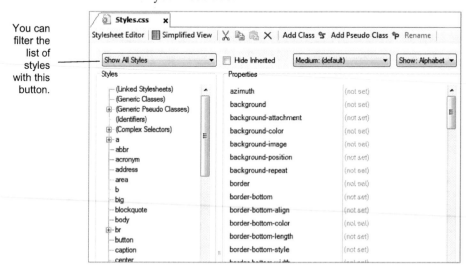

a. In the left pane, expand the style you want to change. The left pane now lists that style's classes. The right pane shows the properties for that style.

b. Select the style you want to change (the parent or one of its classes).

Here's what the Editor shows for our note example:

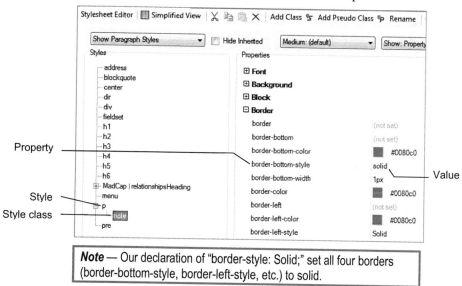

Note — Our declaration of "border-style: Solid;" set all four borders (border-bottom-style, border-left-style, etc.) to solid.

c. In the right pane, click the field to the right of the property to set a value.

2. Click **Save All** to save your work.

3. Close the Stylesheet Editor.

ADDING A STYLE CLASS

Adding a style class allows you to create a custom version of a style.

To add a style class:

1. Open the applicable stylesheet in the Stylesheet Editor (in either Simplified or Advanced View).

2. Select the style you want to add the class to, and select Add Class. The New Style dialog opens.

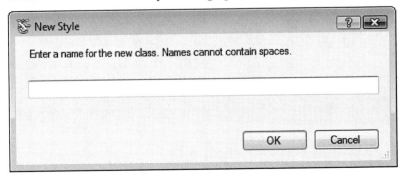

3. Type a name for the new class and click **OK**.

4. Change the formatting as desired for the new class.

5. Click **Save All** to save your work.

6. Close the Stylesheet Editor.

MARKING TEXT FOR REDACTION

Flare's text redaction feature, available starting with Version 5, is handy when you need to conceal confidential or sensitive information in printed output. For example, you might want to black-out names, social security numbers, account numbers, or financial data.

Note — This feature applies only to PDF and XPS print output.

To redact text in print output, simply mark the text you want to redact and select a redaction method for your print output targets.

You choose when to conceal and when to reveal text

Marking text as redacted is especially useful when you want to *selectively* reveal sensitive information. Simply mark the sensitive information as redacted text, then create multiple targets and set the redaction method in each target to conceal or reveal the redacted text. The concealed text is replaced by black rectangles that show where information was contained.

What you can redact

You can redact any type of content: text (characters and entire paragraphs), images, and tables.

Formatting

You can format text for redaction using either local formatting or styles. You can create a character style to apply to selected text or a paragraph style to apply to a text block. As in other cases, if you need to redact only a small quantity of text, local formatting is fine; if you have a lot of text to redact, consider creating a style for text redaction.

☁ To mark text for redaction with local formatting:

1. Select the text to apply redaction to.

2. Select **Format → Font** and click the **Advanced** tab.

3. In the Redacted Text section, select **Redacted** and click **OK**.

   The text you marked is highlighted in gray as shown here. It will be redacted when you build your output.

   > We expect the Pinewood project to generate approximately $350,000 in revenue the first year and $525,000 the second year. Initially, use cost accounting code 4325 for all expenses related to the Pinewood project.

   Text marked for redaction ―――――――

4. Click **Save All** ⊞ to save your work.

   Now that the text is marked, you'll select a method for displaying the redacted text in your output. You do this in the target you use to create the output.

   > **Note** — The target's output type must be PDF or XPS.

Use the following procedure to select a redaction method for a print output target.

🎁 To select the redaction method:

1. In the Project Organizer, expand **Targets** and double-click the desired PDF or XPS target. The Flare Target Editor opens to the last open tab.

2. Click the **Advanced** tab.

3. Select the redaction method to use for this target: **Blackout**, **Highlight**, or **Display as normal text** (no highlighting of any kind).

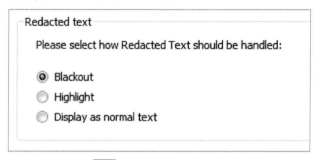

4. Click **Save All** 📄 to save your work.

When you build your output, your selection determines how the redacted text appears, as shown in these examples.

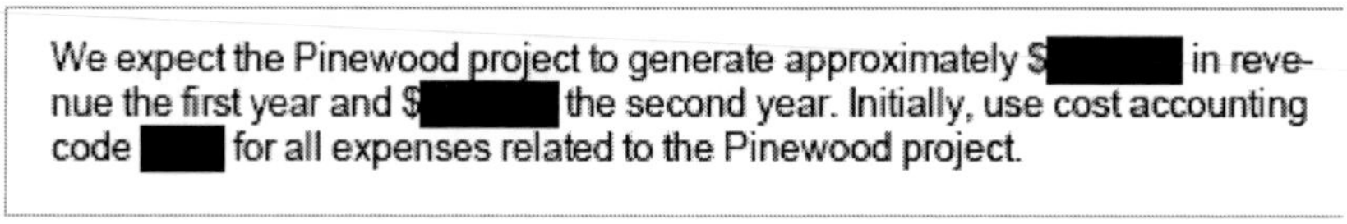

Figure 3-13:
Redacted text —
Blackout method

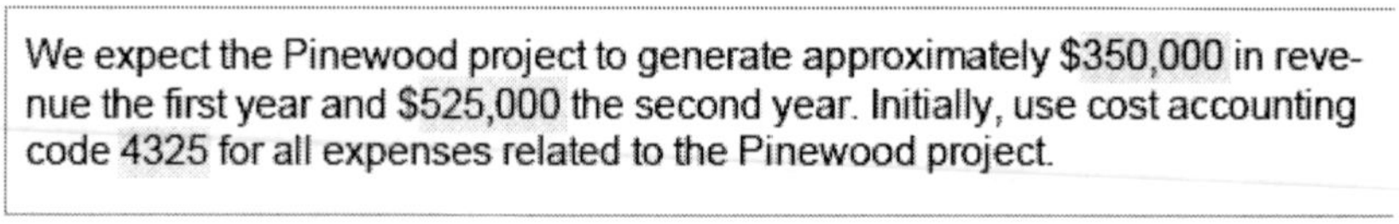

> We expect the Pinewood project to generate approximately $⬛⬛⬛ in revenue the first year and $⬛⬛⬛ the second year. Initially, use cost accounting code ⬛⬛ for all expenses related to the Pinewood project.

Figure 3-14:
Redacted text —
Highlight method

> We expect the Pinewood project to generate approximately $350,000 in revenue the first year and $525,000 the second year. Initially, use cost accounting code 4325 for all expenses related to the Pinewood project.

With the blackout option, the text is actually removed and replaced by black rectangles before Flare builds the output. Although the marked text is removed from the output, it still exists in your topic.

LEARN MORE

This section contains more information about the features you used in this chapter. Refer to it as needed.

THE INSERT TABLE DIALOG

The Insert Table dialog contains options for adding a table to a topic and for setting up the table's characteristics (number of columns, number of rows, table caption, etc.) It contains two tabs: **General** and **Borders**.

The General tab

The General tab contains options for setting the size of the table, its caption, its style, and how columns are sized.

Figure 3-15:
Insert Table
dialog,
General tab

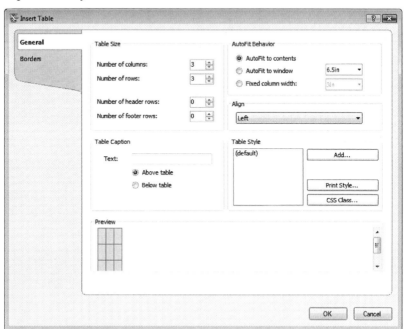

Table 3-2: *Options on the Insert Table dialog, General tab*	In this section ...	Do the following ...
	Table Size	Select the size of the table:
		■ **Number of columns** — Select or type the number of columns.
		■ **Number of rows** — Select or type the number of rows.
		■ **Number of header rows** — Select or type the number of header rows.
		■ **Number of footer rows** — Select or type the number of footer rows. (Helpful for entering footnotes about a table's contents.)
	AutoFit Behavior	Select the method for adjusting column width:
		■ **AutoFit to contents** automatically adjusts the column width to fit the size of the text it contains and wraps the contents to fit the window size.
		Note — For best results, we recommend that you use the **AutoFit to contents** option.
		■ **AutoFit to window** automatically adjusts the column width to fit the window size.
		■ In the drop-down box to the right, if you enter a *percentage*, the table will fill up to that percentage of the window width (even if it means padding the end of a cell with blanks). If you select *automatic*, Flare will not pad the cells with blanks in order to fit the window width. If you set a *length*, the table will not resize wider than the number you set, regardless of the window width.
		■ **Fixed column width** sets all columns to a fixed width, but automatically adjusts the column widths equally to fit the window if resized. To set the column width, open the list to the right of this field, click its down arrow and set the "length."
		Note — In the two drop-down boxes to the right, **default** returns to the default, which is "not set."
	Align	Select the table alignment: Left (default), Center, or Right.

Table 3-2: *(Cont.)*	In this section ...	Do the following ...
	Table Caption	If you want to add a table caption, type it here and select the position of the caption (Above table or Below table).
		Note — If you choose "Below," Internet Explorer might put the caption above the table instead of below.
	Table Style	If you want to use a table stylesheet for this table, select it from the Table Style list. Options include: ▪ **Add** — If the stylesheet you want to use is not listed under Table Styles, click this button to add the table stylesheet to the project. The stylesheet appears in the Table Style list. This option adds the style to the project and to the table you are creating. ▪ **Print Style** — Click this button to select a table stylesheet to use for print output only. ▪ **CSS Class** — Allows you to format the text in your table by selecting a style class from the topic's stylesheet (for example, Styles.css).
	Preview	Select to preview the table's style and the choices you made on this tab (such as table size and caption).

The Borders tab

The Borders tab contains options for applying and formatting borders around the cells of your table.

Figure 3-16:
Insert Table
dialog,
Borders tab

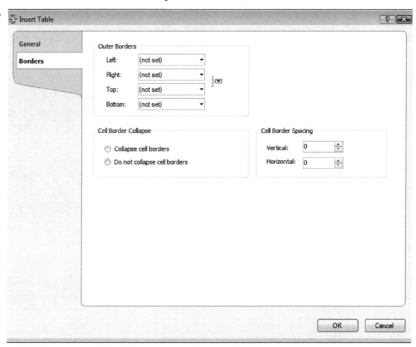

Table 3-3:
Options on
the Insert
Table dialog,
Borders tab

In this section ...	Do the following ...
Outer Borders	Set the borders for the Left, Right, Top, and Bottom of the table individually,
	- or -
	Set the same borders for the entire table by clicking the down arrow shown to the right of the border fields. In either case, this popup appears:

*Click here and select **Length** to set a line thickness.*   *Click to set the line color.*

Length:		(default)
1	px	solid
OK		Cancel

Click to set the unit of measure.   *Click to set the line style.*

(Don't forget to click **OK**.)

Table 3-3: (Cont.)	In this section ...	Do the following ...
	Cell Border Collapse	Select how you want inner borders to appear:

- **Collapse cell borders** – Click this option to join the border lines between cells like this:

- **Do not collapse cell borders** – Click this option to detach cell borders like this:

| | Cell Border Spacing | Increase or decrease the Vertical and Horizontal space (in pixels) between your table cells. Applies only to borders that are not collapsed and tables that do not have outer borders. |

WHAT'S NEXT?

Now that you've formatted your content and added elements such as tables and images, it's time to think about how users will move around in your output. Proceed to Step 4: Create Navigation Aids, to learn about the navigation aids—TOCs, links, bookmarks, cross-references, and indexes—that you can add to your project.

Step 4:
Create
Navigation Aids

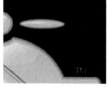

STEP 5: Create Output
5A: Print Output
5B: Online Output

STEP 4:
Create
Nav Aids

STEP 3:
Develop
Content

STEP 2:
Learn the
XML Editor

STEP 1:
Get Started

In this chapter ...
- Create a TOC
- Create links
- Create bookmarks
- Test links
- Add cross-references
- Create index entries
- Format a print index

OVERVIEW

This chapter discusses navigation aids that apply to both online and print output. To learn more about navigation aids that apply to online output only, see Step 5B: Create Online Output.

You can create these types of navigation aids with Flare:

- Table of Contents

- Links

- Cross-references

- Indexes

CREATING A TABLE OF CONTENTS

Flare's Table of Contents (TOC) feature is used for different purposes, depending on whether you're creating print or online output:

- **For online output**, users see the Flare TOC in the output. Users can use the TOC to browse for information and open topics.

- **For print output**, users *do not* see the Flare TOC in the output. Users see only the Table of Contents that Flare built from the headings in topics. With print output, the Flare TOC is used as a topic outline when you build output.

- **For DITA output**, the Flare TOC is used to create the DITAMAP file.

With either output, you decide which topics to include.

A TOC gives your topics structure and can be used to organize content and to work in that structure. With Flare, you can create a TOC in two ways:

- By creating your topics and TOC simultaneously

- By creating your topics, creating your TOC, and linking TOC entries to your topics

Regardless of the method you choose, creating your project's TOC is your first step in building output.

Flare TOC files have an .fltoc file extension.

MULTIPLE TOCS

Flare allows you to create multiple TOCs. Why would you do this?

Suppose you need two TOCs for output that will contain different topics, such as "full" and "light" versions. Or perhaps you plan to build both print and online output, and you want your print output to include an index and a TOC.

Flare always labels one as the Master TOC.

MASTER TOC

When you create a new project, Flare creates a default TOC, which automatically becomes the Master TOC and is named "Master." You'll see it listed like this in the Project Organizer:

Figure 4-1: Master TOC

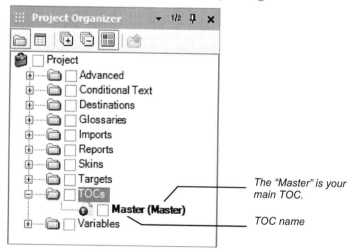

The "Master" is your main TOC.

TOC name

Designating a TOC as "master" allows you to take advantage of the toolbar button [📂 Open Master TOC] **Open Master TOC** and is useful for merging multiple TOCs into one. See "Linking TOCs" on page 163.

> **Best Practice** — Record the name of the Master TOC on the Target Settings form provided in Appendix A.

> **Note** — When you import a project, Flare creates a TOC that is named the same as the import file. This TOC is automatically designated as the Master TOC.

🔔 To designate a TOC as the master:

1. In the Project Organizer, expand the TOCs folder and right-click the TOC file you want to make into the master.

2. Select **Make Master TOC**.

WHAT CAN A *TOC* ITEM LINK TO?

A TOC item can link to any of the following:

- a topic in the current project

- an external file (a file outside of the project where the TOC resides)—even a PDF file!

- another TOC

- a website

- a browse sequence

- a target in another Flare project

- an external Help system

- a MadCap Mimic™ movie

LINKING TOCS

It's typical to link TOC items to topics in the same project, but you can also link a TOC item to another TOC in order to merge the TOCs. For instance:

- If you share common content with other authors, you could create a TOC just for that content. Then you could share the TOC and its topics with the other authors.

- If multiple authors create topics that need to be merged for output, each author could create a TOC for their part of the output. A master TOC would link the TOCs to pull them together. (The TOCs would be merged when you build the output, and the result would be one seamless TOC.)

To see what a TOC item links to:

- Hover your cursor over the TOC item. You will see what the item links to in the Content Explorer.

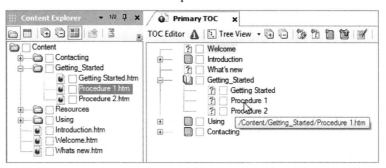

CREATING A TOC

You can create a TOC before you begin creating topics or at any time thereafter. We find it easiest to create a TOC and add topics to your project simultaneously. However, if you prefer, you can add topics to your TOC later by simply dragging and dropping the topics from the Content Explorer.

To create a TOC:

1.　In the Project Organizer, right-click the **TOCs** folder and select **Add Table of Contents** from the menu. The Add TOC dialog opens.

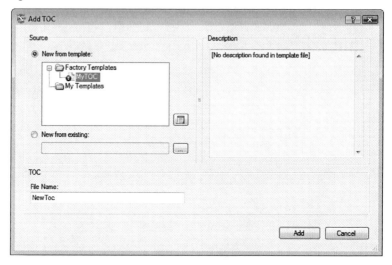

2.　In the File Name field, type a name for the new TOC.

3.　Click **Add**, then **OK** to add the new TOC.

The new TOC is listed in the TOCs folder and opens in the TOC Editor.

To open a TOC:

- In the Project Organizer, expand the TOCs folder and double-click the desired TOC.

The TOC Editor opens in the middle pane and shows the contents of the TOC.

🎩 To add topics to a TOC:

- Drag and drop topics from the Content Explorer into the open TOC.

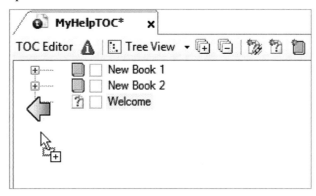

The text that appears in the TOC defaults to the topic title, which by default is the topic's first heading.

OPENING A TOPIC OR THE PROPERTIES DIALOG

When you double-click a TOC item in a TOC, it will either open the topic in the XML Editor or open the Properties dialog for the topic. You control which action will occur with this button on the TOC Editor toolbar:

Toggle the double-click behavior: open topic or display properties

This button acts as a toggle between the two modes.

> **Best Practice** — Set this button so that it opens a topic and leave it that way!

CREATING NEW BOOKS IN A TOC

TOC books allow you to create a hierarchy of topics in a TOC. Use them to organize your topics into a meaningful structure. TOC books can link to the same things that TOC items can, or they can link to nothing at all.

🎁 To create a new TOC book:

- Click **New book** 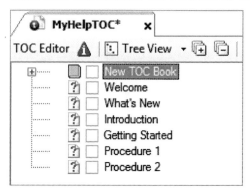 in the TOC Editor toolbar.

Notice that the new TOC book isn't linked to anything yet.
When you create a new TOC book, Flare automatically creates a
new topic (called "New Entry") within it.

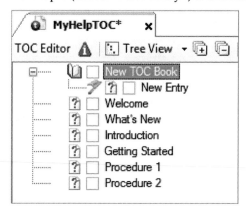

CREATING NEW TOC ITEMS

🎁 To create a new TOC item:

1. Select the TOC folder or TOC item you want to add the item to.

2. Click **New item** in the TOC Editor toolbar.

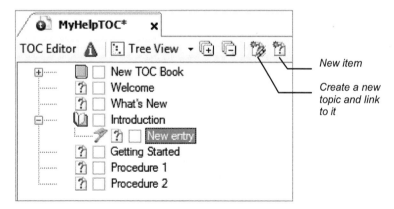

New item

Create a new topic and link to it

Notice that the new TOC item isn't linked to anything yet. You can link a TOC item to a topic at any time by right-clicking and selecting **Link to Topic**. Also, adding a TOC item to an existing TOC item changes the existing item into a TOC book.

> **Note** — To create a TOC item and topic simultaneously and link the two, click
>
> **Create a new topic and link to it** ![icon] instead of the **New item** ![icon] button.

RENAMING A *TOC*

 To rename a TOC:

1. In the Project Organizer, expand the TOCs folder.

2. Right-click the desired TOC and select **Rename** from the menu.

3. Type the new name and press **ENTER**.

REARRANGING ITEMS AND BOOKS IN A *TOC*

Use the following buttons on the TOC Editor toolbar to move TOC books and items left, right, up, or down in the TOC. Moving books and items to the left and right changes their hierarchy in the TOC.

⇦ ⇨ ⇧ ⇩

CREATING LINKS

Flare lets you add various types of links to your topics.

TYPES OF LINKS

A link allows users to quickly jump to additional or related information. You can create links to:

- topics or files inside or outside your project

- information in the same topic

Links can be created for online, print, and DITA output.

> **Note** — In Table 4-1, links in **boldface** are described in this book. Other types of links are described in Flare's Help system.

Table 4-1:
Types of
links

This link ...	Does this ...
Cross-reference	Jumps from text in one topic to another topic or bookmark within a topic. Cross-references can be used in online or print output, but they are especially useful for print output. Unlike text hyperlinks, cross-references can include commands for inserting elements like page numbers and topic titles. Cross-reference link text is updated by Flare when you build output. See ""Adding cross-references" on page 177 for more information.
Text hyperlink	Jumps to a specified location. See ""Creating text hyperlinks," next, for more information.
Text popup	Opens a popup that contains text you specify.
Topic popup	Opens a popup that contains another topic.
Bookmark	Jumps to a bookmark (a marker you create to identify a specific location in a topic). You can link to bookmarks in the same topic with a text hyperlink or in any topic with a cross-reference. See "Creating text hyperlinks," next, and "Creating bookmarks and linking to them" on page 174 for more information.
External link	Links to a file outside your project.
Image hyperlink	Opens a link associated with an image.

	This link ...	Does this ...
Table 4-1: *(Cont.)*	Movie link	Opens a link that plays a movie created with MadCap Mimic, Adobe Flash, Windows Media, or Apple QuickTime.
	Audio link	Opens a link that plays an audio file created with MadCap Echo, Adobe Flash, Windows Media, or Apple QuickTime.
	Toggler	Hides and shows a piece of content. When a user clicks a "toggler hotspot," tagged content is shown or hidden (toggled).
	Drop-down text	Hides and shows a piece of content as a list. When a user clicks this type of link, content is displayed below the link.
	Expanding text	Hides and shows a portion of a paragraph. When a user clicks this type of link, the condensed paragraph is expanded for viewing.
	Concept link ("See Also" or "A-link")	Opens a group of topics related to the current topic.
	Related Topics link	Opens a topic related to the current topic. See "Creating related topics links" on page 172 for more information.
	Relationship Table	Organizes related topics by category (such as related tasks, related concepts, and related reference topics) by placing links in your online output or cross-references in your print output. Although often used with DITA, you don't need to create DITA output to use a relationship table. For more information, search for "relationship tables" in Flare's Help.
	Keyword link ("K-link")	Opens topics related to the current topic by using index keywords shared by both.
	Shortcut control	Launches an application program or window with a relationship to the current topic.

CREATING TEXT HYPERLINKS

A text hyperlink is a commonly used type of link that enables a user to jump to another location, such as:

- a file in the current project

- a place in the current topic (heading, bookmark, or top of topic)

- a place in a different topic (heading, bookmark, or top of topic)

- a topic or file outside your project

- a website

> **Note** — You can also set up an email address as a text hyperlink. When a user clicks the link, his or her email application opens with an email address in the "To" field.

To insert text hyperlinks:

1. Open the topic in which to insert the link.

2. In the topic, select the text you want to use as the link (the hotspot).

3. Select **Insert → Hyperlink** or click **Insert a hyperlink** in the XML Editor toolbar. The Insert Hyperlink dialog opens.

> **Tip** — You can also open the Insert Hyperlink dialog from the Content Explorer by dragging and dropping the topic onto the selected text.

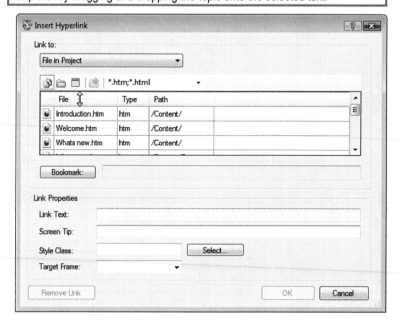

4. Select an option in the **Link to** drop-down and use the following chart to choose what you want to link to.

Use this option ...	To ...
File in Project	Link to a file or bookmark in the project. After selecting this option, click the file you want to link to, which can be a topic, an image, or other file types, or click **Bookmark** and select a location in the document. *Note* — To change the Content Explorer view and the types of files shown, use the options in the Link to section of the dialog box.
Place in this Document	Link to the top of the topic or a heading or bookmark within it. After selecting this option, use the hierarchy displayed to select the place in the topic to link to.
External File	Link to a topic or file (such as a PDF file) outside the project. After selecting this option, click **External Topic** to browse and open the file you want to link to. After you choose an external topic, its path name appears to the right of the External Topic button. *Important* — To be sure that your output will link properly to the file, place a copy of the file in your project's Content folder before linking to it. Files located elsewhere (such as in the project folder) are not copied to the output folder.
Website	Link to an external file, such as a website URL. After selecting this option, enter the complete URL (including the http://) in the Website field.
Email	Link to an email address. After selecting this option, enter the email address and subject in the appropriate fields or select a recent email address. For information about when this could be used, see Flare's Help system.

5. Use the following chart to choose optional link properties (listed in the Link Properties section of this dialog).

Use this option ...	To ...
Link text	Change the text that was selected as a link in the topic.
Screen Tip	Specify text that appears when users hover the cursor over the link.
Style Class	To select a link style to apply to the link text.
Target Frame	Select how the linked destination will open (such as in a new window).

6. Click **OK**. The link is added to the topic. (By default, links appear as blue underlined text.)

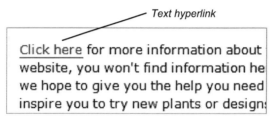

Text hyperlink

CREATING RELATED TOPICS LINKS

With related topics links, users can view information that is relevant to the current topic. Related topics links similar to "See also" in a book index.

To insert a related topics link:

1. Open the topic in which you want to insert the link.

2. Click in the topic where the link will be inserted (typically the bottom of the topic).

3. Select **Insert → Help Control → Related Topics Control**. The Insert Related Topics Control dialog opens.

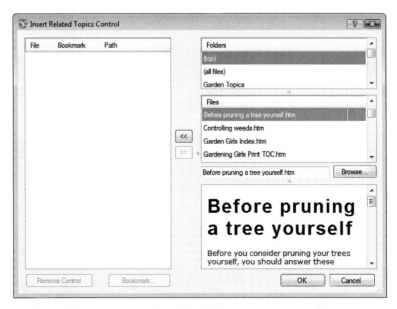

4. In the Folders section, select the following to view topics:

Select ...	To view ...
(top)	Topics in the same folder as the current topic.
(all files)	All topics in the project.
a specific folder	Topics in the Content Explorer folder you chose.

The contents of the Files section changes, depending on what you select in the Folders section.

5. In the Files section, click a topic you want to add as a related topics link and click ⟨⟨. The topic is added to the left side of the dialog. Repeat this step for each topic you want to add to the link.

6. Click **OK**. The link is added to the topic. (If Show Markers is turned on, related topics links appear as shown here.)

Selecting a tree

When selecting a tree, you need to think about these things:

- the shape of the tree

- fall color

- shade

- mature size of the tree

Related topics link

[Related To...]

Best Practice — Apply an "online only" condition tag to the text block that contains the related topic link to prevent it from appearing as an extra line in print output. (When you build print output, Flare automatically removes Help control links from your topics, since they don't apply to print output.)

CREATING BOOKMARKS AND LINKING TO THEM

Bookmarks allow you to place a marker in a topic so you can link to that text from within the topic or from another topic. First, you insert the bookmark, then you insert links to it.

To insert a bookmark:

1. Click in the topic where you want to insert the bookmark (typically at the beginning of a paragraph or heading).

2. Select **Insert → Bookmark**. The Manage Bookmarks dialog opens.

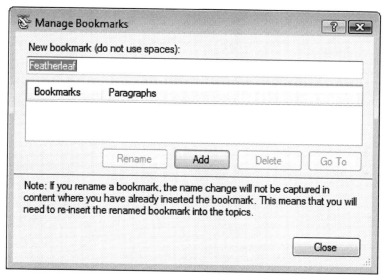

3. In the New bookmark field, type a bookmark name (without any spaces). If you clicked at the beginning of a text block, Flare places the first word in the New bookmark field.

4. Click **Add**. Flare marks the location with a bookmark icon and the bookmark name.

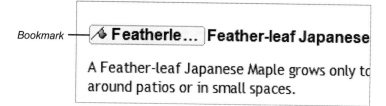

Bookmark

To insert a link to a bookmark in the same topic:

1. Select the text you want to link to.

2. Select **Insert → Hyperlink** or click **Insert a hyperlink** in the XML Editor toolbar. The Insert Hyperlink dialog opens.

3. Select **Place in this Document**.

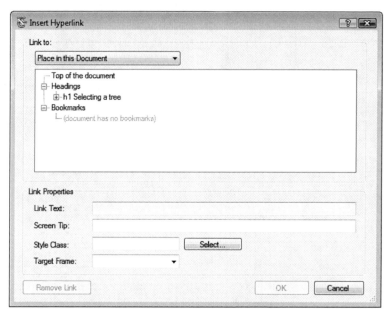

4.   Select the bookmark you want to link to.

5.   Click **OK**. The link is added to the topic. (By default, links
     appear as blue underlined text.)

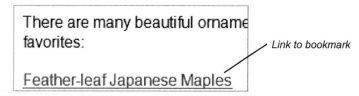

Link to bookmark

TESTING YOUR LINKS

You can test your links as you develop project content or test them
all after you build your output. The choice is yours.

There are two ways to test your links. You can:

- Build your output, view it, and click on each link to be sure that
  it jumps to the proper location (topic, bookmark, URL, email
  address, etc.). Test your links in every topic.

- Preview a topic in the XML Editor and click on each link in that
  topic. See "Previewing a topic" on page 53.

ADDING CROSS-REFERENCES

Like a text hyperlink, a cross-reference lets a user jump to a topic or bookmark in a topic. But unlike text hyperlinks, cross-references have more formatting options and can include commands for inserting items such as page numbers and topic titles in the result.

ABOUT COMMANDS

Using commands allows Flare to automatically update cross-references when the destination's title, page number etc., change.

Let's see how commands work. Suppose you create a cross-reference to a topic that includes a title and page number:

> See "Adding an account" on page 23.

If you change the topic title to "Adding a user account" and build your output, Flare automatically updates the cross-reference with the new title:

> See "Adding a user account" on page 23.

> **Important** — If you change a topic's title, Flare updates cross-references to it.

CROSS-REFERENCES IN PRINT AND ONLINE OUTPUT

You can add cross-references to online output, but they are most useful for print output. By using stylesheet mediums, you can create one cross-reference format for online output (e.g., without page numbers) and another for print output (e.g., with page numbers).

When you create a new project, Flare creates three stylesheet mediums:

- Default
- Print
- Non-print

Cross-references use the MadCap:xref style. For the **default** and **non-print** mediums, the MadCap:xref style is set to:

See "{paratext}"

For the **print** medium, the MadCap:xref style is set to:

See "{paratext}" on page {page}

> **Note** — To use the cross-reference style defined by the print medium, select the print medium on the Advanced tab when you set up your target for print output. For more information about using mediums, see "What are mediums?" on page 89.

INSERTING A CROSS-REFERENCE

To insert a cross-reference:

1. Open the topic in which to insert the cross-reference.

2. In the XML Editor, place your cursor where you want to insert the cross-reference.

3. Select **Insert → Cross-Reference**. The Insert Cross-Reference dialog opens.

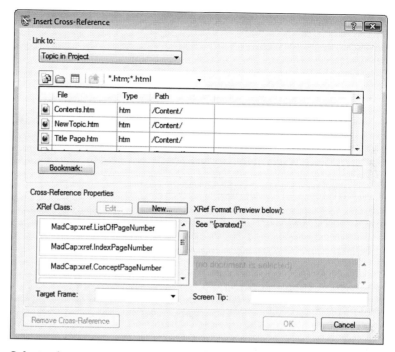

4. Select what you want to link to by doing one of the following:

To link to ...	Do this ...
A file in the open project	Select **Topic in Project**. Then select the file you want to link to. (To select a bookmark in the current topic, click **Bookmark**.) **Note** — To change the Content Explorer view and the types of files shown, use the options in the Link to section of the dialog box.
A heading, bookmark, or the top of the current topic	Select **Place in this document**. Then select where you want to link to.

This example shows the Insert Cross-Reference dialog after choosing a cross-reference to a topic in the open project.

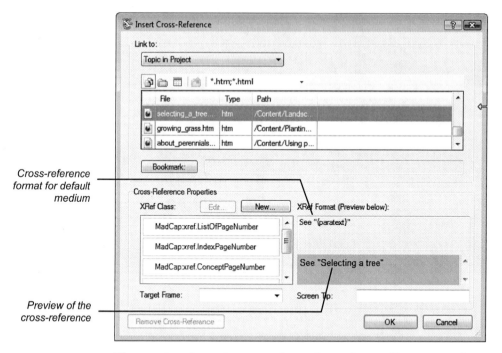

Cross-reference format for default medium

Preview of the cross-reference

The preview format you see depends on the medium currently selected in the XML Editor. Notice the XRef Format (See "{paratext}"). This is the format for the default medium. The format for the print medium is: See "{paratext}" on page {page}.

> **Note** — The {paratext} command displays the *text* of the first *paragraph* (text block) in the linked topic. In the example above, "Selecting a tree" is the first text block. (It also happens to be the title of the topic.)

5. (*Optional*) From the Target Frame list, select an option (such as New Window) for opening the linked file. If you don't select an option, the topic opens in the same window as the topic that contains the cross-reference.

6. (*Optional*) In the Screen Tip field, type the phrase you want to appear when a user hovers the cursor over the cross-reference in the output.

7. Click **OK**. The cross-reference is added to the topic.

> For information about varieties of plants, <u>See "Selecting a tree"</u>

8. Click **Save All** [icon] to save your work.

CHANGING CROSS-REFERENCES

You can change a cross-reference by:

- Changing the file it links to

- Changing the target frame (how the linked topic opens in the output)

- Entering or changing the screen tip

- Changing the format of the cross-reference style, which changes the format for all cross-references that use that style.

Changing a single cross-reference

Use the following procedure to change the linked file, target frame, or screen tip of a single cross-reference.

To change a single cross-reference:

1. Open the topic that contains the cross-reference you want to change.

2. Right-click the cross-reference and select **Edit Cross-Reference**. The Insert Cross-Reference dialog appears.

3. Change the cross-reference as described in Steps 4 – 8 of the procedure for inserting a cross-reference (page 178).

Changing the format of a cross-reference style

There are two ways to change the format of a cross-reference style. Both methods *change the style in your stylesheet.* You can:

- Open a topic that contains a cross-reference that uses the style you want to change, and edit the style.

- Open the Stylesheet Editor and change the MadCap:xref style (or MadCap:xref.stylename, if you've created a class of the MadCap:xref style).

You'll learn the first method here. For more information about using the Stylesheet Editor, see "Changing styles with the Stylesheet Editor" on page 146.

To change the format of a cross-reference style:

1. Open any topic that contains a cross-reference with the style you want to change.

2. Right-click the cross-reference and select **Edit Cross-Reference**. The Insert Cross-Reference dialog appears.

3. In the Cross-Reference Properties section, select the <MadCap:xref> style you want to change.

> **Note** — These instructions show you how to change the format of the MadCap:xref tag. If you create your own cross-reference style (a class of the MadCap:xref tag) and want to change it, select it instead.

4. Click **Edit**. The Edit Cross-Reference Style Class dialog opens.

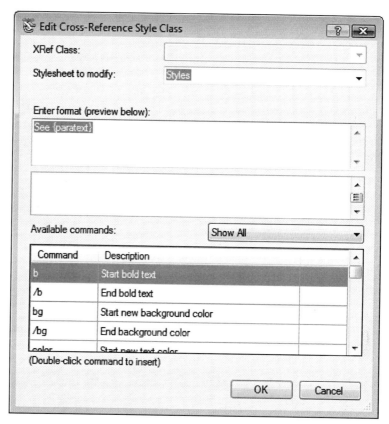

5. In the Stylesheet to modify field, select the stylesheet you want
    to change.

> **Important** — These steps change the MadCap:xref style in all three
> mediums (default, print, and non-print) for the stylesheet you select. (For
> more information about mediums, see "What are mediums?" on page 89.)

6. In the Enter format field, change the format as desired.

To insert ...	Do this ...
Text (e.g., "See" or "on page")	Type the text in the Enter format field.

To insert ...	Do this ...
A command	▪ Click in the Enter format field where you want to insert the command. ▪ In the Available commands list, locate and double-click the command you want to insert.

> **Note** — For commands such as adding boldface, you'll need to insert *both* a start and end tag into the Enter format field.

7. Click **OK**, then **Yes** to confirm that you want to redefine the existing style.

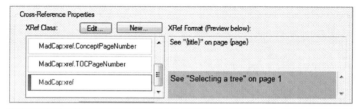

> **Note** — When you change a cross-reference style, you might not see the format change until you update the cross-reference.

UPDATING CROSS-REFERENCES MANUALLY

Updating cross-references manually is optional because Flare does this automatically when you build your output. However, you can update the appearance (format) and content of cross-references in the active topic at any time.

> **Tip** — When you change the format of a cross-reference, it's helpful to see what it looks like without building your output.

To update cross-references manually:

1. Open the topic that contains the cross-reference you want to update.

2. Select **Tools → Update Cross-References**. The Update Cross-References dialog appears, listing all cross-references in the active topic.

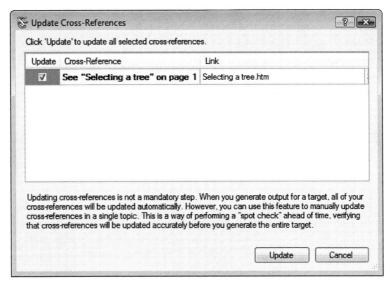

3. Click **Update**. The cross-references are updated in the active topic. Both the format and the content are updated.

ADVANCED FEATURES

You can do more with cross-references, such as:

- Creating context-sensitive cross-references in which the cross-reference link text reflects its proximity to the linked output if it appears on the same, previous, or next page.

- Using stylesheet mediums to format a cross-reference differently for print and online output. For example, a cross-reference can appear as "See 'Adding an account'" in your online output and "See 'Adding an account' on page 56" in your print output.

- Creating classes of the MadCap|xref style.

- Adding format commands.

To learn more about these features, search on "cross-references" in the Flare Help system.

CREATING INDEX ENTRIES

Index entries are created in the same way, whether you're using them for print or online output. To create index terms, you must add index keywords to your topics before building your output. The keywords are added right in the topics.

> ***Tip*** — You can make index keywords conditional (by applying a condition tag) so that you can include only index terms applicable to the desired target. See the procedure called "To add index terms with Index Entry Mode" that follows.

ADDING INDEX KEYWORDS

Here are three ways to add index keywords:

- Add a single keyword to the open topic

- Use Index Entry mode to add phrases and multi-level keywords to the open topic

- Use the Index window to add phrases and multi-level keywords to your index hierarchy and assign them to topics

You might use a combination of these methods, depending on your needs. This chart describes when each method might be helpful.

Table 4-2: When to use each method

Use this option ...	When ...
Add a single keyword	<ul><li>You want to add a single-word index entry.</li><li>The topic is open and active (in view).</li><li>The word you want to add exists in the topic.</li><li>You want to add a word fast.</li></ul>
Index Entry mode	<ul><li>You want to add index entries to snippets.</li><li>You need to create index entries that are phrases.</li><li>The index entry cannot be placed at the top of the topic; but instead must be inserted in a specific place within the topic.</li><li>You need to add a multi-level index entry.</li><li>You want to add multiple index keywords to the same index marker.</li></ul>

Table 4-2: (Cont.)	**Use this option ...**	**When ...**
	Index window	▪ The topic is not open.
		▪ You want an easy way to add the same index marker to the beginning of multiple topics.
		▪ You want to add terms quickly.
		▪ You want the index term to be placed at the beginning of a topic.
		▪ The top-level term already exists in the index and you want to add a second-level entry to it.

No matter which method you use to create index entries, the terms are added to the applicable topic within an index code marker.

> *Note* — Index Entry mode opens the Index window. Once open, you can either type terms in the boxes at the top of the window, or you can enter terms in the index hierarchy at the bottom (the third method, described in the previous chart).

To add a single keyword:

1. Open the topic you want to insert index keywords into.

2. Click in the word (or immediately before or after it) you want to add a keyword for, and press **F10** or select **Tools → Index → Insert** "word" **as Indexed Keyword**.

    The word you clicked is added as an index keyword. If markers are visible, the marker appears where you clicked.

> *Tip* — To turn on markers, see "Viewing index keywords" on page 194.

Index keyword

Growing grass

Growing grass grass isn't very complicat about the conditions that grass needs to be

To add index terms with Index Entry Mode:

1. Open the topic you want to insert index keywords into.

2. Click **Index Entry Mode** ⫼▾ in the XML Editor's top toolbar to turn on Index Entry mode. The cursor changes to an index entry symbol, as shown here:

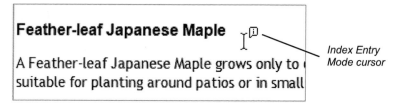

Feather-leaf Japanese Maple

A Feather-leaf Japanese Maple grows only to (suitable for planting around patios or in small

Index Entry Mode cursor

3. Click in the topic where you want to place an index entry.

4. Type the index keyword or phrase.

    The Index window opens and shows your entry as you type it.

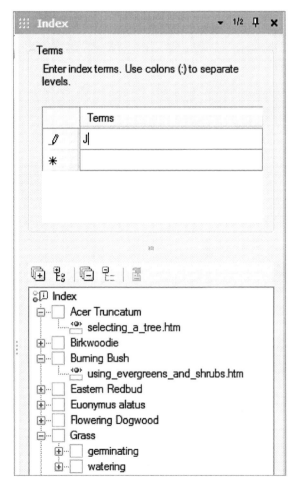

5. Press **ENTER**. The index entry is placed in your topic and the cursor moves to the next blank line in the Index window. (If markers are turned on, you'll see the beginning of the entry where you placed it in the text.)

Index keyword (marker is turned on)

Feather-leaf Japanese Maple

A Feather-leaf Japanese Maple Japanese M... grows only to 6 feet tall, and is quite suitable for

6. To add more keywords to the same index marker, type a keyword on the next line and press **ENTER**. Continue adding index keywords to the same marker, as desired.

> **Note** — To create a multi-level index entry, separate the levels by a colon in the Index window. In the example above, "trees:selecting" causes the term "selecting" to be listed under "trees" in the index.

Two-level index keyword

Feather-leaf Japanese Maple

trees:select... A Feather-leaf Japanese Maple Japanese M... grows only to 6 feet tall, and is quite suitable for planting around patios or in small spaces.

7. When you're done adding entries to the index marker, click your cursor in a different spot in the topic to add another index marker.

8. When you're done adding index markers to the open topic, click **Toggle Index Entry Mode** again, then click anywhere in the topic. Now you'll be able to continue editing in the XML Editor.

9. (*Optional*) When you're done adding index entries, close the Index window.

To add index terms with the Index window:

1. Open the topic you want to insert index keywords into.

2. Select **View → Index Window**.

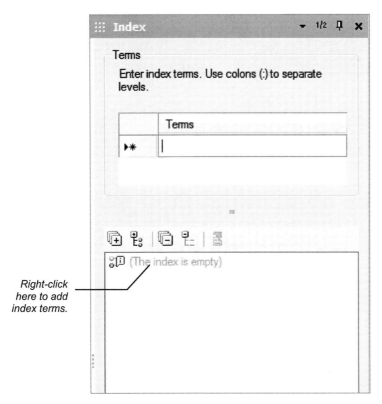

Right-click here to add index terms.

3. If the index already has some entries, right-click **Index**. If it has no entries, right-click **The index is empty**.

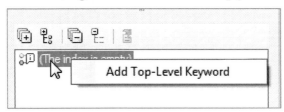

4. Select **Add Top-Level Keyword**. Flare adds a new term to the index with a temporary name ("NewTerm").

Top-level index keyword

5. Type the text for the top level index term.

6. To add a sub-keyword (a second-level entry), right-click the top-level entry and select **Add Sub-Keyword**.

Sub-keyword ———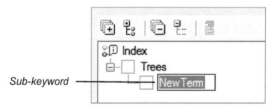

7. Type the text for the sub-keyword.

    Here is an index with a few more index entries that have not been assigned to topics:

    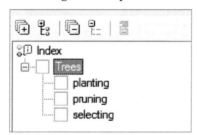

8. To assign a topic to an entry at any level, right-click the entry and select **Assign Topic**. The Open File dialog opens.

9. Select the file you want to assign to this index entry and click **Open**.

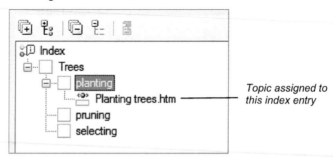

Topic assigned to this index entry

Flare places the index code marker at the beginning of the assigned topic:

Index entry in the assigned topic

If you hover your cursor over the index marker, you'll see that "Trees:planting" is the keyword for this index entry.

Here is an example that shows two topics assigned to the same index entry:

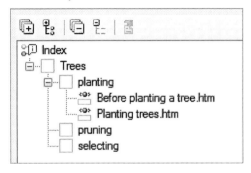

10. (*Optional*) When you're done adding index entries, close the Index window.

APPLYING CONDITION TAGS TO INDEX ENTRIES

Applying a condition tag to an index entry marker applies it to all of that marker's keywords. Just like with topic content, index entries that are tagged with condition tags can be excluded from your output. If excluded, the index is created without those entries.

To apply a condition tag to an index entry:

1. Open the topic that contains the index entry you want to apply a condition tag to.

2. Right-click the index marker and select **Conditions** from the menu. The Condition Tags dialog opens.

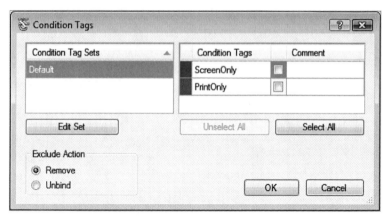

3. Check the condition tag (or tags) you want to apply to the index marker and click **OK**. The condition tag is applied to the marker and the color associated with that condition tag is shown on the marker in the topic.

Index marker with a condition tag applied

> ## Feather-leaf Japanese Maple
>
> ■ Trees:Japan...A Feather-leaf Japanese Maple grows only to 6 feet tall, and is quite suitable for planting around patios or in small spaces.

> **Note** — To learn more about condition tags, see "Using condition tags" on page 348.

VIEWING INDEX KEYWORDS

To see index keywords in a topic, you must have markers turned on.

To turn on markers:

- Click the arrow to the right of **Toggle show tags** `<t> ▾` in the XML Editor's top toolbar, and select **Show Markers**.

CHANGING AND DELETING INDEX KEYWORDS

You can change the text of a marker's index keywords and remove keywords from a marker.

To change or remove a word from an index keyword:

1. Open the topic that contains the keyword you want to change or remove.

2. Make sure that markers are visible. If not, click the arrow to the right of **Toggle show tags** `<t>` in the XML Editor's top toolbar, and select **Show Markers**.

3. Right-click the marker to be changed and select **Edit Index Keyword** from the menu. The Index window opens and shows the keywords contained in that marker.

4. Change or remove keywords as desired and press **ENTER**. Flare changes the marker's keywords. Close the Index window when finished.

DELETING INDEX MARKERS

You can delete entire index markers, but **use caution** when doing so because this removes all keywords contained in that marker.

> **Note** — This procedure applies to all markers, not just index markers.

To delete an index marker:

1. Open the topic that contains the index marker to be deleted.

2. Make sure that markers are visible. If not, click the arrow to the right of **Toggle show tags** `<t>` in the XML Editor' top toolbar, and select **Show Markers**.

3. Right-click the marker to be deleted and select **Delete** from the menu. The marker is removed from the topic.

HOW INDEX ENTRIES APPEAR IN ONLINE OUTPUT

The index terms you add to your topics are shown in online output when you click the **Index** accordion bar. Index terms open the topics in which they were inserted. In the figures that follow, notice that "trees:selecting" was entered as the index keyword, which results in a two-level index entry for selecting trees.

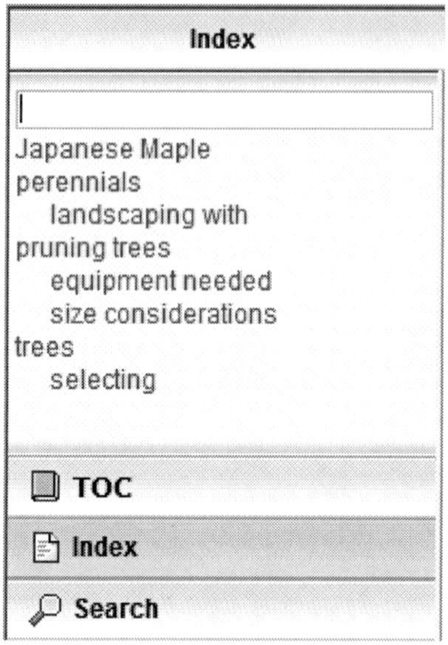

Figure 4-2: *Index in online output*

HOW INDEX ENTRIES APPEAR IN PRINT OUTPUT

The index terms you add to your topics are shown in print output as a traditional index. Here's an example of a print index:

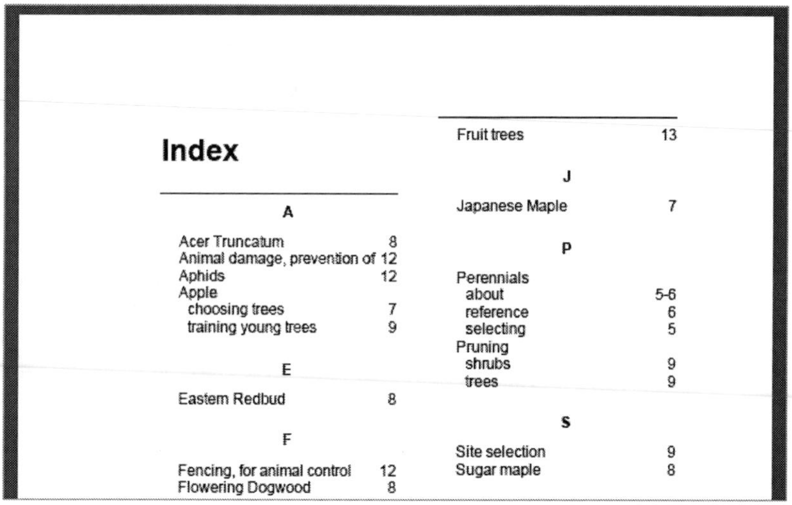

Index

A

Acer Truncatum	8
Animal damage, prevention of	12
Aphids	12
Apple	
choosing trees	7
training young trees	9

E

Eastern Redbud	8

F

Fencing, for animal control	12
Flowering Dogwood	8
Fruit trees	13

J

Japanese Maple	7

P

Perennials	
about	5-6
reference	6
selecting	5
Pruning	
shrubs	9
trees	9

S

Site selection	9
Sugar maple	8

Figure 4-3: *Index in print output*

As the previous figure shows, index entries that contain multiple pages are shown as a range of pages separated by a dash.

FORMATTING A PRINT INDEX

You can format your index with styles by using Flare's Stylesheet Editor, or by adding style rules to your stylesheet (your CSS file). This is an advanced skill to learn after you've learned Flare basics.

Either way, here are some of the things you might want to do to format your index:

Table 4-3: Examples of index formatting

To ...	Do this ...
Change the leader (between the index entry and the page number)	1. In the Content Explorer, double-click your stylesheet to open it in the Stylesheet Editor. Then open Simplified View. (If "Simplified View" appears to the right of the Editor name, click it; otherwise the editor is already in Simplified View.) 2. Double-click the index style whose leader you wish to change (such as p.Index1). 3. On the Properties dialog, click the **Leader** tab. 4. Select the type of leader (**Dot**, **Dash**, **Underline**, or **None**). 5. Repeat Steps 2 – 4 for each index style to be changed (p.Index2, p.Index3, etc.).
Remove the line above the index columns	1. Open your stylesheet in the Stylesheet Editor in Advanced View. (If "Advanced View" appears to the right of the Editor name, click it; otherwise the editor is already in Advanced View.) 2. Click the **MadCap	indexProxy** style. If not already selected, select **Show: Alphabetical List** from the list in the right pane. 3. In the right pane, scroll to the "border-top-style" property and click the field to its right. 4. Select **None** from the list.

Table 4-3:
(Cont.)

To ...	Do this ...
Left (or right) align index headings **Note** — Index headings are centered by default.	1. Open your stylesheet in the Stylesheet Editor in Simplified View. (See Step 1 in the first row of this table.) 2. Scroll to and double-click the **p.IndexHeading** style. 3. On the Properties dialog, click the **Paragraph** tab. 4. Select the alignment as desired (**Left** or **Right**).
Change the spacing before or after index headings	1. Open your stylesheet in the Stylesheet Editor in Simplified View. (See Step 1 in the first row of this table.) 2. Scroll to and double-click the **p.IndexHeading** style. 3. On the Properties dialog, click the **Paragraph** tab. 4. In the Spacing section, under Before and After, select **Length**, then set the spacing in the desired unit of measure (Point, Pixel, Inch, etc.).
Wrap long index entries to the next line	1. Open your stylesheet in the Stylesheet Editor in Advanced View. (If "Advanced View" appears to the right of the Editor name, click it; otherwise the editor is already in Advanced View.) 2. Scroll to and double-click the index style you want to change (such as **p.Index1**). 3. If not already selected, select **Show: Alphabetical List** from the list in the right pane. 4. In the right pane, scroll to the "white-space" property. (It's near the bottom of the list.) Click the field to its right. 5. Select **normal** from the list. 6. Repeat Steps 2 – 5 for each index style to be changed (p.Index2, p.Index3, etc.).
Change the font or font size of index entries	Open your stylesheet in the Stylesheet Editor in Simplified View. (See Step 1 in the first row of this table.)

Table 4-3: (Cont.)

To ...	Do this ...
Change the font or font size of index headings	1. Open your stylesheet in the Stylesheet Editor in Simplified View. (See Step 1 in the first row of this table.) 2. Scroll to and double-click the **p.IndexHeading** style. 3. On the Properties dialog, click the **Font** tab. 4. Select the desired font and font size.
Change the number of index columns	1. Create a page layout with the desired number of columns. (See "Task 3: Add page layouts" on page 221.) *Tip* — When you create the page layout, if you select the "IndexResizable" template, you will automatically get two columns. 2. Link the page layout to the index topic in your TOC. (See "Task 7: Link page layouts to topics in the TOC" on page 233.)

Here's how a print index looks after changing the default formatting:

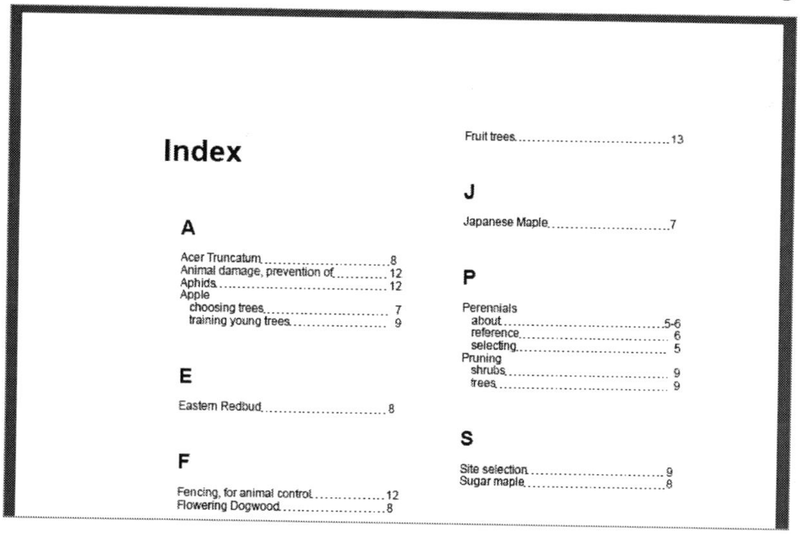

Figure 4-4:
A PDF index with formatting applied

Index

A

Acer Truncatum................................8
Animal damage, prevention of............12
Aphids...12
Apple
  choosing trees................................7
  training young trees.........................9

E

Eastern Redbud...............................8

F

Fencing, for animal control...............12
Flowering Dogwood...........................8

Fruit trees.......................................13

J

Japanese Maple...............................7

P

Perennials
  about...5-6
  reference.......................................6
  selecting..5
Pruning
  shrubs..9
  trees..9

S

Site selection....................................9
Sugar maple......................................8

When you build PDF, XHTML, or XPS output, Flare puts the index terms and page numbers in a two-column table. The index term is left-aligned and the page number is right-aligned, as shown here.

Index term	Page number

The table has no borders. (We show borders here only so you can see the table.)

When you build Word and FrameMaker output, the page numbers are shown next to the index terms separated by a comma (rather than right-aligned).

Figure 4-5:
An index
in MS Word
with no
leader dots
and left-
aligned page
numbers

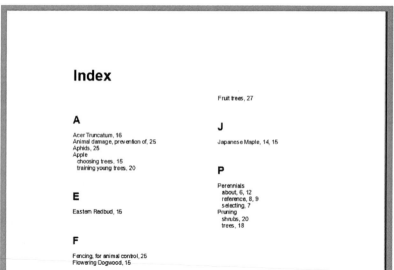

WHAT'S NEXT?

Now your Flare project is ready to be built into output. Refer to:

- Step 5A: Create Print Output (which includes PDFs)

- Step 5B: Create Online Output

- Appendix G: DITA Import and Export

You're almost there!

Step 5A:
Create
Print Output

STEP 4:
Create
Nav Aids

STEP 3:
Develop
Content

STEP 2:
Learn the
XML Editor

STEP 1:
Get Started

In this chapter ...
- ➤ Learn about types of print output
- ➤ Create a simple print document
- ➤ Make upfront decisions
- ➤ Include front and back matter
- ➤ Discover page layouts
- ➤ Build your output

Overview

In this chapter, you'll learn how to build the following types of print output:

- Microsoft Word
- Adobe FrameMaker
- Adobe PDF
- Microsoft XPS
- XHTML

> **Note** — If you're unfamiliar with terms and concepts such as *output*, *build*, *distribute* and *target*, refer to the Document Basics chapter.

When you build print output, Flare puts the print output files in a folder in your project directory. You can then distribute those files to others. The type and number of files Flare creates depends on the type of print output you build.

Keeping Track of Print Output

To make it easier to track various targets and types of output, we've created a Target Settings form (see Appendix A). As you learn to create more targets for your output, you'll find it very helpful to record the names of various Flare project files.

We suggest that you keep a copy of this form handy as you proceed through this chapter and begin making it a habit to fill it out.

Types of Print Output

This section describes the various types of print output, plus information about viewing and distributing your output.

MICROSOFT WORD OUTPUT

You can build Microsoft Word files that can be used with Microsoft Word 2003 and Microsoft Word 2007. The files can be created in one of these formats: DOC, XML, or DOCX (Word 2007 only).

By default, Flare creates a DOC file if you have MS Word 2003 and an XML file if you have MS Word 2007. Output is saved in a single file unless you set up the target to build multiple files. For more information, see the topic "Specifying Chapter Breaks and Page Layouts" in the Flare Help system.

> **Note** — If you want Flare to create a Word Table of Contents or an index, the content *must* be contained in a single file.

Distributing Word output

When you build your Word output, Flare does not embed images into the DOC, DOCX, or XML file. Instead, it stores the images in the Resources\Images folder (located in a sub-folder of the Output folder).

When you distribute your Word output, you must include the DOC, DOCX, or XML file *plus* the contents of the Resources folder, which contain ancillary files such as images.

> **Tip** — If you want to embed images into the document file so you can distribute it without the Resources folder, point your browser to the MadCap knowledge base (http://kb.madcapsoftware.com), search for "embedding images" and follow the instructions in "Article #: OUTPW1010F - Embedding Images in Word output."

ADOBE FRAMEMAKER OUTPUT

You can create FrameMaker documents for Adobe FrameMaker 7.0 and later versions in BOOK and FM formats. FrameMaker output is saved as multiple files, which consist of a BOOK file with associated FM files.

> **Tip** — If you want to save FrameMaker output in a single file, see the topic "Specifying Chapter Breaks and Page Layouts" in the Flare Help system.

Distributing FrameMaker output

When you distribute FrameMaker output, you must include the
BOOK and FM files *plus* the contents of the Resources folder (located
in a sub-folder of the Output folder). The Resources folder contains
ancillary files, such as the images you've inserted into your topics.

ADOBE *PDF* OUTPUT

You can build PDF output by itself or with Microsoft Word or Adobe
FrameMaker output. The output is saved in a single PDF file.

Distributing PDF output

The PDF file is the only file you need to distribute.

MICROSOFT *XPS* OUTPUT

XPS (XML Paper Specification) is a fixed layout, device-independent
document format developed by Microsoft. You can build XPS output
by itself or simultaneously with Microsoft 2007 output. XPS output is
saved in a single XPS file.

Table 5A-1:
Building
XPS
output

To build XPS output ...	You must have ...
By itself	Windows Vista - or - .NET Framework 3.0 installed on your computer (a free download from Microsoft).
Simultaneously with Microsoft 2007 output	Microsoft Word 2007 – and – the "Save as XPS" add-in for Microsoft Office 2007 installed on your computer (a free download from Microsoft).

Viewing XPS output

You can view XPS output from within Flare or externally by opening the XPS output file with Internet Explorer 7 or higher.

Table 5A-2: Viewing XPS output

To view XPS output ...	You must have ...
From within Flare (immediately after building the output)	Internet Explorer 7 or higher. Flare lets you browse for Internet Explorer (if it's not your default browser).
Outside of Flare on a computer running Vista	Internet Explorer 7 or higher.
Outside of Flare on a computer running XP	.NET Framework 3.0 installed on your computer – and – Internet Explorer 7 or higher. Both are free downloads from Microsoft.

Distributing XPS output

The XPS file is the only file you need to distribute.

XHTML OUTPUT

XHTML is a browser-based XML document format that you can view online or print. Regardless of the number of topics, XHTML output is saved in a single file with an .htm extension.

Distributing XHTML output

When you distribute your output, you must include the HTM file *plus* the contents of the Resources folder. The Resources folder contains ancillary files, such as the images you've inserted into your topics.

BEFORE CREATING PRINT OUTPUT

Before you create print output, you should do the following:

- **Create your project**. You can build print output from any Flare project. To create the project, see "Creating a Flare project" on page 43.

- **Create and format your content**. You create and format content for print output as you would for any other output as described in Step 2: Learn the XML Editor, and Step 3: Develop Content.

- **Add navigation aids**. Use Step 4: Create Navigation Aids, to add cross-references, links, and index entries.

- **Verify that you have a target for the type of print output you want to create**. If not, add the target. See "Adding a target" on page 61.

WHAT YOU CAN INCLUDE IN A PRINT DOCUMENT

Your print output can contain any of the following front and back matter parts, which you'll learn more about later in this chapter:

- Table or Contents
- index
- glossary
- endnotes
- list of elements
- list of concepts

DECISION TIME!

Before you continue, think about the document parts your output must contain, how it should be oriented, and its size.

Which front or back document parts do you need?

How should the print output be oriented?

- ✓ Portrait
- ✓ Landscape
- ✓ A combination of both

What size does your document need to be?

- ✓ Letter
- ✓ Legal
- ✓ A4
- ✓ Custom size

Appendix A contains detailed planning worksheets to help you record your decisions.

OUR RECOMMENDATION

In this chapter, you'll learn how to create both a simple print document and a more complex one—one with multiple document parts. For the more complex document, we've provided a tutorial.

We think it's best to climb the learning curve one step at a time. Therefore, we suggest that you create a simple print document as described next before attempting to create a document with front and back matter.

If all you need is a simple print document, read only the next section. Otherwise, take a look at "Creating a more complex print document" starting on page 211.

CREATING A SIMPLE PRINT DOCUMENT

Read this section to create only a simple print document (no title page, TOC, index, or glossary). This is the quickest way to produce print output because it requires the least amount of setup.

To create a simple print document:

- Create a topic outline (a Flare TOC), which tells Flare which topics to print and in what order.

- Edit the target for the type of print output you want.

- Build the output.

Use the following procedure to create a simple print document (one that uses the same page layout throughout) in PDF format.

To create a simple PDF print document:

1. Create a TOC that includes the topics to be printed in the desired print order. See "Creating a Table of Contents" on page 160. Flare uses this TOC as an outline when building the output.

    > **Note** — Your TOC can be as simple as a list of topics if that's all you need.

2. Add a new target. In the Project Organizer, right-click **Targets** and select **Add Target** from the menu. In the Add Target dialog, type a File Name for the target and select **PDF** for the Output Type. Click **Add**, then **OK**. (See "Adding a target" on page 61 for more information.)

    The Flare Target Editor opens to the last open tab.

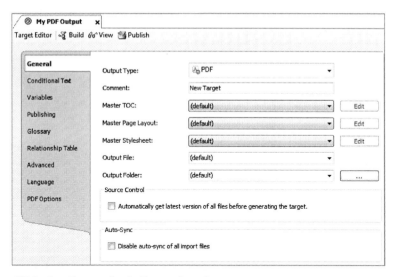

3. Click the **General** tab if not already open.

4. In the Master TOC field, select the TOC to use as an outline (if not already selected).

5. (*PDF and XPS only*) If your output includes redacted text, click the **Advanced** tab and select the redaction method (**Blackout, Highlight, Display as normal text**).

6. (*Optional*) Click the **PDF Options** tab and select the desired PDF options such as image compression, document properties, initial view, and security.

7. Click **Save All** to save your selections.

8. In the Project Organizer under **Targets**, right-click the target you just set up and select **Build <target name>** from the menu.

    Flare builds the output according to the selections you made. If your project is large, this might take several seconds.

9. View the output when prompted or view it later.

    When you're ready to distribute your output, you'll find it in a folder under your project's Output folder. By default, the file is in a folder named for the target used to build output.

Now that you've created a simple print document, let's get more ambitious!

CREATING A MORE COMPLEX PRINT DOCUMENT

We've developed a tutorial to show you how to create a document that's more complex—one with front and back parts.

Keep in mind that there are many ways to accomplish the same result. How you set up print output depends in part on how you arrange content in your Flare topic files. For instance, one person might put a document's title and copyright text into a single topic and another might put them into two separate topics.

In this tutorial, you'll learn one way of setting up a more complex document.

HOW TO USE THIS TUTORIAL

There's a lot to learn here. Because it's so easy to focus intently on the detailed instructions of a tutorial, you can miss the significance of what you're doing. We suggest that you go through this tutorial a few times. The real learning happens after you step back from the details and can see the big picture.

So, let's get to it!

This tutorial teaches you how to create a PDF document that contains a title, copyright text, Table of Contents, two chapters, and an index. We suggest that you **set aside at least two hours** to complete this entire tutorial.

SAMPLE DOCUMENT

Our sample output will have these characteristics:

- portrait orientation

- page size of 8.5 x 11 inches

- page margins of one inch on three sides (top, bottom, outside) and 1.5 inches on the inside. (The Flare page layout templates you're going to use for this tutorial have a 1.5 inch inside margin.)

- two-column index

- chapters starting on an odd page
- chapters ending on an even page (whether the page has content or not)

The following illustrations show what you'll be creating in the tutorial.

Figure 5A-1:
Title page

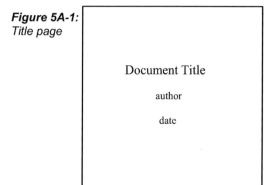

Specs: *First page in the document starts on the right; no header, footer or page number.*

Figure 5A-2:
Copyright page

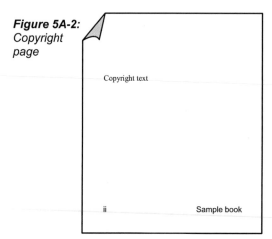

Specs: *Second page in the document starts on the left; no header. Footer contains the words "Sample book." Roman numeral page number.*

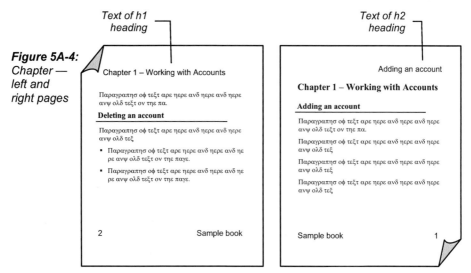

Figure 5A-3:
Table of Contents — left and right pages

Contents

iv   Sample book

Contents

Sample book   v

Specs: Header contains the word "Contents." Footer contains the words "Sample book." Roman numeral page numbers.

Text of h1 heading

Text of h2 heading

Figure 5A-4:
Chapter — left and right pages

Chapter 1 – Working with Accounts

Παραγραπησ οφ τεξτ αρε ηερε ανδ ηερε ανδ ηερε ανυ ολδ τεξτ ον τηε πα.

Deleting an account

Παραγραπησ οφ τεξτ αρε ηερε ανδ ηερε ανδ ηερε ανψ ολδ τεξ

- Παραγραπησ οφ τεξτ αρε ηερε ανδ ηερε ανδ ηε ρε ανψ ολδ τεξτ ον τηε παγε.
- Παραγραπησ οφ τεξτ αρε ηερε ανδ ηερε ανδ ηε ρε ανψ ολδ τεξτ ον τηε παγε.

2   Sample book

Adding an account

Chapter 1 – Working with Accounts

Adding an account

Παραγραπησ οφ τεξτ αρε ηερε ανδ ηερε ανδ ηερε ανυ ολδ τεξτ ον τηε πα.

Παραγραπησ οφ τεξτ αρε ηερε ανδ ηερε ανδ ηερε ανψ ολδ τεξ

Παραγραπησ οφ τεξτ αρε ηερε ανδ ηερε ανδ ηερε ανψ ολδ τεξ

Παραγραπησ οφ τεξτ αρε ηερε ανδ ηερε ανδ ηερε ανψ ολδ τεξ

Sample book   1

Specs: Header text uses h1 style (left page) and h2 style (right page). Footer contains the words "Sample book." Decimal (1, 2, 3) page numbers.

Figure 5A-5:
Index —
left and
right pages

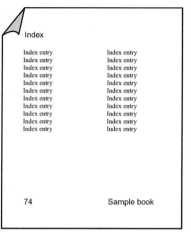

Specs: *Header contains the word "Index." Footer contains the words "Sample book." Decimal (1, 2, 3) page numbers.*

Complete all of the tasks in this tutorial to learn how to set up and build a more complex document with front and back matter. Read on to learn about the tasks you're going to complete.

TUTORIAL TASKS

- **Task 1**: Create a topic for each front and back matter part to be included in the output (e.g., Table of Contents, glossary, index). These topics are placeholders for content.

- **Task 2**: Create a topic outline (Flare TOC), which tells Flare which topics to print and in what order.

- **Task 3**: Add a page layout for each document part.

- **Task 4**: Delete unneeded pages from page layouts.

- **Task 5**: Customize footers.

- **Task 6**: Customize headers.

- **Task 7**: Link page layouts to topics in the Flare TOC.

- **Task 8**: Set up the print target.

- **Task 9**: Build the print output.

TUTORIAL SETUP

Before you begin this tutorial, make sure you have completed these setup tasks:

- Create a project. (See "Creating a Flare project" on page 43.) Select **MyPDF** for the target.

- Add topics with these names (See "Adding a topic" on page 49):

  - **Title**
  - **Chapter 1**
  - **Overview**
  - **Starting your application**
  - **Chapter 2**
  - **Adding accounts**

TASK 1: CREATE PLACEHOLDER TOPICS

In this tutorial, you'll create two special topics:

- Table of Contents

- Index

These topics are different from regular Flare topics because you don't type content (other than a topic heading) into them. Instead, Flare inserts a placeholder, called a **proxy**, into the topic.

When you build your output, the proxy is automatically replaced with the actual content. Flare builds the print Table of Contents from your headings (styles h1 – h6) and the index from index markers you'll place in your topics.

> **Note** — You don't need to do anything special with the title/copyright topic and chapter topics. They're just normal Flare topics into which you would type content.

You'll start by creating a topic for the printed Table of Contents.

1. Select **Project → Add Topic**. On the Add New Topic dialog, do the following:

    a. If not already selected, select **New from template**.

    b. Under the **Factory Templates** folder, select **TopicForTOC.htm**.

    c. Type **Print TOC** for the File Name.

    d. Type **Contents** for the 1st Heading. If this field is not visible, click 〔⤓〕.

    e. Click **Add**, then **OK** to copy the file to your project. The new topic is copied to the Content Explorer.

    > **Best Practice** — Give the TOC a meaningful file name such as **<your project name> Print TOC** to distinguish it from any other TOCs you might have in your project.
    >
    > This is a good example of when you might *type* the 1st heading instead of leaving it blank. If left blank, Flare uses the File name for the 1st heading.

    When you build your output, Flare builds the print Table of Contents from heading styles in your topics.

    > *Tip* — To prevent the h1 heading in the Table of Contents topic from being listed in the print Table of Contents, use a style other than h1 – h6 for the heading. For example, you might create a class of the "p" paragraph style and apply formatting to make it look like the h1 style.

2. With the new topic (Print TOC) open, delete the text shown before the output toc proxy.

    The XML Editor page should now look like this:

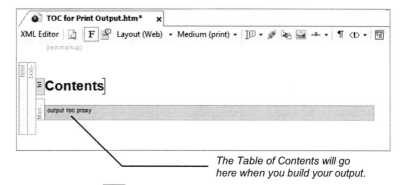

The Table of Contents will go here when you build your output.

3. Click **Save All** to save your work.

Now you'll create a topic to hold the index.

4. Select **Project → Add Topic**. On the Add New Topic dialog, do the following:

    a. If not already selected, select **New from template**.

    b. Under the **Factory Templates** folder, select **TopicForIndex.htm**.

    c. Type **Print Index** for the File Name.

    d. Type **Index** for the 1st Heading. If this field is not visible, click.

    e. Click **Add**, then **OK** to copy the file to your project.

    The new topic is copied to the Content Explorer.

5. With the new topic (Print Index) open, delete the text shown before the output index proxy.

    The XML Editor page should now look like this:

The index will go here when you build your output.

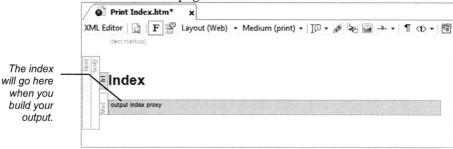

6. Click **Save All** to save your work.

Creating the topic for the index isn't the only thing you need to do to create an index. You also need to add index keywords, which are used to create the index entries. (To create index keywords, see "Creating index entries" on page 186.)

TASK 2: CREATE A TOPIC OUTLINE

In this task, you'll create a topic outline that contains all of the topics you want to include in your output.

Using Flare's TOC feature, you'll add the regular topics (Title Page, Chapter 1, Overview, Starting your application, Chapter 2, and Adding accounts) to the TOC plus you'll add TOC entries for the Table of Contents and index topics you just created.

> **Important** — The TOC entries in the topic outline *do not* become the Table of Contents in your print output. *Flare uses them only to locate the topics to include and build them in the proper order.* The Table of Contents generated from the TOC proxy is built from heading styles h1 – h6 in your topics. To exclude specific heading styles from the print Table of Contents, change the "mc-heading-level-property" in your stylesheet to zero (0) for each heading style to exclude. (Search for "mc-heading-level" in Flare's Help.)

Now you'll create the topic outline for your print (PDF) output.

1. In the Project Organizer, expand the TOCs folder and double-click **Master (Master)**. The TOC Editor opens with the beginnings of a TOC, which includes a starter topic called "Topic."

2. In the Master TOC, right-click **Topic** and select **Delete** from the menu.

3. Click **Save All** to save your changes.

   Now you have an empty TOC, and you're ready to build your topic outline.

4. Open the Content Explorer to view the list of topics in your project. You should have the eight topics you created

(Chapter 1.htm, Chapter 2.htm, Overview.htm, Starting your application.htm, Adding accounts.htm, Print Index.htm, Print TOC.htm, and Title.htm) plus the starter topic (Topic.htm) that Flare added when you created your project.

Let's get rid of the starter topic.

5. In the Content Explorer, right-click **Topic.htm** and select **Delete** from the menu. Click **OK** in response to the confirmation message. (If the Link Update dialog appears, click **Remove Links**.)

    Now you'll add your topics to the TOC in the order you want them to appear in your print output.

6. Drag **Title.htm** to the TOC Editor. Next, drag each topic to the TOC Editor and drop them in the order shown here:

    Print TOC
    Chapter 1
    Overview
    Starting your application
    Chapter 2
    Adding accounts
    Print Index

    Your Master TOC should now look like this.

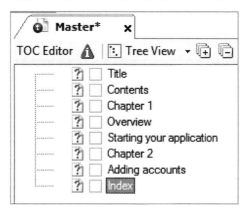

    If it doesn't match, use the "Move item …" buttons in the TOC Editor's toolbar to place all topics the same level.

Now you'll learn how to change the hierarchy of topics in the TOC.

7. In the TOC Editor, select the topic called **Overview** and click **Move item to the right**  in the TOC Editor toolbar. Notice that the Chapter 1 topic becomes a book when Overview is nested beneath it.

    Next move the topics **Starting your application** and **Adding accounts** to the right using the same method.

    Your TOC Editor window should now look like this:

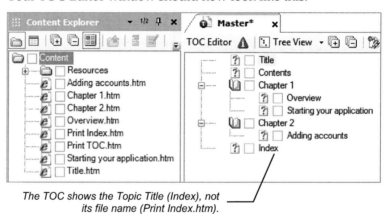

The TOC shows the Topic Title (Index), not its file name (Print Index.htm).

The order in which the topics are arranged in the TOC Editor dictates their order in the output.

8. Click **Save All** to save your work.

    Next, you'll rename the TOC. This next step isn't necessary, but it will help you keep things straight as your project grows.

9. In the Project Organizer, expand the **TOCs** folder (if necessary), right-click **Master (Master)** and select **Rename** from the menu. Then type **Outline for PDF output** and press **ENTER**. Click **Update Links** when prompted.

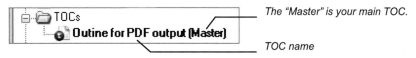

The "Master" is your main TOC.

TOC name

Let's close all open documents before moving on to Task 3.

10. Select **Window → Close All Documents**. The middle pane is now empty.

> **Note** — To create multiple output documents with different topic outlines, you can create one TOC for each topic outline or you can apply condition tags to TOC items.

Next you'll specify **page layouts**, which are files that store your layout choices.

TASK 3: ADD PAGE LAYOUTS

You'll create a page layout from a page layout template provided by Flare, starting with the Title page.

1. Select **Project → Add Page Layout**. The Add New Page Layout dialog opens.

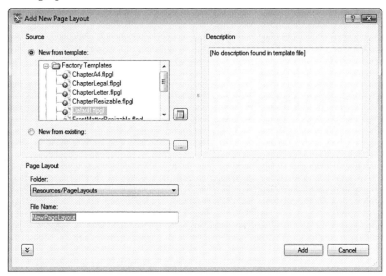

2. Make sure that **New from template** is selected.

3. Under Factory Templates, select the **FrontMatterResizable.flpgl**
    template. (See page 241 for a description of each template.)

    > **Note** — The template you're selecting is a page-layout template. Don't
    > confuse this with a topic template.

4. Type **Title Pg Layout** in the File Name field.

5. Click **Add**, then **OK** to copy the new page layout.

    The file is copied to your project's PageLayouts subfolder under
    the Resources folder in the Content Explorer. (You can ignore
    the default page layout if you see one listed. You won't use it in
    this tutorial. Flare places it there when you create a new project.)

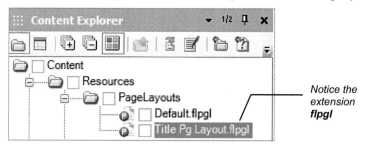

Notice the
extension
flpgl

The page layout you created opens in the Page Layout Editor.

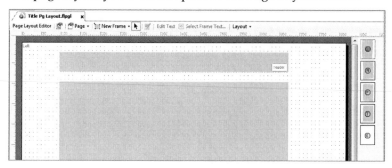

Now you need to create three more page layouts—one for the
TOC, one for chapters, and one for the index.

6. Repeat Steps 1 – 5 in this procedure three times, using this chart as a guide. On the Add New Page Layout dialog:

Select this template ...	Type this File name ...
FrontMatterResizable.flpgl	TOC Pg Layout
ChapterResizable.flpgl	Chapter Pg Layout
IndexResizable.flpgl	Index Pg Layout

When you're done, your four page layouts are listed in the Content Explorer, as shown here:

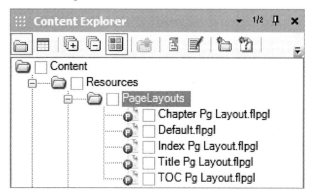

Each page layout should be open in individual tabs in the middle pane.

TASK 4: DELETE PAGES FROM PAGE LAYOUTS

Page layout templates provide a starting point only. You'll probably need to customize the page layouts the first time you create print output. After that, you can reuse them each time you print the same output.

> **Tip** — You can also copy page layouts, so that once you set up the layouts for one output document, you can replicate the layouts for others.

Page layouts can contain up to six page types: First, Title, Left, Right, Normal, and Empty. (See page 241 for more information about page types.) You won't need some of the pages on some of the layouts.

You'll work in the Page Layout Editor to customize the page layouts you just created. First, you'll remove the pages you don't need.

> **Best Practice** — Remove the pages you don't need to keep your page layouts tidy and eliminate uncertainty about which pages you're using.

1. If you don't see all four tabs in the middle pane, click ⟋⟍ ⌄ to the right of the Page Layout Editor tabs to view a list of open files.

2. Select **Title Pg Layout.flpgl** from the list or click its tab to make it active.

3. At the right side of the Page Layout Editor, right-click the **Title** page ⊤ and select **Remove Page**.

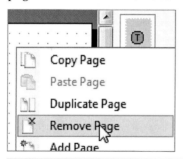

> **Note** — To store title page and copyright text in *different* topics, create a layout that has only T (title) and E (empty) pages as discussed in the Flare Help system. To *combine* title page and copyright text into one topic, use the F (first) page for the title and the L (left) page for the copyright page as we show in this tutorial.

4. Remove the **R** (right) page and the **E** (empty) page using the same process.

    What remains is the **F** (first) page and the **L** (left) page, which you'll use for the copyright text.

5. Remove these pages from these page layouts:

From this page layout ...	Remove these pages ...
TOC Pg Layout.flpgl	(F) and (T)
Chapter Pg Layout.flpgl	(F)
Index Pg Layout.flpgl	(F)

You didn't delete the **E** (empty) pages for these layouts because we want Flare to start each part (chapter, index, etc.) on an odd (right) page. If your layout includes the **Empty** page, Flare will pad the end of the previous chapter with an empty page if necessary in order to begin this chapter on an odd page.

6. Click **Save All** to save your work.

There are two more tasks for you to do to finish setting up the page layouts—customizing the header and footer frames.

TASK 5: CUSTOMIZE FOOTERS

You'll continue working with the Page Layout Editor to customize the footer frames of the page layouts you just created.

Let's start with the chapter page layout (see Figure 5A-4 on page 213). Once you've set up the left and right footers, you'll copy them to the other layouts to save yourself some time.

For this tutorial, this is what you want the left footer to look like.

1	Sample book

1. Click the **Chapter Pg Layout.flpgl** Page Layout Editor tab and
    complete the following tasks:

    a. Click the **Left** page. Scroll down to the footer frame and
        select it.

        The footer frame contains a centered page number, which is
        not what you want for this tutorial, so you need to edit it.

    b. Press **F2** to open the Frame Contents window.

        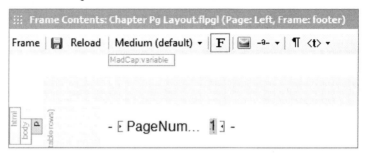

        You'll use the Frame Contents window to add and change
        content in page layout frames. It contains some of the XML
        Editor tools just for this purpose. Notice that the frame
        contains the variable PageNumber (but not in a two-column
        table), so you'll delete it.

    c. In the Frame Contents window, triple-click the text block to
        select the PageNumber variable and the dashes that
        surround it. Then press **Delete**.

        Flare normally aligns all of the text within a footer as either
        left, right, centered, or justified. However, this tutorial
        example is more complex (but also quite typical). We want
        the page number left aligned and the words "Sample book"
        right aligned. How can you do this? With a two-column
        table in the footer!

d.   Select **Table → Insert → Table**, and set these properties on
the General tab of the Insert Table dialog:

Set this property ...	To ...
Number of columns	2
Number of rows	1
Number of header rows	0
Number of footer rows	0
AutoFit Behavior	Fixed column width
Fixed column width	3.00 in

> **Note** — Here's how we calculated 3 inches for the column width:
>
> | | 8.5 inches | (page size) |
> |---|---|---|
> | − | 1.0 inch | (right margin) |
> | − | 1.5 inch | (left margin) |
> | = | 6.0 inches | (space for text) |
>
> Divided by 2 columns = 3 inches per column

e.   Click **OK**.

Now you'll insert the page number variable into the table.

f.   Click inside the left cell of the table and select **Insert →
Variable**. The Variables dialog opens.

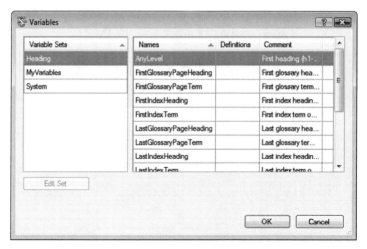

g. Select **System** for the Variable Set and **PageNumber** for the variable name, then click **OK**. The PageNumber variable is shown in the cell of the table.

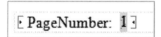

Don't worry about the format or starting page number for now. You'll set these in Task 7 when you link your page layouts to topics in the topic outline.

h. Click in the right cell of the table and type **Sample book**. Then click **Align Right** ≡ on the Text Format toolbar. (If not in view, open the toolbar by clicking **Open the Text Format Toolbar** F .) Your footer should now look like this:

i. Save the frame by clicking **Save File** 🖫 in the Frame Contents window, then close the Frame Contents window.

Leave the Chapter Pg Layout's Left page footer frame in view. You're going to use it again.

2. Since all left pages of this tutorial use this same footer, you'll copy and paste the footer you just created to other left pages.

Copying is faster than recreating the footer everywhere you need it.

To copy the footer:

a. On the **Chapter Pg Layout Left** page, select the footer frame and press **CTRL + C** to copy it.

b. Click the **Title Pg Layout.flpgl** tab, click the Left page, scroll down and select the footer frame, then press **Delete**. Now press **CTRL + V** to paste the frame you just copied.

c. Click **Save All** and close the Title Pg Layout. You're done setting it up.

d. Paste the Chapter Pg Layout Left-page footer frame to these layouts in the same manner. (Don't forget to delete the frame you don't want before pasting the new one.)

In this page layout ...	Paste into these pages ...
Chapter Pg Layout	Empty page
TOC Pg Layout	Left page and Empty page
Index Pg Layout	Left page and Empty page

3. Next you're going to create the right page footer by copying the left page footer and swapping the contents of the table cells.

This is what you want the footer to look like.

Sample book   1

Complete the following tasks:

a. Click the **Chapter Pg Layout** tab and copy its Left page footer frame. Select the **Right** page, delete its footer, and paste in the Left page footer frame. Then press **F2** to open the Frame Contents window.

b. Switch the contents of the cells so the words "**Sample book**" are in the left table cell and the page number is in the right table cell.

    c. Save the frame 💾 and close the Frame Contents window.

    d. Copy and paste the right footer frame into the **Right** pages of the **TOC Pg Layout** and the **Index Pg Layout**.

4. Click **Save All** 💾 to save your work.

Now that both the left and right footers are set up for all pages in your page layouts, you'll set up the header frames.

TASK 6: CUSTOMIZE HEADERS

Both the Table of Contents and Index have headers that contain text you type (no variables). We'll set up the Table of Contents header first. We want the word "Contents" to appear on both left and right pages.

1. Click the **TOC Pg Layout.flpgl** tab and complete the following tasks:

    a. Click the Left page, scroll up and select the header frame, and press **F2**.

    b. In the Frame Contents window, type **Contents**. Then save the frame 💾 and close the Frame Contents window.

    c. Copy the Left page header frame you just created, and paste it into the Empty page. (This way, if Flare needs to pad the end of a chapter with an empty page, the page will have a header.)

    d. Click the **Right** page, select the header frame, and press **F2**.

    e. In the Frame Contents window, type **Contents**. Then save your work and close the Frame Contents window.

    f. Close the **TOC Pg Layout**. You're done setting it up.

Next, you'll set up the header for the Index.

2. Click the **Index Pg Layout.flpgl** tab and complete the following tasks:

   a. Click the Left page, scroll up and select the header, and press **F2**.

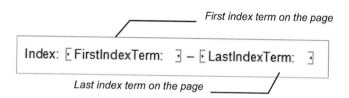

First index term on the page

Last index term on the page

   The variables for first and last index terms came from the index template. Although these variables can be used when creating PDF output, you're not using them for this tutorial, so you'll delete them.

   b. In the Frame Contents window, select the entire text block and press **Delete**.

   c. Type **Index**. Then save the frame and close the Frame Contents window.

   d. Copy the Left page frame you just saved and paste it into the Empty page.

   e. Click the **Right** page, select the header, and press **F2**.

   f. Repeat steps 2b and 2c listed previously.

   g. Close the **Index Pg Layout**. You're done setting it up.

   One more layout to finish—the Chapter Pg Layout.

   The Chapter Pg Layout needs headers that show h1 heading text on left pages and h2 heading text on right pages.

3. Click the **Chapter Pg Layout.flpgl** tab and complete the following tasks:

   a. Click the **Right** page and scroll to the upper right to see what's in the header frame.

Although it's partially covered, the right page header frame
contains the variable Heading.Level1, which places the text
of the first h1 heading on the page in your running header.
We'll delete this and insert Heading.Level 2 (the variable for
the h2 heading).

b.   Select the header frame, press **F2**, right-click the variable,
and select **Delete** from the menu. Now select **Insert →
Variable**.

c.   From the Variables dialog, select **Heading** for the Variable
Set and **Level2** for the Name, and click **OK**. Then save the
frame 💾 and close the Frame Contents window.

d.   Now click the **Left** page, scroll to the left to see the header
frame.

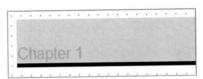

The ChapterResizable template contains a variable that
places a "Chapter" number in the left page header.

What Flare calls a chapter is not necessarily what you might
call a chapter. Flare's "chapter number" represents the order
of the topic files in your topic outline. In this example, Flare
would consider the Title page topic to be "Chapter 1" and
the Table of Contents to be "Chapter 2." It would consider
the real Chapter 1 to be "Chapter 3."

In this example, we want the text of the first heading in
Chapter 1 to appear in the header of left pages. You'll insert
the Level 1 variable to do this.

e.   Select the header frame, press **F2**, select all, and press **Delete**.

f.   Select **Insert → Variable**.

g. From the Variables dialog, select **Heading** for the Variable
Set and **Level1** for the Name, then click **OK**. Save the frame
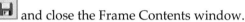 and close the Frame Contents window.

Notice that Heading.Level 1 now appears in the header
frame.

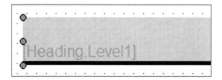

h. Select the header frame you just set up and copy it. Click the
Empty page and paste the frame into it.

4. Click **Save All** 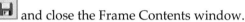 and close the Chapter Page Layout.

Whew! You're done setting up page layouts. It seems like a lot of
work, but once you get comfortable with using Flare's page layout
features, you'll find that shortcuts (such as copying and pasting
frames) make setup quicker. Plus, once your page layouts are set up
the way you want them, you won't have to do it again unless you
want to change them.

> ***Tip*** — You can copy page layouts to the Content\Resources\PageLayout folder
> of another Flare project to use them with other documents.

TASK 7: LINK PAGE LAYOUTS TO TOPICS IN THE TOC

Now you'll tell Flare where each document part begins (chapter
breaks) and which page layout to use for each document part. We're
using the term "document part" to mean each major section, such as
a title page, Table of Contents, chapter, glossary, or index. Flare uses
the term "chapter" generically to refer to these document parts.

In this task, you'll link the applicable page layout to the first topic in
each "chapter." When you build your output, Flare uses that layout
for the remaining topics until it encounters another chapter break.

If you have TOC entries for topics within a chapter, you need to link only the first TOC entry that uses the page layout you are assigning to that chapter.

Let's look at the TOC outline you created in Task 2.

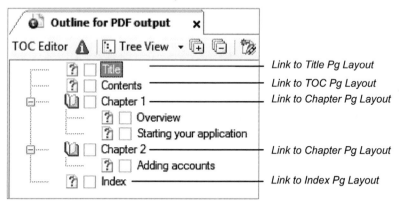

Notice that you *don't* need to link the topics called "Overview" and "Starting your application" to page layouts because they will use the Chapter Pg Layout, which is linked to the Chapter 1 topic. Also notice that you *do* need to link the first topic in Chapter 2 to Chapter Pg Layout, but you don't need to link its second topic, "Adding accounts."

Okay, let's see how to set chapter breaks and link to page layouts.

1. In the Project Organizer, expand the **TOCs** folder and double-click **Outline for PDF output (Master)**.

2. In the TOC Editor, select **Title**, then **Display properties for the selected item** on the top toolbar. The Properties dialog opens.

3. Select the **Printed Output** tab.

This section applies only if you're using master pages for print output. Ignore it if you're using page layouts.

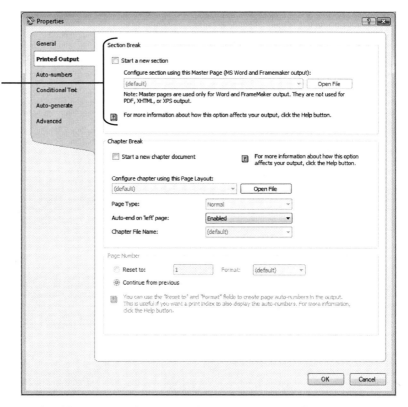

4. In the Chapter Break section, check **Start a new chapter document** to create the chapter break. You must check this box in order to assign a page layout to this TOC entry.

> **Note** — For Word documents, when you check **Start a new chapter document**, Flare inserts a section break before the chapter whose properties you are setting up. The section break is Odd or Even depending on if you select Right or Left for the Page Type.

5. In the Configure chapter using this Page Layout section, select **Title Pg Layout**.

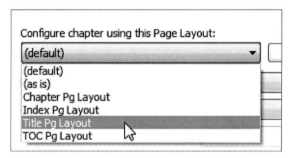

6. From the Page Type list, select **First**. (This is the page type we want Flare to use for the first page of the Title "chapter.")

7. In the Page Number section, select **Reset to** and verify that the number is **1**. Then select **roman (i, ii, iii)** from the Format list.

8. Click **OK**.

9. You do the rest, using the following chart for help.

For TOC entry ...	Assign page layout ...	Select page type ...	Set the page numbers to ...
Contents	TOC Pg Layout	Right	Continue from previous
Chapter 1	Chapter Pg Layout	Right	Reset to 1 Format: Decimal (1, 2, 3)
Chapter 2	Chapter Pg Layout	Right	Continue from previous
Index	Index Pg Layout	Right	Continue from previous

Notice that you're using "Right" for the page type. That's because you want each chapter to start on an odd page. By selecting "Right," you're telling Flare to use the Right page type for the first page of each chapter.

10. Click **Save All** to save your work.

11. Close the TOC.

TASK 8: SET UP THE PRINT TARGET

Now you'll define what you want to build—your print output—by setting up the print target. You're almost there!

1. In the Project Organizer, expand **Targets** and double-click **MyPDF (Primary)**. The MyPDF target opens in the Target Editor.

2. Click the **General** tab (if not already visible).

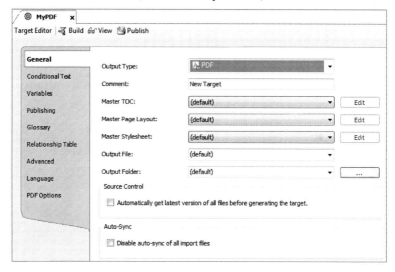

3. When you created your project, you should have selected PDF as the output type. If you didn't, select **PDF** as the Output Type now.

4. In the Master TOC field, select **Outline for PDF output**, which is your topic outline.

5. (*Optional*) Click the **PDF Options** tab and set PDF options as desired.

   For this tutorial, no other options need to be set.

6. Click **Save All** to save your work.

7.   Close the Target Editor.

Because you saved the target settings, you can build your output at any time. Let's try that now.

TASK 9: BUILD THE PRINT OUTPUT

Building the print output is the easiest part of this process. Although it's the last task before distributing your output, you'll likely build your output many times before you're done setting up layouts and developing your project's content.

> *Tip* — Build your output as you set up your page layouts, so you can see the results and make sure that you're getting what you want.

1.   In the Project Organizer, under Targets, right-click **MyPDF (Primary)** and select **Build 'MyPDF'** from the menu.

     A Build Progress window opens as Flare builds the output for the target you selected. If your project is large, this might take several seconds.

2.   Click **Yes** to view the output when prompted. Your default PDF viewer opens and displays your output.

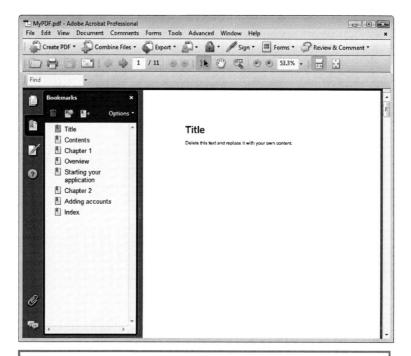

Tip — In the Contents and Index pages of the PDF file, you'll notice a thin black line above the Table of Contents and index entries. In the Styles stylesheet, the proxy styles used in the index and Table of Contents are defined as having a one-pixel black line at the beginning of the proxy content. To change this, see "Changing styles with the Stylesheet Editor" on page 146. Change the "border-top-style" property to "None" for the "MadCap|indexProxy" and "MadCap|tocProxy" styles.

Congratulations! You've survived the construction of a more complex print document!

When you're ready to distribute your PDF file, you'll find it in a folder under your project's Output folder. The file is in a folder named for the target you built (**MyPDF** in this tutorial).

To view and distribute other types of print output, see "Types of print output" on page 202.

LEARN MORE

This section contains more information about the features you used in the tutorial part of this chapter. Refer to it as needed.

PAGE LAYOUTS

In Flare, a **page layout** is a file you create to specify the layout for the pages in a part of your document. You'll create one layout for each unique combination of these page characteristics, including:

- Page orientation
- Page size
- Page number format
- Inclusion of a header on the first page
- Header contents and placement
- Footer contents and placement

For many writers, this means creating one layout for each of the following document parts:

- Title page
- Table of contents
- Chapter (one page layout for each different chapter format)
- Glossary
- Index

> **Best Practice** — Use page layouts rather than master pages to define headers and footers for print output. They provide the functionality and flexibility often needed for print output. Use master pages to define headers and footers in online output.

Page layout templates

To simplify print output, Flare includes templates for standard page layouts. You'll create a page layout by using one of these templates as a starting point. (These are not the same as *topic* templates, which you use when creating a new topic.)

Flare provides the following page-layout templates.

Table 5A-3: Flare page layout templates

Page layout template	Use this template for ...
ChapterA4	Page sizes that conform to the A4 international standard, which is 21 x 29.7 cm (8.27 x 11.69 in.).
ChapterLegal	Legal documents (8.5 x 14 in.).
ChapterLetter	Letter-size documents (8.5 x 11 in.). Frames in this layout are not anchored.
ChapterResizable	Letter-size documents (8.5 x 11 in.) that use frames.*
Default	The body of a document or simple letter-size documents that need a header, body, and footer. Margins are set to one inch all around.
FrontMatterResizable	Front matter pages, such as Tables of Contents (8.5 x 11 in.).*
GlossaryResizable	Glossaries (page size is 8.5 x 11 in.).*
IndexResizable	Indexes (page size is 8.5 x 11 in.).* This option includes the variables "Heading.FirstIndexTerm" and "Heading.LastIndexTerm" in the header. These variables are available only for PDF, XPS, and XHTML output.
NormalResizable	The body of a document or simple letter-size documents that need a header, body, and footer. This option is identical to the "default" layout except that frames are anchored.* Margins are set to one inch all around.

* Frames are anchored. Anchored frames maintain their distance from the edge of the page if you change the page size of the layout.

Page types

For each page layout, you can define six types of pages (First, Right, Left, Title, Normal, and Empty). The page buttons on the right represent each page type contained in a page layout.

Figure 5A-6:
Page layout showing frames and page types

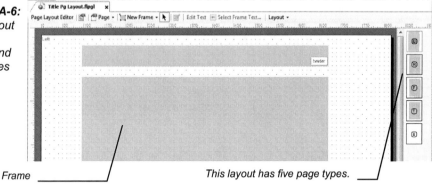

Frame _____   *This layout has five page types.* _____

Page buttons

Clicking a page button opens that page in the Page Layout Editor.

Table 5A-4:
Page Layout Editor Page buttons

This button …	Opens …
Ⓛ	The Left page type.
Ⓡ	The Right page type.
Ⓕ	The First page type.
Ⓣ	The Title page type.
Ⓝ	The Normal page type.
Ⓔ	The Empty page type.

Page frames

Each page type contains **frames** that act as placeholders for content. Page layouts can contain these types of frames:

- Header

- Footer

- Body

- Decoration (not supported by Word or FrameMaker)

- Image

Frames also indicate where the content should be placed on the printed page. To arrange content, you can insert, move, and resize frames. You can also set up a frame's characteristics. For example, a frame can have one or more columns, a background color, and borders.

> **Tip** — Within each frame, content is bounded by the frame size. If you're setting up headers and footers, make sure the frame is large enough to hold the content. (If you're using variables, you might not know this until you build output.) If your headers or footers are cut off, stretch the length of the frames, or reduce the size of the font until the content fits the frame size.

There is much more you can do with frames in Flare. We're just scratching the surface to get you started.

Editing frames

You can edit the contents of all frames except body frames. You edit frames in the Frame Contents window, which has some of the same features as the XML Editor.

Body frames

You cannot change the content in body frames. When you build your output, Flare automatically places your topic content into the body frames.

However, you can insert more body frames on a page to control the flow of content and how it is formatted.

Arrows indicate the direction in which the
text flows from one body frame to another.

Figure 5A-7:
Multiple
body
frames on
a page

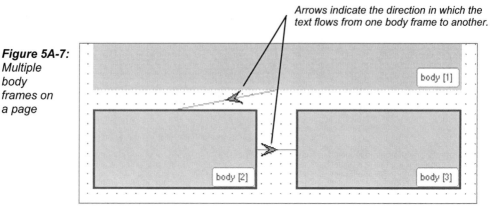

Header and footer frames

You set up header and footer frames with the content you want. To
get content into headers and footers:

- Type text into them

- Insert snippets

- Insert variables (such as page numbers or heading text from
  topics)

WHY PRIMARY TARGETS MATTER

Your project can have many targets, but one target is always
designated as "primary." "Primary target" is Flare's way of singling
out one target. Why is this important?

When you're viewing topics in the XML Editor window, Flare uses
the primary target's settings to determine what you see. For
example, if the primary target uses a page layout, you'll see that
layout's headers and footers in the XML Editor. For more
information about viewing topics in print layout mode, see "Task 7:
Viewing layout modes" on page 87.

For convenience, Flare provides toolbar buttons to open, build, view,
or publish the primary target. You may find these buttons easier to
use if you work more with one target than others.

> **Note** — To change which target is primary, right-click the target in the Project Organizer and select **Make Primary** from the menu.

WHAT'S NEXT?

At this point, you could continue adding content to your project. Since setup is done, you can also re-build the document at any time. Just remember:

- **If you add topics to your project**, you must add linked TOC entries for those topics.

- **If any of those topics will begin a new chapter**, you must designate them as chapter breaks in the TOC and link them to page layouts (see Task 7 starting on page 233).

You've now gone through an entire project cycle, from creating the project to building output! If you keep working with Flare and try other, more advanced features, it won't be long before you're a bona fide Propeller Head or even a Propellus Maximus (these are titles granted to frequent posters on the Flare user forum).

In addition:

- To develop online output, take a look at Step 5B: Create Online Output.

- To create DITA output, see Appendix G.

- To explore other features of Flare, check out the appendixes.

Step 5B:
Create Online Output

STEP 5: Create Output
5A: Print Output
5B: Online Output

STEP 4:
Create
Nav Aids

STEP 3:
Develop
Content

STEP 2:
Learn the
XML Editor

STEP 1:
Get Started

In this chapter ...
➤ Learn about online output types
➤ Add breadcrumbs
➤ Add a master page
➤ Add and edit a skin
➤ Set up a target
➤ Build online output
➤ Test and troubleshoot
➤ Distribute online output

Overview

This step explains how to create and distribute online output, such as Help systems and knowledge bases.

Before you begin using the procedures in this chapter, make sure you have done the following:

- **Create your project**. You can create online output from any Flare project. To create the project, see "Creating a Flare project" on page 43.

- **Create and format your content**. You create and format your content as you would for any other output as described in Step 2: Learn the XML Editor, and Step 3: Develop Content.

- **Add navigation aids**. Use Step 4: Create Navigation Aids, to add links and create index entries for navigation.

> **Note** — If you're unfamiliar with terms and concepts such as *output, build, distribute* and *target*, refer to the Document Basics chapter.

Keeping Track of Online Output

To make it easier to track various targets and types of output, we've created a Target Settings form (see Appendix A). As you create more targets, you'll find it very helpful to record the names of the Flare project files each target uses.

We suggest that you keep a copy of this form handy as you proceed through this chapter and begin making it a habit to fill it out.

TYPES OF ONLINE OUTPUT

With Flare, you can create the following types of online output.

Table 5B-1:
Types
of online
output

Output Type	Description
DotNet Help	A Help format created by MadCap Software (Figure 5B-1).
	For more information, see "About DotNet Help Output" in Flare's Help system.
HTML Help	An HTML-based Help format created by Microsoft that is used to develop Help systems for Windows desktop applications (Figure 5B-2).
	For more information, see "About HTML Help Output" in Flare's Help system.
WebHelp	A web-based Help format that can be run on any Internet browser or platform (Figure 5B-3).
	For more information, see "About WebHelp Output" in Flare's Help system.
WebHelp AIR	A web-based Help format created by Adobe that can be run via a single file from a desktop rather than a server (Figure 5B-3).
	To create online documents in WebHelp AIR:
	▪ You and users must install Abobe AIR (go to http://get.adobe.com/air/ for a free download).
	▪ You must install Java Runtime Environment (go to http://java.sun.com/javase/downloads/index.jsp for a free download).
	For more information, see "About WebHelp AIR Output" in Flare's Help system.
WebHelp Plus	A web-based Help format that provides enhanced functionality (Figure 5B-3).
	For more information, see "About WebHelp Plus Output" in Flare's Help system.
WebHelp Mobile	A standalone web-based Help format designed for viewing on mobile devices. WebHelp Mobile should reside on a web server; it is not intended to be part of an application (Figure 5B-4).
	For more information, see "About WebHelp Mobile Output" in Flare's Help system.

Figure 5B-1:
DotNet
Help
sample

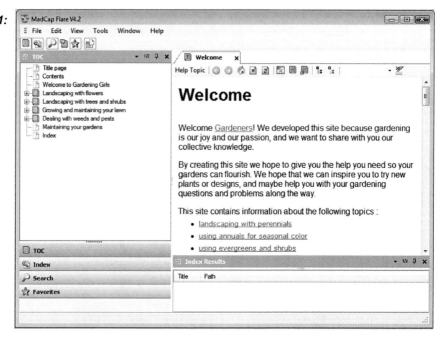

Figure 5B-2:
HTML
Help
sample

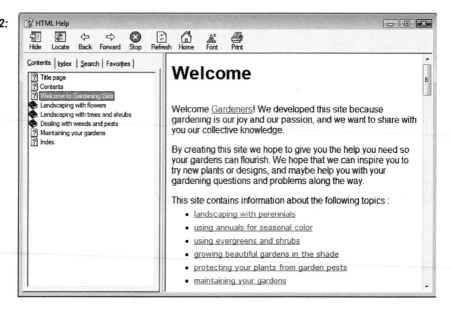

Figure 5B-3:
WebHelp,
WebHelp AIR,
and WebHelp
Plus sample

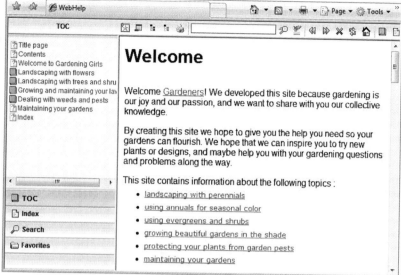

Figure 5B-4:
WebHelp
Mobile sample

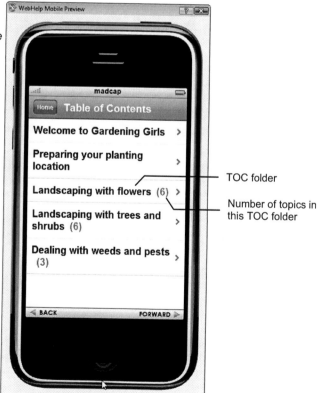

The Basic Steps

Here's a list of the steps you'll take to create online output:

- Create a TOC. See "Creating a Table of Contents" on page 160.

- Add index keywords in topics. See "Creating index entries" on page 186.

- (*Optional*) Add a master page to include a header, footer, and breadcrumbs in your online output.

- Set up your target.

- Build your online output.

- Test and troubleshoot.

- Distribute online output.

> **Note** — When creating online output, you may want to create browse sequences, which are a type of navigation aid. To learn about them, search the Flare Help system for "browse sequences."

About Breadcrumbs

Breadcrumbs are an optional navigation aid that show the path through the TOC to the topic currently open in a Help system session. The breadcrumb trail appears just above the open topic in the output as shown in the following screen.

Figure 5B-5: Breadcrumb trail

breadcrumbs

To show breadcrumbs, you must use a breadcrumbs proxy in a master page and select that master page when you set up your target. If you add a master page to your project (described next) by selecting the MasterPage Factory Template, you automatically get a breadcrumbs proxy.

> **Note** — If you don't want the breadcrumb trail, simply delete it from the master page. From the Content Explorer's Resources\MasterPages folder, open the master page, right-click the proxy, and select **Edit → Delete**.

ADDING A MASTER PAGE

Master pages let you add headers, footers, and breadcrumbs to all topics in online output.

To add a master page:

1. Select **Project → Add Master Page**. The Add New Master Page dialog opens.

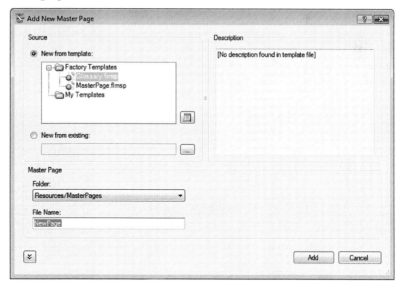

2. If not already selected, select **New from template**.

3. Under the **Factory Templates** folder, select **MasterPage.flmsp**. (The breadcrumbs proxy is automatically used with this template.)

4. In the File Name field, type a name for the master page.

> **Best Practice** — Record the name of the Master Page on the Target Settings form provided in Appendix A.

5. Click **Add**, then **OK** to copy the master page.

    The master page file (.flmsp) is added to the Resources\MasterPages folder in the Content Explorer and the XML Editor opens with the new master page shown.

6. (*Optional*) To include a header in your online topics, place your cursor *before* the **topic body proxy** and type text or include content. (You can place it either before or after the breadcrumbs proxy.)

    > **Note** — You can insert any type of content in online output headers and footers, including images, snippets, variables, and even text hyperlinks.

7. (*Optional*) To include a footer in your topics, place your cursor *after* the **mini-toc proxy** and type text or include content.

8. (*Optional*) To remove a proxy from the master page, right-click it, then select **Edit → Delete**.

9. Click **Save All** to save your work.

    After you create a master page, you must select it when you set up your target. (See "Setting up an online target" on page 256).

> **Note** — You can add multiple master pages to your project, but you can associate only one master page with each target in your project.

ADDING AND EDITING SKINS

A skin defines the appearance of online output—its interface. A skin file stores the interface settings, such as the buttons that will appear, colors, and accordion bars (or tabs if HTML Help).

New projects include a default skin, which you can edit. You can also add skins. For WebHelp Mobile output, you'll need to add a mobile skin to your project before you build output.

To add a skin:

1. Open the Project Organizer and right-click the **Skins** folder.

2. Select **Add Skin**.

3. On the Add Skin dialog, select a skin from the factory template list, type a File Name for the skin, and click **Add**.

To edit a skin:

1. Open the Project Organizer and expand the Skins folder.

2. Double-click the skin you want to edit. The Skin Editor opens.

3. Select the interface features you want (such as TOC, Index, Search, and Favorites) and the buttons you want (such as Back, Forward, Home).

4. On the Styles tab, change styles as desired (colors, fonts, etc.) for the parts of the interface (accordion items, buttons, text, background colors, etc.).

   Here's an example of HTML Help.

With the Skin Editor, you can choose which buttons you want to appear here.

Figure 5B-6:
Example of an HTML Help skin

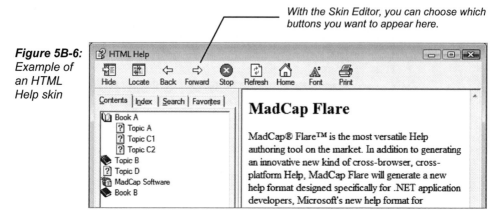

For more information about using skins, search for "skins" in the Flare Help system.

SETTING UP AN ONLINE TARGET

Now that you've finished creating the content, TOC, and index keywords, you'll tell Flare what you want to build—the output—by setting up an online target.

PRIMARY TARGETS

Your project can have many targets, but one target is always designated as "primary." "Primary target" is Flare's way of singling out one target so you can use toolbar buttons to open, build, view, or publish that target. You may find this easier if you work more with one target than others.

When you preview a topic in the XML Editor, the primary target's settings determine what you see.

Use the following procedure to set up a target.

To set up a target:

1. In the Project Organizer, expand the **Targets** folder and double-click the target you want to set up (or right-click the **Targets** folder and select **Add Target**.)

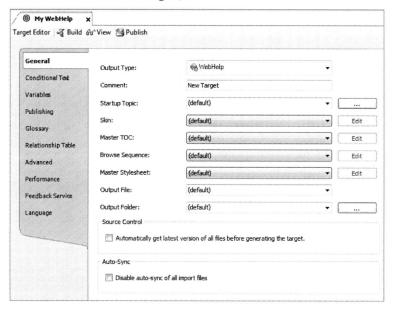

2. Click the **General** tab to open it (if necessary).

3. When you created your project, you should have selected the desired online output type. If you didn't, select the Output Type now. (See "Types of online output" on page 249 for online output types.)

4. In the Startup Topic field, select the topic you want opened when a user opens the online output. (If you're creating a WebHelp Mobile target, you cannot define a startup topic.)

5. In the Master TOC field, select the desired TOC for this target.

6. In the Master Stylesheet field, select the stylesheet used to apply styles to this target. If you select **default**, the Styles stylesheet will be used with this target.

7. In the Output File field, type a name for the file that will launch the online output (Help system or knowledge base).

> **Best Practice** — Check with the software developer to see if there are any requirements for the Output File name. If not, an easy way to keep track of your projects is to enter your project name and the target type (plus the appropriate file extension) as your Output File name. Example: "YourProjectWebHelp.htm"
>
> Don't forget to record the target name, TOC name and Output File name on the Target Settings form in Appendix A. (You'll need to remember the Output File name when you distribute your output.)

In Flare, the Output File is also called the Main Entry file. For RoboHelp™ users, this is the start page.

8. (*Required with WebHelp Mobile*) In the Skin field, select the desired skin. If you don't see a mobile skin in the list, add one to your project. (See page 255.)

9. (*Optional*) To exclude content tagged with a condition tag, click the **Conditional Text** tab.

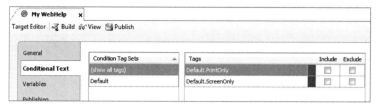

On this tab, check the condition tags you want to exclude from your output.

> **Important** — Unless excluded, all content tagged with a condition tag *is automatically included* in output.

10. (*Optional*) If you are using variables in your topics, click the **Variables** tab if you want to change the value of variables for this target only.

11. (*Optional*) If you are creating a target for context-sensitive help, click the **Advanced** tab and select an Alias File. See "Adding an alias file" on page 330.

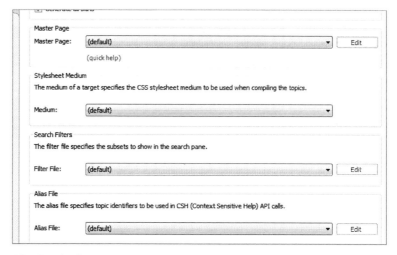

12. *(Optional)* If you are using a master page, click the **Advanced** tab and select the Master Page you want to use to build this target.

13. Click **Save All** to save your work.

Because you saved the target settings, you can build the online output at any time, even immediately. Let's try that now.

BUILDING ONLINE OUTPUT

Building online output is a snap. However, you'll probably build often as you develop content to see how it will look.

> **Best Practice** — Build frequently, especially when you're using condition tags. Doing so will help you verify that the TOC structure is correct—plus you can fix any broken links as you develop content.

WHAT CONTENT IS INCLUDED IN OUTPUT?

All project content is included in output unless you specifically exclude it! Even topics that are not included in your TOC are included in your output. That means that those topics can be found when a user searches for terms in your Help system, knowledge base, or Mobile output.

Why create a topic that you don't want included in output? There can be any number of reasons. Maybe the topic is a work-in-progress for some future version, or maybe you want a place to keep notes about your project, but you don't want that information available in output for users to see.

There are two things you can do to prevent topics from being included in output or from being searched.

How to exclude a topic from being searched

To exclude a topic from being searched (but not from output), right-click the topic in the Content Explorer, select **Properties → Topic Properties** tab and clear the checkbox "Include topic when full-text search database is generated" in the Properties dialog.

How to exclude a topic from output

To exclude the topic from output, apply a condition tag to the topic and exclude that condition tag in your target.

Procedure for building output

To build online output:

1. In the Project Organizer, under Targets, right-click the desired target and select **Build 'target name'** from the menu.

    A Build Progress window opens as Flare builds the output according to the selections you made. If your project is large, this might take several seconds.

2. Click **Yes** to view the output when prompted. Your online output is displayed. Here's a sample of WebHelp output on a computer running Windows Vista.

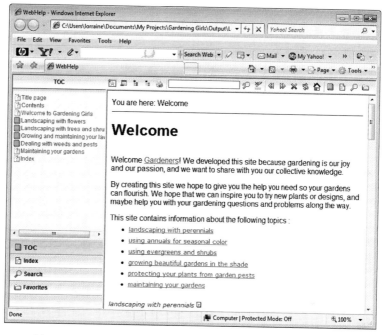

Nice work!

For samples of how your online output will look, see "Types of online output" on page 249.

TESTING AND TROUBLESHOOTING

When you built your output, Flare checked it for errors. During a build, errors will be listed in the Build Progress window.

One of the most common types of errors is broken links. This and other problems are described in Appendix E: Troubleshoot, which starts on page 337, along with information about using the internal analyzer that comes with Flare.

When you make any changes to your content, remember to re-build your output.

> ***Best Practice*** — Always test your links after building online output to verify that they connect to the correct content.

WHAT IS PUBLISHING?

Publishing is *optional*. It is simply is a way of distributing online output—typically WebHelp—after it is built. When you publish, you define a destination where Flare should place the output. The destination can be a website, Intranet location, FTP server, or local hard drive folder. You define that destination from the Publishing tab of the Target Editor.

We discourage the use of publishing for beginners unless you are publishing to your local hard drive! It is much safer to distribute online files manually as we describe than to place them directly on the Web. Besides, software developers and webmasters might prefer that you *not* copy files directly to the web server. Read on to learn about alternatives to publishing.

DISTRIBUTING ONLINE OUTPUT

Distributing your output simply means sending your project to others after it is built. However, *how* you distribute and *what* you distribute differs depending on the type of output you have created and your preferences.

HOW TO DISTRIBUTE

In most cases, you will provide the software developer with the output files so they can be linked to an application. When using the application, users will access your output via the Help menu or context-sensitive help buttons.

With Flare, you can distribute online output in these ways:

- By using an FTP application to upload output files to an FTP site.

- By using Windows Explorer to copy output to another location, such as a folder on a network. This method is quick and easy!

- By burning your output files to a CD.

- By publishing your output to a website or Intranet location (not recommended for beginners) or to a hard drive. See "What is publishing?" previously for details.

WHAT TO DISTRIBUTE

To distribute your output, you must supply:

- The name of the Output File (the file that launches the online output—defined when you created the target). See "Setting up an online target" on page 256 for details.

- Specific files and folders as defined in Table 5B-2.

> **Note** — You distribute only *output* files; you don't distribute your project's source files (the files contained in the Content folder under your project name).

Use Table 5B-2 as a guide to when you're ready to distribute your output.

Table 5B-2: What to distribute

To distribute ...	Include ...
DotNet Help	All *output* files and folders under Ouput\<your user name>, starting with the folder named for the target, plus the MadCap Help Viewer (a free download from MadCap Software).
HTML Help	The CHM file (such as YourProject.chm).
WebHelp	All *output* files and folders under Ouput\<your user name>, starting with the folder named for the target.
WebHelp Plus	All *output* files and folders under Ouput\<your user name>, starting with the folder named for the target.
WebHelp AIR	The AIR file (such as YourProject.air). Users must also install Adobe AIR™ (a free download at http://get.adobe.com/air/).
WebHelp Mobile	All *output* files and folders under Ouput\<your user name>, starting with the folder named for the target.

Where are the project's output files?

Here is where you can find your project's output files if you use the default locations for storing your project files.

- **For Vista** — In Windows Explorer, open the **My Projects** folder in the **Documents** folder. The output files for each target are located in the Output folder under your project name.

  Example:
  Documents\My Projects\Gardening Girls\Output\<user name>\<target name>

- **For XP** — In Windows Explorer, open the **My Projects** folder in the **My Documents** folder. The output files for each target are located in the Output folder under your project name.

Figure 5B-7:
Default location of project output as seen in Windows Explorer

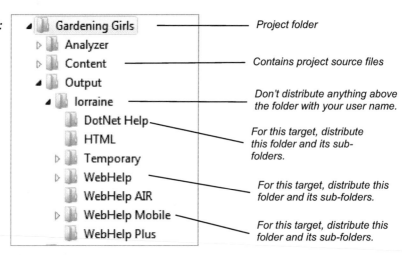

About the Output File

The Output File was created when you defined the target. This is the file that launches your online output. The Output File uses the following file extensions:

Table 5B-3:
Output
File
extensions

Extension	Type of output
.mchelp	DotNet Help
.chm	HTML Help
.htm	WebHelp, WebHelp Plus, and WebHelp Mobile
.air	WebHelp AIR

You'll need to give the software developer the name of the Output File and its location. The application needs to run this file.

For each type of online output listed above, you can find the Output File in the following folder (if you accepted the default project location when you created your project):

My Projects\<project name>\Output\<user name\<target name>

WHAT'S NEXT?

At this point, you could continue adding content to your project. Since setup is done, you can also re-build the document at any time. Just remember that **if you add topics to your project, you should add linked TOC entries for those topics**.

You've now gone through an entire project cycle, from creating the project to building output! If you keep working with Flare and try other, more advanced features, it won't be long before you're a bona fide Propeller Head or even a Propellus Maximus (these are titles granted to frequent posters on the Flare user forum).

In addition:

- To develop print output, take a look at Step 5A: Create Print Output.

- To create DITA output, see Appendix G.

- To explore other features of Flare, check out the appendixes.

Appendix A:
Planning
Worksheets

In this chapter …
> Part 1: Source of content
> Part 2: Types of output
> Part 3: Content reviews
> Part 4: Start a new project
> Part 5: Target settings

PART 1: SOURCE OF CONTENT

Use this worksheet to define where your content will come from. Copy this worksheet as needed.

If your content is …	Decide …
Not in electronic form	▪ Which topics will you create? _____ _____ _____ _____ _____ _____ _____ ▪ Which images will you create? _____ _____ _____ _____
Word or FrameMaker documents	How will you maintain the content? ☐ By using Flare ☐ By using your source application If maintaining with source application, do you want Flare to *automatically* re-import? (The alternative is that *you initiate* the re-importing.) ☐ Yes ☐ No
HTML files	Do you want to keep the style of your source content or use a Flare stylesheet? ☐ Keep style of source content ☐ Use a Flare stylesheet Name of Flare stylesheet: _____

If your content is ...	Decide ...
DITA files	How will you maintain the content? ☐ By using Flare ☐ By using your source application If maintaining with source application, do you want Flare to *automatically* re-import? (The alternative is that *you initiate* the re-importing.) ☐ Yes ☐ No Do you want to import all files into one folder? ☐ Yes ☐ No Do you want Flare to preserve element IDs when it converts DITA content? ☐ Yes ☐ No

Part 2: Type of Output

Use this worksheet to define the output to be built by Flare. Copy this worksheet as needed.

To create …	Decide …
Online output	▪ Type of output: (*Check all that apply. Indicate if you want to create multiple outputs of one type—for different versions, etc.*) □ WebHelp □ WebHelp Mobile □ WebHelp Plus □ HTML Help □ WebHelp AIR □ DocNet Help ▪ How will you structure the Help TOC (books, sub-books, with topics in each)? We recommend that you write this structure on a separate sheet and list the topics in each. ▪ How do you want your final output to look? Body text font: _____ Size: _____ Color: _____ Heading 1 font: _____ Size: _____ Color: _____ Heading 2 font: _____ Size: _____ Color: _____ ▪ Which interface (skin) will you use? □ Default Help interface: Name: _____ Location: _____ □ Custom interface (not covered in this book): Name: _____ Location: _____ ▪ (WebHelp only) Which buttons do you want on the toolbar? _____ ▪ (HTML Help only) Which Help buttons do you want? _____ ▪ Which features do you want? (TOC, Index, Search, etc.) _____ (Features appear as tabs in HTML Help and as accordion bars in Mobile and WebHelp.) ▪ Which mobile skin do you want to use? _____

To create …	Decide …
Print output	▪ Type of output: □ Word document □ FrameMaker document □ PDF file □ XHTML file □ XPS file (requires either Vista, Microsoft .NET Framework 3.0, or Word 2007 with the Office 2007 "Save as XPS" add-in) ▪ For the output selected above, choose which of the following will be included: □ TOC □ Mini-TOC □ Glossary □ Endnotes □ List of concepts □ List of elements (table of figures or images) □ First page header: _____ □ Right page header: _____ □ Left page header: _____ □ First page footer: _____ □ Right page footer: _____ □ Left page footer: _____ *(If you checked multiple front and back matter parts, you might need a separate page to document the headers and footers for each part.)* Start each document part on the right (odd) side? □ Yes □ No End each document part on a left page that is empty if necessary? □ Yes □ No ▪ For the output selected above, identify: Page size: _____ Page orientation: □ Portrait □ Landscape Page margins: Left: _____ Right : _____ Top: _____ Bottom: _____ Unit of measure (inches, pixels, points, etc.): _____

To create ...	Decide ...
DITA output (code)	▪ How will you structure the Help TOC (books, sub-books, with topics in each)? We recommend that you write this structure on a separate sheet and list the topics in each.

PART 3: CONTENT REVIEWS

Use this worksheet to determine how content will be reviewed. Copy this worksheet as needed.

Select one	If reviewers use ...	Reviews will proceed like this ...
☐	Flare or X-Edit (Full, Contribute or Review)	▪ You send reviewers Flare topics. ▪ Reviewers view topics with Flare or X-Edit and annotate them. ▪ You view comments in Flare and accept or dismiss them in your Flare topics.
☐	Word or FrameMaker	▪ You give reviewers Word or FrameMaker documents in electronic or print forms that contain the topics to be reviewed. ▪ You type changes directly into your Flare topics.
☐	Printed documents	▪ You print topics from Flare or give reviewers a PDF that contains the topics to be reviewed. ▪ You type changes directly into your Flare topics.

PART 4: START NEW PROJECT

Use this worksheet before you begin using the Start New Project Wizard. Copy this worksheet as needed.

> **Note** — If you choose to create the project and import the content simultaneously, you do not need to use the Start New Project Wizard. For simplicity, we don't cover that feature in this guide. However, the Flare Help system does an excellent job describing how to use it. Just search for "Creating a project by importing."

If you want to ...	Decide ...
Store your project in a location other than the default folder **Note** — The Windows XP default is My Documents\My Projects. The Windows Vista default is \<user name\>\Documents\My Projects.	Where your project will be stored: _____ _____
Use your project with a source control application	Identify the type of source control application: ☐ Visual Source Safe Location of INI file: _____ Folder used to store Flare project: _____ ☐ Team Foundation Server Location: _____ ☐ Other: _____ Location: _____

PART 5: TARGET SETTINGS

Use this form to record the settings for the target to be built by Flare. Copy this form as needed.

Product Names/Acronyms:

Target	Master TOC	"Master" Page Layout	Master Page (Advanced tab)	Medium	Condition Tags	Output File (Main Entry File)
					Excl:	
					Excl:	
					Excl:	
					Excl:	
					Excl:	
					Excl:	

SAMPLE TARGET SETTINGS FORM (TWO PRODUCTS)

Product Names/Acronyms: Widget Professional (WPRO) Widget Home (WHME)   Both products (WIDG)

Target	Master TOC	"Master" Page Layout	Master Page (Advanced tab)	Medium	Conditionals	Output File (Main Entry File)
WPRO PDF	WPRO Print TOC	WIDG Pg Layout	—	WIDG PrintMed	**Excl:** Comments, WHome, Online	WPRO help topics.pdf
WPRO WebHelp	WPRO Online TOC	—	WIDG Master Page	—	**Excl:** Comments, WHome, Print	WPRO Ver2-1 Help.htm
WPRO Word	WPRO Print TOC	WIDG Pg Layout	—	WIDG PrintMed	**Excl:** Comments, WHome, Online	WPRO help topics.doc
WHME PDF	WHME Print TOC	WIDG Pg Layout	—	WIDG PrintMed	**Excl:** Comments, WPro, Online	WHME help topics.pdf
WHME WebHelp	WHME Online TOC	—	WIDG Master Page	—	**Excl:** Comments & WPro, Print	WHME Ver2-1 Help.htm
WHME Word	WHME Print TOC	WIDG Pg Layout	—	WIDG PrintMed	**Excl:** Comments, WPro, Online	WHME help topics.doc

Stylesheet for all: WIDG Help Styles
Startup topic for WPRO and WHME WebHelp: Welcome
Skin for WPRO and WHME WebHelp: WIDG Skin

Appendix B:

Import
Content

In this chapter ...
> What you can import
> Import Word and Frame files
> Import HTML files

OVERVIEW

In Step1: Get Started, you learned how to create content (topics) from scratch. Now you'll learn how to import content into a Flare project. Not only is importing a fast way to add content, but it also makes the most sense if content already exists. Why re-create content if you don't have to?

You can import content into Flare:

- By creating a Flare project to hold the content and then importing the content, or

- By creating a Flare project and importing the content at the same time.

Since you've already learned how to create a Flare project, we'll discuss only the first scenario. Let's start by looking at what you can import into Flare.

WHAT YOU CAN IMPORT

You can import the following into Flare:

- Microsoft Word documents, 2003 and newer (DOC, DOCX, and RTF files)

- Adobe FrameMaker documents (BOOK, FM, and MIF files)

- HTML files

- RoboHelp projects (MPG and XPJ files)

- XHTML files (from other Flare projects)

- Microsoft HTML Help projects (HHP files)

- DITA files (DITA and DITAMAP files; see Appendix G)

When Flare imports content, it converts it to XHTML format.

> **Note** — You can also import an existing Flare project from a source control application.

WHAT THIS APPENDIX INCLUDES

In this appendix, we'll cover three import options:

- Importing Word files

- Importing FrameMaker files

- Importing HTML files

You may also find it handy to copy and paste small pieces of text into your topics, which is done without importing. See "Copying and pasting text into a topic" on page 99 for details.

WHAT YOU WON'T FIND IN THIS APPENDIX

As we said earlier, this book addresses the needs of new Flare users who have little experience with document authoring tools.

Consequently, we don't discuss how to do these tasks:

- **Import a RoboHelp project**. RoboHelp users transitioning to Flare can find instructions by searching for "robohelp project" in the Flare Help system.

- **Import DITA files** (see Appendix G).

- **Import XHTML files from another Flare project**. For information, search for "importing xhtml" in the Flare Help system.

- **Link project files from other Flare projects** ("global project linking"). To learn about this feature, search for "global project linking" in the Flare Help system.

GETTING STARTED

It's likely that you have Word, FrameMaker, or HTML files, but not all three to import. So there's no need to read this entire appendix.

Use this chart to help you decide which sections to read.

Table B-1: What sections to read

If you have …	Do this …	See these sections …
Content in Word files	Import the Word files Use heading styles to break the content into topics	Importing from Word and FrameMaker files, next A bird's-eye view of the import process (page 281) Dividing one document into many topics (page 283) Choices for importing styles (page 284) Choices for maintaining content (page 285) Importing a Word document (page 287)
Content in FrameMaker files	Import the FrameMaker files Use heading styles to break the content into topics	Importing from Word and FrameMaker files (page 281) A bird's-eye view of the import process (page 281) Dividing one document into many topics (page 283) Choices for importing styles (page 284) Choices for maintaining content (page 285) Importing a FrameMaker document (page 295)
Content in HTM or HTML files (such as website content)	Import the HTML files	Importing HTML files (page 306)

IMPORTING FROM WORD AND FRAMEMAKER FILES

With some import programs, you simply transfer text and start maintaining it in its new form. You can do this with Flare, but we suggest you consider using one of Flare's most powerful features: linking Flare topics to the program (source) that created them.

What does this mean? It means you can **import content from Word or FrameMaker and then update it in Word or FrameMaker**. That's it!

When source and destination files are linked, you can re-import the content at any time or choose to have Flare automatically check for updates to the source. The bottom line is that you don't have to use Flare's XML Editor to make updates if you prefer doing so in Word or FrameMaker.

A BIRD'S-EYE VIEW OF THE IMPORT PROCESS

Now that you know what's possible, let's take a high-level look at the entire process, starting with what to do before you import the content.

Before importing

DECISION TIME!

Before you import a document, decide:

- ✓ Which documents will you import?

- ✓ Where do you want to divide the content into topics?

- ✓ How do you want Flare to handle styles when it converts your Word or FrameMaker documents?

- ✓ Will you maintain the content with Flare or with your original source program (Word or FrameMaker)?

After you've made these decisions, **prepare your content for importing**. The cleaner your source files are, the smoother the import will be. We suggest that you take these steps:

- **Use styles to control formatting** rather than local formatting in your source files. Don't use toolbar buttons and shortcut keys to apply formatting such as bold and italics.

- **Clean up the styles in your Word or FrameMaker document** (if necessary). It's easy to have a proliferation of style variations. See "Choices for importing styles" on page 284 for more information about why this is important.

- **Make sure that the text of each topic is contiguous**. Choose a paragraph style (typically a heading style) that will be used to divide topics in Flare. Then edit your document to make sure that *the content of each topic* is preceded by that heading style. See "Dividing one document into many topics" to learn more.

> **Important** — The time you invest in cleaning up your content upfront is worth it! It will mean fewer surprises when you import it.

Import tasks

Importing content from Word or FrameMaker into Flare is a two-part process:

- First, you'll **set up the rules** for importing the content. This involves telling Flare the decisions you made about importing, such as if you want to link your Flare topics to source files and which style marks the beginning a each topic.

  > **Note** — Import rules are stored in a Flare import file, which is saved in the Imports folder of the Project Organizer. For Word imports, the file's extension is .flimp; for FrameMaker imports, its extension is .flimpfm.

- Next, you'll **import the content** into your project, using the import rules.

Our recommendation

Before you import *all* your content files, we recommend that you set up the import file and try importing a small sample file. Select a sample file that's somewhat representative of your other content files.

If you're not satisfied with the result, you might have to clean up your source files further, or tweak the import settings in your Flare import file until you have all the settings the way you want them. There are many import settings and it might take a few test imports to decide exactly how you want to set it up.

> *Tip* — You can change a Flare import file from the **Project Organizer**. Simply open the **Imports** folder and double-click the name of the Flare import file you want to change.

Let's look more closely at some of the choices you'll make when you set up the import file.

DIVIDING ONE DOCUMENT INTO MANY TOPICS

As mentioned earlier, if a source file will be imported into more than one Flare topic, you must decide *where* you want to divide the source content.

A Word or FrameMaker document typically contains paragraphs of text separated by headings. Generally, Heading 1 is used for a major topic, and lower-level headings (Heading 2 or Heading 3) are used to divide sub-topics in the Heading 1 topic.

Before you import files, **choose a paragraph style (typically a heading style) at which to break topics**. Then **edit your document** to make sure that the content for each topic is preceded by the heading style you chose.

> *Note* — Multiple topics don't have to be contained in one physical source document. You can easily import multiple source files, even if each file contains content for only one topic.

An example

Suppose you chose the Heading 2 style as the dividing point between your topics. When you import your document, each unit of content between each Heading 2 style will be converted into a Flare topic, as shown in the following illustration.

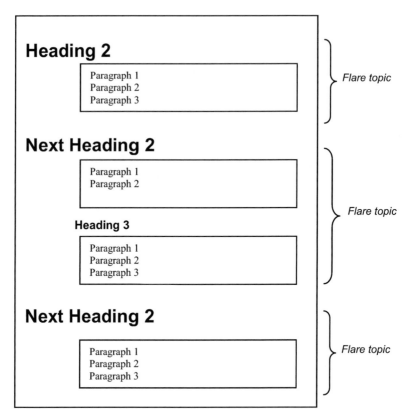

When you import this document, you'll end up with three Flare topics, as shown above.

CHOICES FOR IMPORTING STYLES

You should carefully consider the state of your documents' styles when deciding if you want to preserve them during import. Examine your source document(s) and ask:

- If you use local ("inline") formatting to control the appearance of your Word or FrameMaker files, do you want Flare to preserve that formatting?

- Are there lots of variations of styles? For example, do you have Heading 1, Heading 1 + bold, Heading 1 centered, Heading 1 underlined? Or are the styles clean (one type of Heading 1; one type of Heading 2, etc.)?

Then use this chart to help you decide the correct Flare import option.

***Table B-2:** Choices for importing styles*

If ...	Use this import option ...
You want to retain the styles in your source document *and* you don't have a proliferation of style variations - or - You want to retain the local formatting in your source document (Word files only)	**Preserve MS Word (or FrameMaker) Styles** With this option, Flare converts all Word or FrameMaker styles, including every style variation and custom style, to cascading stylesheet (CSS) styles.
You want to use *only* the styles from a Flare stylesheet in your project	**Don't Preserve MS Word (or FrameMaker) Styles**

CHOICES FOR MAINTAINING CONTENT

Before you import your content, you'll need to decide where you will maintain it. You have two choices:

- **Option 1** — Use Flare to maintain your content after import. You will import your content just once and maintain it in Flare after that.

- **Option 2** — Use Word or FrameMaker to maintain your content after import. With this option, your Flare topics will be linked to the source files from which they were created, and **you will not change your topics in Flare.**

So how will Flare topics get updated if you choose Option 2? Time for more decisions ...

Decision Time!

If you choose Option 2, you will select one of these options:

✓   Have Flare check your source files and remind you when they have changed. It's then up to you to update your Flare topics by re-importing your Word or FrameMaker files.

✓   Have Flare check your source files for changes when you build the output, automatically re-import them, and update the corresponding Flare topics before building the output. This option is called **Easy Sync**.

Use this chart to help you decide on the right options for you.

Table B-3: Options for maintaining content

Choose ...	When ...
Option 1: Maintain content in Flare	You don't need to keep the source files current.
	Changes are made by only one or two people (who have access to Flare).
Option 2: Maintain content in Word or FrameMaker	Some of the people editing content have Word or FrameMaker, but not Flare.
Easy Sync (available with Option 2)	You make frequent changes to your content.
	Changes are made by many people.

About Easy Sync

With Easy Sync, you don't have to guess if and when your content has changed. All changes to the source files will be incorporated before the Flare output is built.

Important — When you use Easy Sync, don't change your topics in Flare! They will be lost with the next automatic re-import.

What if you change your mind after importing the content?

No problem! You can switch between linking your files and not linking them by using the Link Generate Files to Source Files checkbox on the Source Files tab in the Import Editor. If you unlink the source files, you must then begin updating your content with Flare instead of with Word or FrameMaker.

> ***Tip*** — You can also turn Easy Sync on and off for complete control over when changes are re-imported into Flare.

IMPORTING A WORD DOCUMENT

You can import Word documents in DOC, DOCX, or RTF (Rich Text) format that were created with Microsoft Word 2003 or 2007.

Flare can import the following items from Word files:

- text

- images

- formats

- index entries

- links

- cross-references

About Word drawing objects and images

Flare handles drawing objects and images in Word as follows:

- Flare puts imported images into your project's Resources folder, which is available in the Content Explorer.

- Flare does *not* import drawing objects, such as callouts, lines, and arrows.

- The text of floating text boxes can be imported, but the text will be anchored instead of floating.

If your Word file contains drawing objects, consider taking the
actions listed on the following chart before you import your
Word files.

Table B-4:
Actions to
take before
importing
Word
drawing
objects

If your Word file contains …	Do this …
Callouts and other drawing objects that annotate images	<ul><li>Incorporate callouts into the image files before import *or*</li><li>Use MadCap Capture to re-create the drawing objects.</li></ul> **Tip** — If you want to edit callouts after import, use Capture to create a graphics file that you can import. Because Capture stores graphic elements in layers, you can easily edit callouts later.
Drawings that do not annotate images	Import the drawings as raster or vector images in any of these formats: BMP, EMF, EXPS, GIF, HDP, JPG, JPEG, PNG, SWF, TIF, TIFF, WDP, WMF, XAML, or XPS.

How Flare creates TOCs from a Word document

Flare creates a new TOC from the topics you import. The TOC has
the same name as the Word import file (your settings file).

However, if you created a TOC in Flare before importing your Word
document, Flare does *not* add your imported topics to the existing
TOC. To consolidate the new TOC with an existing one, you can link
the new TOC to the existing TOC or you can copy TOC items. Search
on "linking a toc" in the Flare's Help.

How to import content from Word documents

Follow these instructions to import content from a Word document
into a Flare project. This procedure includes instructions for creating
the Word import file *and* importing the content.

To import content from a Word document:

1. Make sure that the Flare project in which to import content is open with the Project Organizer in view.

2. If you have previously imported Word documents into this project, skip to Step 3, next.

   If you have not previously imported Word documents into this project, you must create a Flare import file to store your import settings (rules for importing). Do the following:

   a. In the Project Organizer, right-click the **Imports** folder.

   b. Select **Add MS Word Import File** from the menu. The Add MS Word Import File dialog opens.

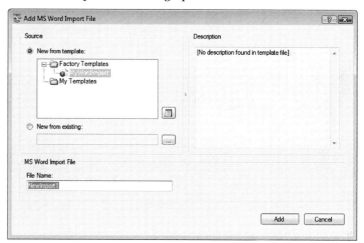

   c. If not already selected, select **New from template**.

   d. To use a template provided by Flare, select **MyWordImport** under the **Factory Templates** folder. To use one of your own templates, select **My Templates** for the folder and select the template you want to use from the list of templates on the right.

   e. Type a File Name. (Flare will add an extension of .flimp to the Word import file.)

f.   Click **Add,** then **OK** to confirm the copy action. The File
     Name you typed is listed in the Imports folder and the Word
     Import Editor opens.

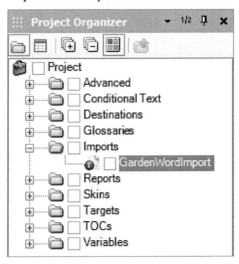

g.   Skip to Step 5 below.

3.   If you have previously imported documents into this project,
     expand the **Imports** folder.

4.   Double-click the Flare import file you want to use for this
     import.

     The Word Import Editor opens.

5.   On the Source Files tab, do the following:

     a.   Click **Add Files** and select the Word documents you want to
          add. (You can choose DOC, DOCX, or RTF files.)

          > **Note** — DOCX (Word's XML format) is available only with
          > Word 2007.

     b.   If you want to update your content from Flare instead of
          from Word after import, clear the **Link Generated Files To
          Source Files** checkbox. (See "Choices for maintaining
          content" on page 285 for options.)

> **Note** — If your imported topics are linked to your source files, a link
> icon 🕮 appears next to the topic's file name on the XML Editor tab. (If
> you're using source control, the source control icon appears instead.)

c. If you've selected multiple Word documents to import, you
can change the order in which they're listed by clicking
Move Up and **Move Down**.

> **Note** — The document order shown here determines the topic order
> in the TOC that Flare creates.

6. If you're splitting your documents into multiple topics, do the
following:

a. Click the **New Topic Styles** tab. On the left, Flare shows the
styles used in the Word documents being imported.

b. In the Used Word Styles column, double-click the style that
will mark the beginning of each new topic. The style appears
in the right column.

7. If you want Flare to incorporate changes from your linked Word
documents each time you build your Flare output, do the
following:

a. Verify that the **Link Generated Files To Source Files**
checkbox (Source Files tab) is checked.

b. Click the **Options** tab, then check **Auto-reimport before
'Generate Output'**. (This feature is called "Easy Sync" in the
Flare Help system.)

8. *(Optional)* On the Options tab, select these options if you have
topics that are shorter than 50 characters, want to avoid creating
empty topics, or want to split long topics in Word documents:

To ...	Use this option ...
Split long topics based on the number of characters (instead of using heading styles) and have Flare create a link called "Topic Continued" at the end of each page that is continued. You can also edit the link's format of the link.	Add "Topic Continued" links when appropriate

To ...	Use this option ...
Split long topics based on the number of characters and have Flare create a link called "Topic Continued From" at the top of each page that continues a split topic. You can also edit the format of the link.	Add "Topic Continued From..." links when appropriate
Split long topics when a specified number of characters in the topic is reached. Enter the number of characters to use as a threshold. If a topic exceeds the threshold, it will be split.	Split Long Topics
Prevent Flare from creating topics for empty sections in your Word documents. Enter the threshold of empty characters. If a source topic exceeds the threshold, Flare will not create a topic for it.	Avoid Creating 'Empty' Topics
Important — Clear this option if you have any topics that are shorter than 50 characters (the default threshold). If selected, Flare consolidates topics that are shorter than the threshold instead of creating separate topics. (Instead of clearing this option, you could also increase the threshold.)	
Specify a length for the file names Flare will create when it splits long topics.	Approximate Filename Length
Set imported tables to Auto-Fit to Contents so no table width is set.	Convert all tables to "Auto-Fit to Contents"

Note — To learn more about these options, search for "creating topics" in the Flare Help system.

9. If you want the imported topics to be linked to a Flare stylesheet, click the **Stylesheet** tab and do the following:

    a. Click **Stylesheet** and select a stylesheet to apply to the imported topics. (If you select a stylesheet from the list of those contained in your project, Flare creates a new stylesheet from it, and appends the number "1" to its name.)

b. Select the appropriate button to either preserve or not preserve Word styles. (See "Choices for importing styles" on page 283.)

c. To create Flare styles for local formatting (not controlled by Word styles) in your Word document, check **Convert inline formatting to CSS styles**; otherwise, clear this option. (This option is available only if you preserve Word styles.)

> **Note** — In Word, you can apply formats by using toolbar buttons and menu options instead of character styles. In Flare, you'll hear the terms "local" formatting and "inline" formatting to describe this.

10. (*Optional*) If you want your Word *paragraph* styles to take on the characteristics of your Flare styles, map the styles by doing the following:

a. Click the **Paragraph Styles** tab.

b. For each Word style you want to map, select the style in the MS Word Style column, select a style (in the Flare Styles column) to map to it, then click **Map**. The Flare styles you select appear to the right of the Word styles you mapped them to, as shown here:

MS Word Style	Flare Style
Bodytext	p.Bodytext
Heading 1	h1.Heading 1
Heading 3	h3.Heading 3
Procedure	

Word style ——— (pointing to Heading 3)

The Flare style it is mapped to. (In this example, we preserved Word styles.)

> **Note** — If you chose to preserve Word styles (on the Stylesheet tab), and you then map a Word style to a Flare style, Flare creates a style class of the Flare style. For example, if the Word style is called "Heading 1" and it's mapped to the Flare style "h1," the style class is "h1.Heading 1."

Here's another example where we mapped paragraph styles but did *not* preserve Word styles. Notice how the resulting Flare style name is purely a Flare style name (h1), not a

combination of the Word style (Heading 1) and the Flare
style. (Flare did not create a new style.)

MS Word Style	Flare Style
Bodytext	p
Heading 1	h1
Heading 2	h2

Word style —— (points to Heading 2 / Word style column)

The Flare style it is mapped to.
(In this example, we did not
preserve Word styles.)

11. (*Optional*) If you want your Word *character* styles to take on the
characteristics of your Flare styles, map the styles by doing the
following:

   a. Click the **Character Styles** tab.

   b. For each Word style you want to map, select the style in the
   MS Word Style column, select a style in the Flare Styles
   column to map it to, then click **Map**.

12. Do one of the following:

   - If you want to import the content now, proceed to Step 13,
   next.

   - If you don't want to import the content now, click **Save All**
   , then close the Word Import Editor.

13. Select **Import** (under the tab name). Then click **Yes** when
prompted to save changes to the Flare import file.

The Accept Imported Documents dialog opens, listing the
documents to be imported (on the left) and a preview of the
currently selected document (on the right).

14. If you're satisfied with how the topic previews look, click **Accept** to import the files. The files are added to your Flare project.

15. Close the Word Import Editor.

Where are my imported topics?

You may notice that your imported topics aren't listed in the Content Explorer with your other project topics. That's because Flare put your imported topics together in a folder in the Content Explorer. That folder has the same name as the Word import file you created.

Figure B-1: Where Flare stores your imported Word topics

Imported topics

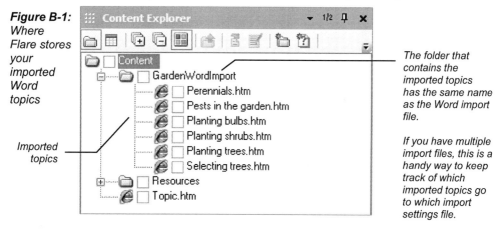

The folder that contains the imported topics has the same name as the Word import file.

If you have multiple import files, this is a handy way to keep track of which imported topics go to which import settings file.

IMPORTING A FRAMEMAKER DOCUMENT

You can import FrameMaker documents that were created with FrameMaker Versions 7.0 and newer in BOOK, FM, or MIF formats.

As already discussed, when you import a document, you can split it into multiple topics. Flare uses FrameMaker's heading styles as the division points.

Flare can import the following items from FrameMaker files:

- text
- images
- formats
- variables
- conditionals
- auto-numbering
- index entries
- hypertext links
- cross-references

Flare does *not* import FrameMaker master pages, so if you import a document that has master pages, you'll need to create Flare page layouts instead.

> **Best Practice** — If you have a FrameMaker book, it is better to import the book rather than individual files. Flare will identify and import the files that are part of the book.

About FrameMaker images

Flare handles images in FrameMaker as follows:

- Flare puts imported images in the same folder as imported topics. If you prefer, you can later move the images to the Resources\Images folder, which is the default folder for new images.

- Flare imports the text of anchored frames (such as text callouts) as an image.

- After import, you might need to resize or re-position images, since Flare does not anchor them in frames.

Before importing FrameMaker documents

When Flare imports your FrameMaker files, it uses the file name of the first FrameMaker source file as the file name of the first topic file it creates. If you want the file name to be the same as the text of the first heading, you must insert a marker in your first FrameMaker source file before you import the file.

> **Best Practice** — Insert a marker in every FrameMaker source file to be imported, not just the first one. (After all, you might later decide to rearrange the order in which you import the FrameMaker files.)

Add the marker at the *end* of the first heading in each FrameMaker file you want to import, not at the beginning of the heading. The marker should be a custom marker type called "Filename." For the text of the marker, type the file name for the first topic to be created from this source file. (For specific instructions, search the Flare Help system for "Specifying custom file names for FrameMaker imports.")

How to import content from FrameMaker documents

Follow these instructions to import content from a FrameMaker document into a Flare project. This procedure includes instructions for creating the FrameMaker import file *and* importing the content.

 **To import content from a FrameMaker document:**

1. Make sure that the Flare project in which to import content is open with the Project Organizer in view.

2. If you have previously imported FrameMaker documents into this project, skip to Step 3, next.

   If you have not previously imported FrameMaker documents into this project, you must create a Flare import file to store your import settings (rules for importing). Do the following:

   a. In the Project Organizer, right-click the **Imports** folder.

b. Select **Add FrameMaker Import File** from the menu. The
    Add FrameMaker Import File dialog opens.

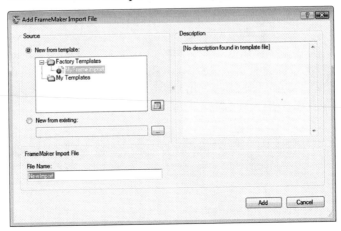

c. If not already selected, select **New from template**.

d. To use a template provided by Flare, select **MyFrameImport**
    under the **Factory Templates** folder. To use one of your own
    templates, select **My Templates** for the folder and select the
    template you want to use from the list of templates on the
    right.

e. Type a File Name. (Flare will add an extension of .flimpfm to
    the import file.)

f. Click **Add**, then click **OK** to confirm the copy action. The File
    Name you typed is listed in the Imports folder and the
    Frame Import Editor opens.

g.   Skip to Step 5, below.

3.   If you have previously imported documents into this project,
     expand the **Imports** folder.

4.   Double-click the Flare import file you want to use for this
     import.

     The Frame Import Editor opens.

5.   On the **Source Files** tab, do the following:

     a.   Click **Add Files** and select the FrameMaker documents you
          want to add. (You can choose BOOK, FM, or MIF files.)

          > **Best Practice** — If you're importing a FrameMaker book, it is better
          > to import the book rather than individual FM files. Flare will identify and
          > import the files that are part of the book.

     b.   If you want to update your content from Flare instead of
          from FrameMaker after import, clear the **Link Generated
          Files To Source Files** checkbox. (See "Choices for
          maintaining content" on page 285 for options.)

          > **Note** — If your imported topics are linked to your source files, a link
          > icon ⚇ appears next to the topic's file name on the XML Editor tab. (If
          > you are using source control, the source control icons appear instead.)

c. If you've selected multiple FrameMaker documents to import, you can change the order in which they're listed by clicking **Move Up** and **Move Down**.

> **Note** — The document order shown here determines the topic order in the TOC that Flare creates.

6. If you're splitting your FrameMaker documents into multiple topics, do the following:

a. Click the **New Topic Styles** tab. FrameMaker opens. Styles you use in the FrameMaker documents being imported are shown on the left.

b. In the Used FrameMaker Styles column, double-click the style that will mark the beginning of each new topic. The style is listed in the right column.

7. (*Optional*) On the **Options** tab, select from among the following tasks:

To ...	Do this ...
Import the text contents of anchored frames (such as text callouts)	Check the **Generate Images for Anchored Frames when needed** box. The text will be imported as images. (Images contained in anchored frames will be imported as images whether or not you check this box.) > **Important** — If you don't check this option, your text callouts will not be imported into Flare.
Incorporate changes in your linked FrameMaker documents each time you build Flare output	Verify that the **Link Generated Files To Source Files** box is checked (on the Source Files tab). Check the **Auto-reimport before 'Generate Output'** box. (This feature is called "Easy Sync" in the Flare Help system.)
Preserve the size of resized images in your FrameMaker documents	Check the **Preserve Image Size** box.

To ...	Do this ...
Enable passthrough markers (if used) in your FrameMaker documents	Check the **Enable 'Passthrough' Markers** box and select the format (text, fragment, or XML) of the passthrough markers. FrameMaker passthrough markers indicate text (such as JavaScript code) that requires special treatment when imported.
Create Flare table styles from the formats used in tables in your FrameMaker topics	Check the **Convert Table Styles** box. Table formatting will be imported even if you don't select this option.

8. (*Optional*) On the **Options** tab, select these options if you have topics that are shorter than 50 characters, want to avoid creating empty topics, or want to split long topics in FrameMaker documents:

To ...	Do this ...
Split long topics when a topic reaches a specified number of characters	Check the **Split Long Topics** box and enter the number of characters to use as a threshold. When a topic exceeds the threshold, it will be split.
Create a link called "Topic Continued" at the end of each Flare page that is continued	Check the **Add "Topic Continued" links when appropriate** box. You can also edit the format of the link.
Create a link called "Topic Continued From" at the top of each Flare page that continues a split topic	Check the **Add "Topic Continued From..." links when appropriate** box. You can also edit the format of the link.
Specify a length for filenames Flare will create when it splits long topics.	Type a length in the **Approximate Filename Length** field.

To ...	Do this ...
Prevent Flare from creating topics for empty sections in your FrameMaker documents	Check the **Avoid Creating 'Empty' Topics** box and enter the threshold of empty characters.

When a source topic exceeds the threshold, Flare will not create a Flare topic for it.

> *Important* — Clear this option if you have any topics that are shorter than 50 characters (the default threshold). If selected, Flare consolidates topics that are shorter than the threshold instead of creating separate topics. (Instead of clearing this option, you could also increase the threshold.)

> *Note* — To learn more about these options, search for "creating topics" in the Flare Help system.

9. On the **Stylesheet** tab, do the following:

   a. Apply a stylesheet to the imported topics. Either select a stylesheet from list of stylesheets in this project, or click the **Stylesheet** button and select a stylesheet outside of your project.

   b. Select the appropriate button to either preserve or not preserve FrameMaker styles. (See "Choices for importing styles" on page 283.)

   c. To specify the characteristics for each style's property group, click the **Conversion Styles** button to open the Import Styles Editor. Click the field to the right of each characteristic to select a value.

10. (*Optional*) If you want your FrameMaker *paragraph* styles to take on the characteristics of your Flare styles, map the styles by doing the following:

    a. Click the **Paragraph Styles** tab.

b. For each FrameMaker style you want to map, select the style in the FrameMaker Style column, select a style (in the Flare Styles column) to map to it, then click **Map**. The Flare styles you select appear to the right of the FrameMaker styles you mapped them to, as shown here:

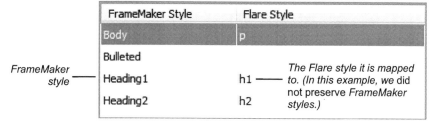

FrameMaker Style	Flare Style
Body	p.Body
Bulleted	
Heading1	h1.Heading1
Heading2	h2.Heading2

FrameMaker style —

The Flare style it is mapped to. (In this example, we preserved FrameMaker styles.)

> **Note** — If you chose to preserve FrameMaker styles (on the Stylesheet tab), and you then map a FrameMaker style to a Flare style, Flare creates a style class of the Flare style. For example, if the FrameMaker style is called "Heading1" and it's mapped to the Flare style "h1," the style class is "h1.Heading1."

Here's another example where we mapped paragraph styles but did *not* preserve FrameMaker styles. Notice how the resulting Flare style name is purely a Flare style name (h1), not a combination of the FrameMaker style (Heading1) and the Flare style. (Flare did not create a new style.)

FrameMaker Style	Flare Style
Body	p
Bulleted	
Heading1	h1
Heading2	h2

FrameMaker style —

The Flare style it is mapped to. (In this example, we did not preserve FrameMaker styles.)

11. (*Optional*) To make your FrameMaker *character* styles take on the characteristics of your Flare styles, map the styles by doing the following:

a. Click the **Character Styles** tab.

b. For each FrameMaker style you want to map, select the style in the FrameMaker Style column, select a style in the Flare Styles column to map to it, then click **Map**.

12. (*Optional*) To make your FrameMaker *cross-references* take on the characteristics of a Flare style, map the styles by doing the following:

a. Click the **Cross-Reference** tab.

b. For each FrameMaker style you want to map, select the style in the FrameMaker Style column, select a style in the Flare styles column to map to it, then click **Map**.

13. Do one of the following:

- If you want to import the content now, proceed to Step 14, next.

- If you don't want to import the content now, click **Save All** , then close the Frame Import Editor.

14. Select **Import** (under the tab name). Then click **Yes** when prompted to save changes to the Flare import file.

The Accept Imported Documents dialog opens and lists the documents to be imported (on the left) and a preview of the currently selected document (on the right).

15. If you're satisfied with how the topic previews look, click **Accept** to import the files. The files are added to your Flare project.

16. Close the Frame Import Editor.

Where are my imported topics and images?

You may have noticed that your imported topics aren't listed in the Content Explorer with your other project topics. That's because Flare put your imported topics together in a folder in the Content Explorer. This folder has the same name as the FrameMaker book file (if you imported a FrameMaker book) or as the first document listed at the top of the Source Files tab.

Flare placed your imported images in the same folder as the imported topics. (If you prefer, you can move the images to the Resources\Images folder, which is the default folder for new images.)

Figure B-2: *Where Flare stores your imported Frame-Maker topics*

Imported topics

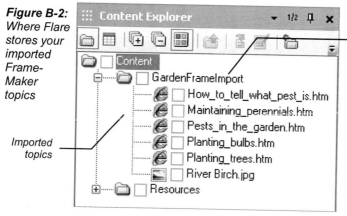

The folder that contains the imported topics has the same name as the FrameMaker import file.

If you have multiple import files, this is a handy way to keep track of which imported topics go to which import settings file.

IMPORTING HTML FILES

What if you have content that's in HTML format, such as website content? How can you get that content into a Flare project? It's quick and easy to do this with Flare.

Notes

Don't confuse HTML files and Flare files with an .htm extension. Flare files conform to the XML specification, HTML files do not.

If you copy an HTM file from another Flare project, it does not need to be imported.

When you import an HTML file, the style of your text looks the same as it did in your source HTML file.

Follow these instructions to import HTML files into a Flare project. The files are automatically converted to XHTML format.

To import one or more HTML files:

1. Select **Project → Import HTML Files**. The Import HTML Files Wizard opens.

2. Click **Add Files** and select the HTML files you want to add.

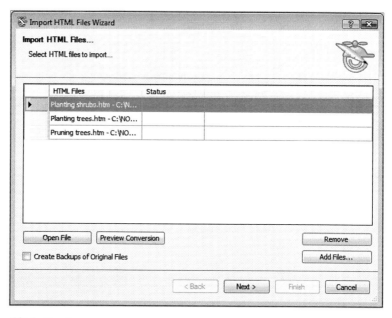

3. Click **Next**.

4. Select these options as desired:

To ...	Do this ...
Import the files to the Content Explorer's Content folder	Select **Import to project content folder**.
Import the files to another folder in the Content Explorer	Select **Import to folder**, click **Browse**, and select the folder to import the files to.
Import supporting resource files (such as images and style sheets)	Select **Import resources** and choose one of the following: ■ **Keep existing structure** to retain the folder structure of the source files. ■ **To project resources folder** to copy the supporting files to the Content Explorer's Resources folder. ■ **To folder**, and click **Browse** to select another project folder to import the files to.

5. Click **Finish**.

A conversion message box appears while the files are converted to XHTML format. When the process is complete a message appears to confirm that the files were successfully converted.

Appendix C:
XML Editor Reference

In this chapter …
> Toolbars
> Cursor types
> Rulers
> Shortcuts when working with text
> Navigational shortcuts
> IntelliSense

TOP TOOLBAR

Click ...	To ...
Preview compiled topic	See how the topic will look when compiled. To learn more, see "Previewing a topic" on page 53.
F Open the Text Format toolbar	Open or close the Text Format toolbar, used to format the text in your topics.
Open the Review toolbar	Open or close the Review toolbar, used to send topics out for review, import a reviewed topic, insert annotations (comments), show annotations, and switch between edit and review mode.
Layout (Web) ▾ or Layout (Print) ▾ Layout Mode	Toggle between **Web Layout** and **Print Layout** modes. (See "Task 7: Viewing layout modes" on page 87.) Click the down arrow to select two additional choices: • **Edit Page Layout Document** — Opens the Page Layout Editor so you can edit the page layout associated with this topic. • **Edit Master Stylesheet** — Opens the Stylesheet Editor so you can edit the stylesheet associated with this topic (if there is one).
Medium: (default) ▾ Medium (default, non-print, print)	Select a medium to use when viewing your topic. (Flare uses the "default" medium for web layouts and the "print" medium for print layouts.) The XML Editor shows the topic in the styles associated with the medium you select. For more info, see "What are mediums?" on page 89.
I⊡ ▾ Index Entry Mode	Toggle index entry mode on or off. Also contains a drop-down list of options for creating index keywords. To learn more about index entry mode, see "Adding index keywords" on page 186.
Insert a hyperlink	Open the Insert Hyperlink dialog box to add a hypertext link. Links can open topics within your project or external to your project, files, email addresses, websites, documents, or headings and bookmarks within the active topic.

Click ...	To ...
Insert a Cross-Reference	Open the Insert Cross-Reference dialog box to add a cross-reference to your topic. By default, the cross-reference inserts the word "See" plus the text of the block you are cross-referencing within quotes.
	You can create a cross-reference to a topic in the project, a file, a document, or a heading or bookmark within the active topic.
Insert a picture	Open the Insert Picture dialog box to insert a picture or graphics file. You can also type a screen tip that will appear when you hover your cursor over the picture.
Quick character ...	Select an ASCII character to insert. You can also enter the Unicode code for a symbol that you would like to be able to select with the Quick Character option.
Toggle show space	Toggle on or off the display of spaces and the end of block character for the active topic.
Show tags	Toggle on or off the display of the *active* topic with its XML tags. (This is not editable code. If you want to edit a topic's code, you need to use a text editor such as Notepad or Flare's Internal Text Editor.)
	The drop-down list contains additional choices for various items such as variable names, bookmark names, and conditional indicators.
Send this file to the text editor	Open the active topic in Flare's Internal Text Editor so you can edit the topic's XML tags and content.

BOTTOM TOOLBAR

Click ...	To ...
Smaller Font (*Web Layout only*)	Lower the magnification of fonts in the *active* topic. Each time you click, the magnification is lowered by 10%. (You cannot reduce the magnification to below 100 %.)
	Note — This option does not reduce the size of images.

Click ...	To ...
[100] Reset font scaling to 100% *(Web Layout only)*	Reset the magnification of fonts in the *active* topic to 100%. (Does not change the font size.)
[+] Larger Font *(Web Layout only)*	Raise the magnification of fonts in the *active* topic. Each time you click, the magnification is raised by 10%.
[100%] ▼ *(Web Layout only)*	Select a percentage by which to magnify the fonts in the *active* topic.
[⏮] Go to the first page *(Print Layout only)*	Show the first page of the topic.
[◁] Go to the previous page *(Print Layout only)*	Show the previous page of the topic.
[▷] Go to the next page *(Print Layout only)*	Show the next page of the topic.
[⏭] Go to the last page *(Print Layout only)*	Show the last page of the topic.
Page: [1] ↕ of 2 *(Print Layout only)*	Select the page number you want to view.
Zoom/scale *(Print Layout only)* **Note** — This button changes to reflect the current zoom/scale choice.	Specify how to magnify the page for the *active* topic: [100] **100 %** — Scales the content to 100% magnification. [🗋🗋] **100 % (2 pages)** — Shows two pages, each scaled to 100%.

Click ...	To ...
	Fit Width — Scales the content to fit the window width.
	One Page — Scales the content to show one page.
	Two Pages — Scales the content to show two pages.
	Four Pages — Scales the content to show four pages.
	Eight Pages — Scales the content to show eight pages.
Hide/show Conditional Indicators	Toggle on or off the highlighting of condition tags that have been applied to text in the *active* topic. See "Using condition tags" on page 348 for information about using condition tags in your topics.
Toggle show blocks	Toggle on or off tag bars in the *active* topic. Tag bars show the tag for each block in your topic. To learn more about tag bars, see page 92.
Toggle show spans	Toggle on or off span bars for the *active* topic. Span bars appear across the top of the content area and show the tags for formats applied to text. For example, if you apply bold to a word, a span bar labeled "b" appears above your topic. To learn more about span bars, see page 92.
Toggle show table rows	Toggle on or off table row (structure) bars in the *active* topic. (You must click inside a table to see its row bars.) There is one numbered bar for each row. You can resize or rearrange a table's rows by dragging its row bars. To learn more about table structure bars, see page 92.
Toggle show table columns	Toggle on or off column (structure) bars in the *active* topic. (You must click inside a table to see its column bars.) There is one bar for each column. The bars show the width of each column in pixels. You can resize or rearrange a table's columns by dragging its column bars. To learn more about table structure bars, see page 92.
Toggle show the horizontal ruler	Toggle on or off a horizontal ruler across the top of the *active* topic. Click the ruler to select the units of measure (pixels, points, centimeters, or inches) used.

Click ...	To ...
⊞ Toggle show the vertical ruler	Toggle on or off a vertical ruler at the left side of the *active* topic. Click the ruler to select the units of measure (pixels, points, centimeters, or inches) used.

Cursor Types

There are other cursor shapes that we don't discuss here, but these are the most common ones. Refer to Figure C-1 when reading about cursor types.

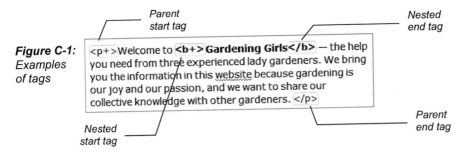

Parent start tag
Nested end tag
Nested start tag
Parent end tag

Figure C-1: *Examples of tags*

Cursor looks like this ...	When it's ...
[	Placed at a start tag. A start tag might be at the beginning of a text block or within a text block (an inline tag). For example, you might have applied bold to text within a text block. That text will be nested with its own tag set, as shown in Figure C-1.
]	Placed at an end tag.
I	Floating over text in a text block.
|	Anchored within a text block. (You clicked the mouse or used the keyboard to move the cursor in a text block.) When the cursor looks like this, you can edit text at the location of the cursor.

Cursor looks like this ...	When it's ...
	Placed at the start of a nested tag.
	When the cursor looks like this, you can insert text in the parent tag after the nested end tag.
	Placed between the end tag for a text block and the next start tag. For example, the cursor might be positioned after an end paragraph tag </p> and before the next start paragraph tag <p+>.
	When the cursor looks like this, you can insert text at the beginning of the next start tag.
	This cursor appears only when you use the keyboard (not the mouse) to navigate in your topic.
	Placed on the **Resize Picture** button at the lower right corner of an image. When the cursor looks like this, you can resize the image.
	Placed over a span bar (top structure bar).
	Right-click the structure bar to open a menu of choices that pertain to the text associated with the span bar.
	Placed over a tag bar (left structure bar), a table row bar, or a table column bar.
	Right-click the structure bar to open a menu of choices that pertain to the text block associated with the tag bar.

Note — The first seven cursors in this table appear only when you're not viewing tags.

RULERS

Rulers in the XML Editor work the same as in most word processing programs.

Figure C-2:
Horizontal
and vertical
rulers

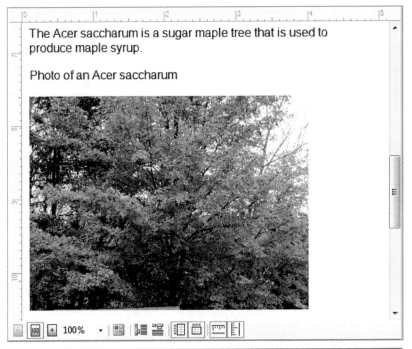

The Acer saccharum is a sugar maple tree that is used to produce maple syrup.

Photo of an Acer saccharum

100%

Note — A ruler can be in view for one open topic, but not in view for another.

To show or hide the horizontal ruler:

- Click **Toggle Show the horizontal ruler**.

To show or hide the vertical ruler:

- Click **Toggle Show the vertical ruler**.

To change a ruler's units of measure:

1. Click the ruler.

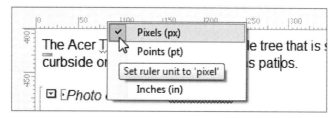

2. Select the units of measure you want (pixels, points, centimeters, inches).

SHORTCUTS WHEN WORKING WITH TEXT

SELECTING TEXT

To select ...	Do this ...
A word	Double-click the word.
A block of text	Triple-click anywhere within the text block - or - Hover your cursor over the block's tag bar and click the bar when the cursor changes to a hand.
The entire topic	Select **Edit** → **Select All** - or - Click five times in fast succession.

DELETING TEXT

To ...	Do this ...
Delete the character to the right of the insertion point	Press **DELETE**.

To ...	Do this ...
Delete the character to the left of the insertion point	Press **BACKSPACE**.
Delete several consecutive words	Select the words. Then press **DELETE**, select **Edit →** **Delete**, or click the **Delete** ☒ button.
Delete an entire text block	Select the text block and press **DELETE** - or - Hover your cursor over the block's structure bar. When the cursor changes to a hand 🖑, right-click the structure bar and select **Delete** from the menu. *Note* — The start and end tags for the text block are also deleted.

COPYING AND PASTING TEXT

You can copy (**CTRL + C**) and paste (**CTRL + V**) text as you would in most word processing applications, but you can also right-click the tag bar (left) to open a context menu that contains copy and paste options. (For more info, see "Copying and pasting text into a topic" on page 99.)

MOVING TEXT WITHIN A TOPIC

Use the following procedures to move a word, several consecutive words, or entire blocks of text.

To move a one word or several consecutive words:

1. Select the words to be moved. (See the chart on page 317 for assistance.)

2. Cut the selected text (**CTRL + X**) and paste it (**CTRL + V**) where desired within the topic.

To move a text block:

Do one of the following:

- Select the text block to be moved. (See the chart on page 317 for assistance.) Cut the text block (**CTRL + X**) and paste it (**CTRL + V**) where desired within the topic.

- Make sure that tag bars are in view. (If not, click the **Toggle show blocks** button.) Then do one of the following:

  - Drag and drop the text block's tag bar to the desired place in the topic.

  - Hover your cursor over the text block's tag bar until the cursor changes to a hand , then right-click the structure bar and select **Move** to choose movement options.

> **Note** — To learn more about tag bars, see "Toggling tag and span bars" on page 94.

NAVIGATIONAL SHORTCUTS

To move to ...	Do this ...
The top of the topic	Press **CTRL + HOME**.
	A blinking left bracket [appears before the first word in the block.
The end of the topic	Press **CTRL + END**.
	A blinking right bracket] appears after the last word in the block.
The next page of print output (*in Print Output mode*)	Press **PAGE DOWN**.
The previous page of print output (*in Print Output mode*)	Press **PAGE UP**.
The end of the block of text your cursor is in	Press **END**.
	A blinking right bracket] appears after the last word in the block.

To move to ...	Do this ...
The end of the current paragraph	Press **ENTER**. This option also starts a new paragraph.
The next word	**CTRL + →**
The previous word	**CTRL + ←**

USING INTELLISENSE

IntelliSense is an XML Editor feature that predicts ways to complete the word or phrase you are typing. As you type, IntelliSense displays a popup that shows words and phrases you've already used (matching phrases). If you see the word or phrase you want inserted, you can quickly select it, thus saving you typing time.

You can also view and select these things:

- **variables** contained in the open project

- **frequent phrases** (phrases you've used frequently in the open project)

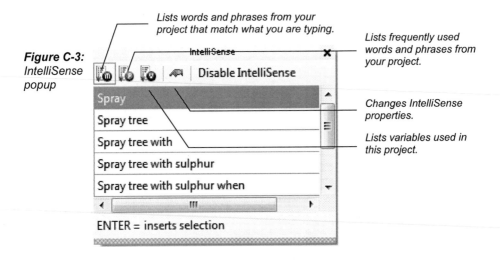

Figure C-3: IntelliSense popup

Lists words and phrases from your project that match what you are typing.

Lists frequently used words and phrases from your project.

Changes IntelliSense properties.

Lists variables used in this project.

CHANGING INTELLISENSE SETTINGS

By changing IntelliSense settings, you can change the results that appear in the IntelliSense popup for matching and frequent phrases. For example, you can a set a minimum and maximum for the number of words that should appear in the popup, and you can set a value for the number of times a phrase should occur to be considered frequent.

IntelliSense is preset with defaults for these settings. If those don't meet your needs, you can learn more by searching for "IntelliSense dialog" in the Flare Help system.

> **Note** — To use IntelliSense, Microsoft SQL Server must be installed.

Once the IntelliSense popup appears, here's what you can do.

To select a suggestion:

1. (*Optional*) Select the IntelliSense button for frequent phrases or project variables.

2. To insert a word, phrase, or variable, do one of the following:

    - Double-click the row.

    - Click the row once and press **ENTER**.

To dismiss the popup:

To ignore the IntelliSense suggestions and dismiss the popup, do one of the following:

- Keep typing the word.

- Close IntelliSense.

If you find yourself dismissing the popup often, try changing the IntelliSense settings. If you decide that IntelliSense is not helpful for your project, you can disable it.

DISABLING AND ENABLING INTELLISENSE

IntelliSense is enabled by default, but can be easily disabled by clicking the **Disable IntelliSense** Disable IntelliSense button on the IntelliSense popup.

> **Note** — To re-enable IntelliSense, select **Edit** → **IntelliSense** → **Enable IntelliSense**.

Appendix D:
Context-Sensitive Help

In this chapter ...

➤ Learn about context-sensitive help
➤ Create a header file
➤ Create an alias file
➤ Set up an alias file
➤ Test your context-sensitive help

OVERVIEW

This appendix pertains to Help systems only. Further, it applies only if the application you are writing Help for will have help buttons on its windows and dialogs.

Creating context-sensitive help involves collaboration between you (the help author) and the software developers of the application you are writing Help for. When you develop context-sensitive help, you'll work closely with software developers to make it happen.

WHAT IS CONTEXT-SENSITIVE HELP?

Context-sensitive help links an application's window or dialog to a help topic that explains it. Users can access a help topic by clicking a help button or pressing **F1** from the associated window or dialog.

With context-sensitive help, a software developer places help buttons on the windows and dialogs where Help is needed. As the help author, you'll write the help topics that the help buttons will open—plus you'll indicate ahead of time which topics go with which dialogs. This process is called **mapping**, and it uses two kinds of files:

- Header file

- Alias file

HEADER FILE

Header files (also called map files) assign a unique identification number (map number) to each window and dialog that will open a help topic. The choice of which windows and dialogs will have context-sensitive help is a decision you and the software developers will make and depends on the content of your Help system.

Header files are text files, readable in Notepad. They have an extension of .h or .hh, which is added automatically by Flare.

Software developers may provide the header file, but if not, you can use Flare to create it, and then add topic IDs used by an application and map numbers to it. If you create the header file, you'll need to discuss with the software developers what it should contain, because the map numbers must match the topic IDs used in the application. For more information about this, see "Creating a header file" on page 328.

Here's an example of a header file. (Header files typically have more than five lines, but for the sake of space, we show just five here.)

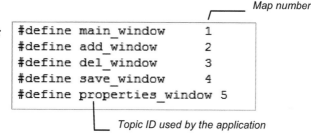

Figure D-1:
Header file

ALIAS FILE

An alias file is used to assign each map number to a topic in your Flare Help project. You'll create alias files from Flare in a format readable only by Flare (you cannot view them in Notepad). Alias files have an .flali extension.

In addition to assigning windows and dialogs to help topics, you can also assign a **skin** to each help topic so you can change the appearance of the context-sensitive help. For example, you might want context-sensitive topics to open in a smaller window than your regular help topics.

Think of an alias file as the "go-between" that connects a software application and your Help system.

AN EXAMPLE OF MAPPING

Suppose that your application contains an Add dialog, a Change dialog, and a Properties dialog, each of which need to open context-sensitive help. In addition, assume that ...

Table D-1:
Example
of mapping

This dialog's help button ...	Should open this topic ...
Add dialog	Adding a widget
Change dialog	Changing a widget
Properties dialog	Widget properties

The header and alias files in our example would contain:

HOW FLARE USES CONTEXT-SENSITIVE HELP

Let's look at how Flare uses help buttons to open Flare help topics:

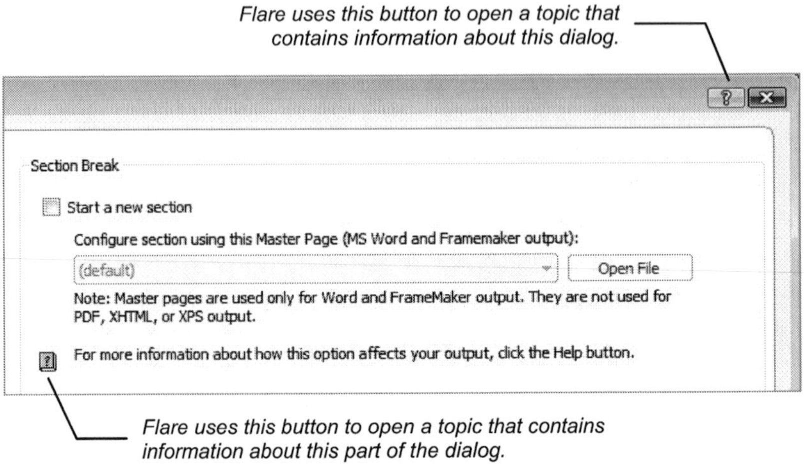

Flare uses this button to open a topic that contains information about this dialog.

Figure D-2:
Help
buttons on
a dialog

Section Break

Start a new section

Configure section using this Master Page (MS Word and Framemaker output):

(default)   Open File

Note: Master pages are used only for Word and FrameMaker output. They are not used for PDF, XHTML, or XPS output.

For more information about how this option affects your output, click the Help button.

Flare uses this button to open a topic that contains information about this part of the dialog.

YOUR TASKS

To create context-sensitive help in Flare, you'll need to complete these tasks:

- **Planning**. Talk to the software developer and decide which windows and dialogs require context-sensitive help and whether context-sensitive help topics will open in windows that are sized or positioned differently than regular help topics.

- Verify that your **project contains a header file**.

  If the software developer gives you a header file, you must import it into your project. (You can find instructions for importing a header file in the Flare Help system by searching on "header files" and opening the topic called "Importing Header Files.") Alternately, you can copy the header file into the Project Organizer's Advanced folder (<project name>\project\advanced).

  If the software developer doesn't give you a header file, create a header file in Flare. See "Creating a header file" next.

- **Add an alias file** to your project. See "Adding an alias file" on page 330.

- **Set up the alias file**. This involves creating topic IDs and map numbers (only if you didn't get a header file from the software developer), mapping topic IDs to help topics, and optionally assigning a skin to topic IDs. See "Setting up an alias file" on page 331.

- **Select the alias file when you set up the target**. To do this, open the target in the Target Editor, click the **Advanced** tab, and select the alias file.

- *If you create the header file,* **give it to the software developer**. (For instructions, search on "header files" in the Flare Help system and open the topic called "Providing a Developer with a Header File.")

- **Test the context-sensitive help links** using Flare.

- **Build the output** and **give output files to the software developers**.

CREATING A HEADER FILE

If you do not get a header file from the software developer, you'll need to create one. This requires two steps:

- (*Optional*) **Add a header file to your project**. Skip this step if you already have a header file in the Advanced folder of the Project Organizer.

  Flare creates a default header file when you create a new project. If you want to use that header file, you don't need to add another one to your project.

Figure D-3:
Default
header file

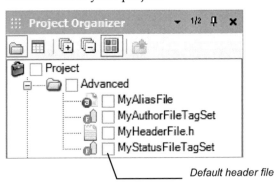

Default header file

The default header file contains one line:

Figure D-4:
Contents of
the default
header file

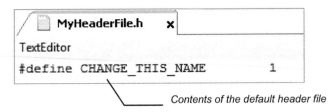

Contents of the default header file

- **Add content to the header file**—This involves creating one line for each window or dialog that will link to a help topic. Each line contains a topic ID (such as add_acct_dialog) and a unique map number. *You'll add content to the header file when you set up the alias file.*

ADDING A HEADER FILE TO YOUR PROJECT

If you don't want to use the default header file, complete the following procedure to add a new header file.

To add a header file to your project:

1. Select **Project → Advanced → Add Header File**. The Add Header File dialog opens.

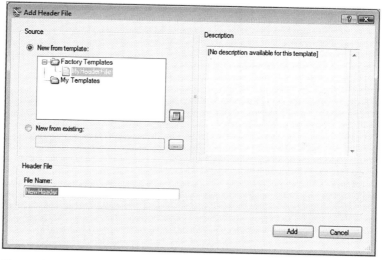

2. If not already selected, select **New from template**.

3. Under the **Factory Templates** folder, select **MyHeaderFile**.

4. Type a File Name for the header file.

5. Click **Add**, then **OK** to copy the header file to the project.

   The header file is copied to your project in the Project Organizer's Advanced folder.

ADDING CONTENT TO THE HEADER FILE

Adding content means adding a line for each window or dialog that will open a help topic. Each window or dialog will be a separate line, and each line will contain a **topic ID** and a unique **map number** for that window or dialog as show in Figure D-1.

Flare automatically adds content (topic IDs and map numbers) to the header file when you assign help topics to windows and dialogs in the Alias Editor, as described next.

ADDING AN ALIAS FILE

Before adding an alias file, make sure that your project already has a header file (see the previous topic).

To add an alias file to your project:

1. Select **Project → Advanced → Add Alias File**. The Add Alias File dialog opens.

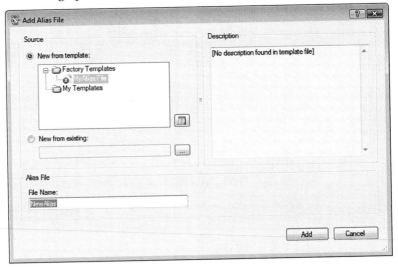

2. If not already selected, select **New from template**.

3. Under the **Factory Templates** folder, select **MyAliasFile**.

4. Type a File Name for the alias file.

5. Click **Add**, then **OK** to copy the alias file to the project.

    The alias file opens in the Alias Editor and is copied to your project in the Project Organizer's Advanced folder.

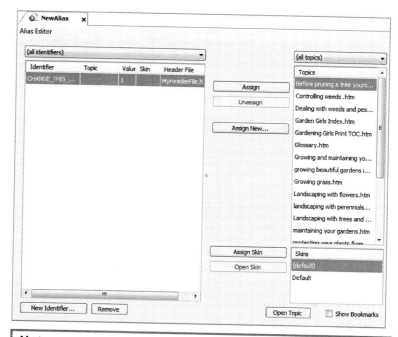

Note — You can set up the alias file now or later.

6. If you don't want to set up the alias file now, close the Alias Editor.

SETTING UP AN ALIAS FILE

Setting up an alias file involves these tasks:

- (*If you created the header file*) **Creating topic IDs and unique map numbers**. You don't need to complete this task if you received a header file from a software developer.

- **Mapping.** This involves assigning help topics to windows and dialogs, which simultaneously creates the topic IDs and map numbers in the header file.

- (*Optional*) **Assigning a skin to topic IDs**.

Use the following procedure to set up an alias file.

To set up an alias file:

1. If the alias file is not open in the Alias Editor, open it now by double-clicking it in the Advanced folder of the Project Organizer.

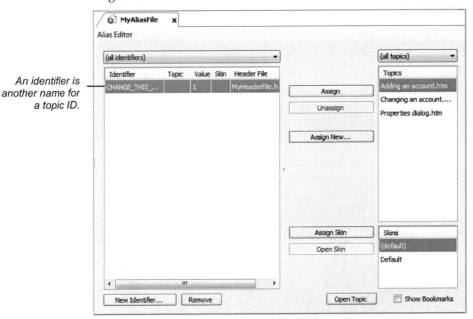

An identifier is another name for a topic ID.

The left side of the Alias Editor lists the contents of your header files: identifier (topic ID) and value. It also has places for you to assign a topic and a skin to this identifier. If you have more than one header file, it lists the identifiers from all of them.

2. If you have more than one header file, click the down arrow to the right of "all identifiers" and select the appropriate header file from the list.

> **Note** — If you received a header file from the software developer, the left side of the Alias Editor will contain many lines (one for each topic ID/map number combination). Otherwise, the left side will show only what's in the header file you created ("CHANGE_THIS_NAME" if it's a new header file that you've done nothing with).

New and default header files contain a placeholder identifier
("CHANGE_THIS_NAME").

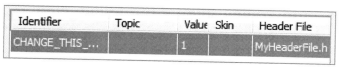

Identifier	Topic	Value	Skin	Header File
CHANGE_THIS_...		1		MyHeaderFile.h

3. Complete the tasks listed in the following chart as applicable.

To ...	Do this ...
Change the text of an identifier	<ul><li>Click the identifier.</li><li>Type the new name. (Use underscores instead of spaces to separate the words.)</li></ul><table><tr><td>Identifier</td><td>Topic</td><td>Value</td><td>Skin</td><td>Header File</td></tr><tr><td>ADD_ACCT_DIA...</td><td></td><td>1</td><td></td><td>MyHeaderFile.h</td></tr></table>
Create a new identifier (a new row)	<ul><li>Click **New Identifier**. A new row appears on the left with an assigned value and a temporary name (NEW1).</li></ul><table><tr><td>Identifier</td><td>Topic</td><td>Value</td><td>Skin</td><td>Header File</td></tr><tr><td>ADD_ACCT_DIA...</td><td>Adding an ...</td><td>1</td><td>CSH ...</td><td>MyHeaderFile.h</td></tr><tr><td>NEW1</td><td></td><td>1000</td><td></td><td>MyHeaderFile.h</td></tr></table>
Change the value	<ul><li>Click the value and type the new value.</li></ul>
Delete an identifier	<ul><li>Select the identifier and click **Remove**.</li></ul>
Map a topic to an identifier listed on the left	<ul><li>Select the identifier.</li><li>Select a topic (from the right) to map to the identifier.</li><li>Click **Assign**.</li></ul><table><tr><td>Identifier</td><td>Topic</td><td>Value</td><td>Skin</td><td>Header File</td></tr><tr><td>ADD_ACCT_DIA...</td><td>Adding an ...</td><td>1</td><td></td><td>MyHeaderFile.h</td></tr></table>
Map a skin to an identifier listed on the left	<ul><li>Select the identifier.</li><li>Select a skin (bottom right) to map to the identifier.</li><li>Click **Assign Skin**.</li></ul><table><tr><td>Identifier</td><td>Topic</td><td>Value</td><td>Skin</td><td>Header File</td></tr><tr><td>ADD_ACCT_DIA...</td><td>Adding an ...</td><td>1</td><td>CSH ...</td><td>MyHeaderFile.h</td></tr></table>

4. To create a new identifier and map a topic to it:

    a. Select a topic (from the right) to map to the identifier.

    b. Click **Assign New**. The Assign New Identifier dialog opens.

    c. Type the new identifier name. (Use underscores instead of spaces to separate the words.)

    d. Type a value.

    e. Click **OK**.

        The identifier appears on the left and is mapped to the topic that you selected.

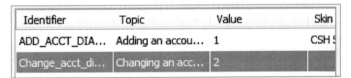

5. When you're done creating identifiers and mapping topics, click **Save All** 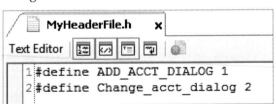 to save the changes you made to the alias and header files.

    Notice that Flare automatically updates the header file when you change the alias file.

SETTING UP THE TARGET

You'll set up your target as you normally would, except for one additional task: click the Target Editor's **Advanced** tab and select the alias file from the list at the bottom of the tab. (For more information see "Setting up an online target" on page 256.)

TESTING YOUR CONTEXT-SENSITIVE HELP

It's a good idea to test your context-sensitive help links in two ways:

- **From the software application** after you've built your Help system and given it to the software developer to link into the application. Click the help button from each window or dialog that is linked to a help topic.

- **From Flare** (discussed next).

TESTING CONTEXT-SENSITIVE HELP FROM FLARE

Use the following procedure to test context-sensitive links after you have mapped topics to identifiers and built the Help.

To test your help links from Flare:

1. Build the output for the Help system (see Step 5B: Create Online Output).

2. Right-click the Help target and select **Test CSH API Calls <target name>** from the menu.

   The Context Sensitive Help (CSH) API Tester dialog appears.

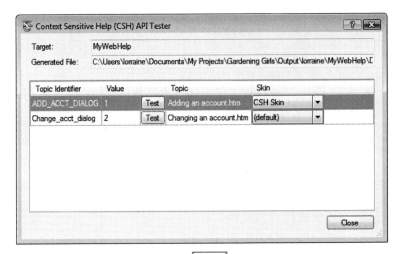

3. For each Topic Identifier, click [Test]. The help topic linked to the identifier opens in a separate window. If the correct topic does not appear, you'll need to check its mapping in the alias file.

   If you see the message "found no topic identifiers in target," check to make sure that the alias file is set up and that you selected it on the Advanced tab of the Target Editor for your Help target.

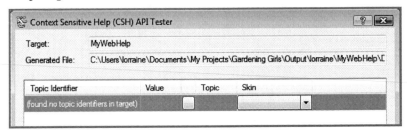

4. When you are done testing links, click **Close**.

Appendix E:
Troubleshoot

In this chapter ...
➤ Broken links
➤ Unlinked TOC items
➤ Image issues with Internet Explorer
➤ Build errors
➤ Analyzer

Overview

Here are some common problems that can occur in your projects:

- Broken links

- Broken bookmark links

- Build errors

- Unlinked TOC items

- Unlinked TOC books. (This is not a problem if you choose not to link TOC books by design.)

> **Note** — Don't confuse unlinked items with broken links. A *broken link* is one that no longer works because the file or path to it is no longer valid. An *unlinked TOC item* is not linked to anything.

Here's another, less common problem that we've experienced:

- Images that don't show up in WebHelp output viewed with Internet Explorer

Continue reading to find out why these problems occur and how to fix them.

Broken Links and Unlinked Items

Flare attempts to help you avoid broken links. For example, if you try to delete a file (topic, image, page layout, master page, stylesheet or skin, for example) that something else links to, Flare lets you know and asks how you want to handle the links.

Figure E-1:
Flare warns you when you try to delete files that are linked

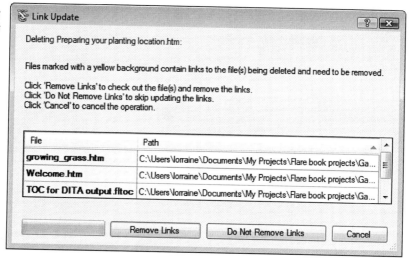

However, you can still end up with broken links in your project. Here are some reasons why.

POSSIBLE CAUSES

Broken links can occur if you:

- Move a linked topic or project file to a different folder from Windows Explorer.

- Delete a linked topic or project file from Windows Explorer.

> *Important* — Do not move or delete topic or project files from Windows Explorer! Do this only from Flare's Content Explorer.

- Delete a file that was linked to another file (topic, table of contents, or target, for example), and you selected **Do Not Remove Links** when prompted.

HOW BROKEN LINKS AND UNLINKED ITEMS APPEAR IN THE TOC

The TOC Editor marks broken links with this symbol ✗ and unlinked items and books with this symbol ✎. Unlinked books are not necessarily a problem. You might intentionally choose to not link TOC books to topics.

Figure E-2:
Broken links and unlinked items in a TOC

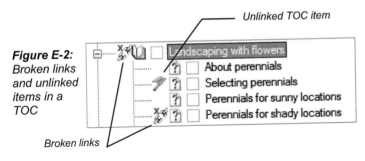

The following table describes how you can view a summary of and locate problems in your TOC.

Table E-1:
Tasks related to broken links and unlinked items

To ...	Click this ...
View a summary of broken links and unlinked items	2 Broken Link(s) in the TOC Editor toolbar
Show or hide unlinked books	
Navigate to the next broken link or unlinked item in your TOC	
Navigate to the previous broken link or unlinked item in your TOC	

> **Tip** — The navigate buttons are especially useful when your TOC is long or the TOC books are collapsed.

UNLINKED TOC ITEMS

You'll end up with *unlinked TOC items* if you add a new TOC item by clicking **New item** in the TOC Editor toolbar and then forget to link the TOC item to a topic.

> **Best Practice** — To avoid unlinked TOC items, create a TOC item and topic simultaneously by clicking **Create a new topic and link to it** ⬚ in the TOC Editor toolbar.

To fix an unlinked TOC item:

1. Right-click the TOC item and select Properties from the menu.

2. In the Properties dialog General tab, click the **Select Link** button.

3. Navigate to and select the topic, click **Open**, then click **OK**.

   The item is linked and the unlinked symbol disappears.

PROBLEMS WITH IMAGES

It's typical to add images (photographs, screen captures, and illustrations) to topics. Flare supports these image formats: BMP, EMF, EXPS, GIF, HDP, JPG, PNG, SWF, TIF, TIFF, WDP, WMF, XAML, and XPS.

However, be careful when converting an image from one format to another before you insert it into a Flare topic. You can easily corrupt an image file without even knowing it.

If one or more of your images don't appear when you view WebHelp output with Internet Explorer, it's likely that you have one or more corrupt images in your project. It's our experience that if you insert a corrupt image into your Flare project, Internet Explorer may display the image sometimes, and sometimes not!

It can be very difficult to determine which image is the culprit because all images appear normal when viewed in the XML Editor. But here's a clue: **If Windows Explorer encounters a corrupt image, all images after that disappear.** Firefox, however, seems unaffected by the same images and displays all output as expected.

Build Errors

When Flare builds your output, it checks for errors. If it finds any, the following message appears:

Figure E-3:
Build error

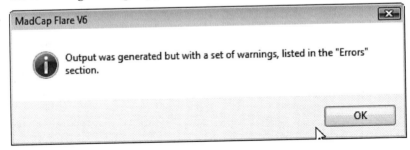

Click the **Errors** tab to view the errors.

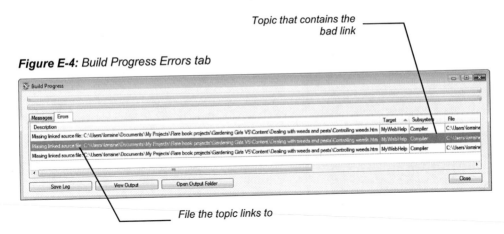

Figure E-4: Build Progress Errors tab

You can also click **Save Log** to save these messages in an error report. Then click **OK** to confirm that the log was saved in the Project Organizer's Reports folder.

> *Best Practice* — Save errors in a log so you can keep it open while fixing topics. (You cannot open topics to fix errors until you close this dialog.)

OPENING THE ERROR LOG FILE

Use the following procedure to open an error log that you saved after building output.

To open the error log:

1. In the Project Organizer, expand the **Reports** folder and double-click the log file you previously saved. The log file opens in the middle pane.

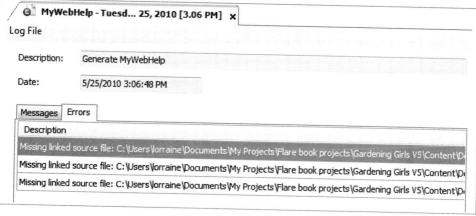

2. Scroll to the right (if necessary) to view the file that contains the bad link (in the "File" column).

3. Double-click the row in the error log that lists the file with the bad link. Fix the link, using this chart as a guide.

If the problem is a ...	Do this ...
Missing linked source file in a TOC	<ul><li>Right-click the TOC item.</li><li>Select **Link to Topic.**</li><li>Select the topic to link to.</li><li>Save the TOC.</li></ul>

If the problem is a ...	Do this ...
Missing related topic	▪ Right-click the **Related Topics** Help control.
	▪ Select **Edit Related Topics Control**.
	▪ On the right side of the Insert Related Topics Control dialog, select the correct file to link to.
	▪ Click **OK**. Save the topic.
Missing linked source file in a topic	▪ Right-click the bad link.
	▪ Select **Edit Hyperlink.**
	▪ On the Insert Hyperlink dialog, reselect the topic (file, document, etc.) to link to.
	▪ Save the topic.

To analyze your project for errors *before* building output, read the next section.

ANALYZING YOUR PROJECT

Flare offers two analyzers that help diagnose problems in your projects:

- **Internal analyzer** (provided with Flare)
- **External analyzer** (MadCap Analyzer, purchased separately)

This section discusses the internal analyzer.

WHAT YOU CAN ANALYZE

With the internal analyzer, you can examine your Flare project for the following problems:

- Broken links
- Topics that aren't linked to a TOC (to a TOC you select or to any TOC in your project)
- Topics that do not contain any index markers

- Incoming links (links that point to the current file from other files)

- Project annotations (a list of files that have annotations)

- Database errors (project files that are not scanned for errors because they are incompatible with the analyzer)

> **Important** — If your project has database errors, submit a bug report to MadCap Software Technical Support. To do so, click **Feature Requests** at the bottom of the Start Page.

ANALYZING YOUR PROJECT

Use the following procedure to analyze your project with Flare's internal analyzer.

To analyze your project:

1. Select **View → Project Analysis**. The Project Analysis window opens in the left pane.

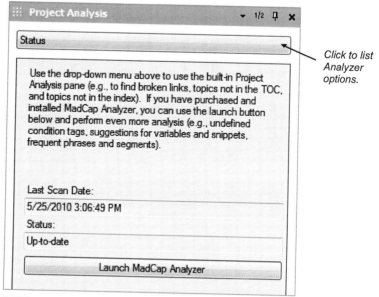

Click to list Analyzer options.

> **Tip** — Expand the left pane to see more of the Project Analysis window.

2. Select an option from the list.

To ...	Select this from the list ...
See when your project was last analyzed	**Status**
Check your project for broken links and bookmarks	**Broken Links**
See which topics have not been linked to a TOC	**Topics not in Selected TOC** Then select the TOC from the Filter list.
See which topics don't have index entries	**Topics not in Index** Then select the TOC from the list.
View a list of files that point to the file that is active in the middle pane	**Incoming Links** Then click Browse Links.
View a list of files that contain annotations	**Project Annotations**
View a list of files with database problems	**Database Errors**

3. (*Optional*) Double-click a file to open its topic.

4. To open MadCap Analyzer (a separate software product), select **Status** from the list and click **Launch MadCap Analyzer**. Analyzer opens in a new window.

> **Note** — This book describes how to analyze a project with Flare's internal analyzer. It does not cover MadCap Analyzer.

5. When you're done analyzing your project, close the Project Analysis window.

Appendix F:
Single-
Sourcing

In this chapter ...
- ➤ Create Condition tags
- ➤ Create Snippets
- ➤ Create Variables

Overview

Single-sourcing can be summarized in one phrase: **Create once, use many!** With Flare, you create content once and reuse it in any number of topics and outputs.

Flare provides these features for single-sourcing your content:

- **Condition tags**, which mark content for a particular target.

- **Snippets**, which are small units of content you reuse in multiple topics.

- **Variables**, which store changeable content (such as customer names and version numbers) that you can use in multiple topics. When you build your output, Flare substitutes the variable value everywhere it is used.

- **Multiple targets** from the same content (commonly called "multi-channel publishing"). Targets are described in the Document Basics chapter, Step 5A: Create Print Output, Step 5B: Create Online Output, and Appendix G: DITA Import and Export.

Read the rest of this chapter to find out how to use condition tags, snippets and variables in your Flare project.

Using Condition Tags

A condition tag is a marker you apply to content so that content shows up in some of your outputs but not in others.

Condition tags let you create output that contains variations of a project's content. In a *single* project, you can store the common content and the variations of it. No need to spend time and money creating different documents that duplicate common content for different needs.

With condition tags, you tag only the variations of content, not the common content that is reused for all outputs. When you set up your target, you specify which condition tags to exclude for that target.

> **Note** — You can apply condition tags to topics, snippets, images, stylesheets, blocks of content (paragraphs), text within blocks, table rows and columns, TOC entries, index keyword markers, and project files (targets, skins, glossaries, etc.).

AN EXAMPLE

Suppose you need to create two Help systems, one for an insurance program in NY and another for an insurance program in CA. Here's what you'd do:

1. Create all the content for both Help systems in one project (instead of two separate projects).

2. Create one condition tag called "Insurance NY" and another called "Insurance CA."

3. Apply the "Insurance NY" condition tag to the content that belongs only in the Help system for NY insurance users.

4. Apply the "Insurance CA" condition tag to the content that belongs only in the Help system for CA insurance users.

5. Create two targets: one for Insurance NY and one for Insurance CA.

6. Set up the Insurance NY target to exclude the Insurance CA condition tag.

7. Set up the Insurance CA target to exclude the Insurance NY condition tag.

TERMS YOU SHOULD KNOW

Before you continue, let's clarify the difference between a couple of Flare terms:

- **Condition tag set** — A named group of condition tags. Condition tag sets are listed in the Project Organizer's Conditional Text folder. You can create as many sets as you want.

> **Note** — To create a condition tag set, select **Project → Add Condition Tag Set**.

- **Condition tag** — A color-coded marker that you apply to content. Condition tags are contained in a condition tag set. You can create multiple tags in a single set.

CREATING CONDITION TAGS

Use the following procedure to add or change a condition tag (not a condition tag set).

To create a condition tag:

1. Open the Project Organizer.

2. Expand the **Conditional Text** folder, which shows existing condition tag sets. Flare includes a default condition tag set.

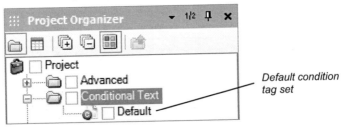

Default condition tag set

3. Double-click the condition tag set you want to add tags to. The Condition TagSet Editor opens, showing existing tags for the tag set.

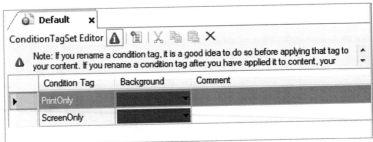

The default condition tag set contains two condition tags: "PrintOnly" and "ScreenOnly." Each condition tag has a unique color that highlights the content tagged with it.

4. Add or change tags as described in this table:

To ...	Do this ...
Add a new tag	- In the Condition TagSet Editor's toolbar, click **New item** . A new row appears, and Flare assigns a temporary name.
Rename a tag	- Select the tag's row and press **F2**. - Select the existing name and type a new name for the tag.
Change a tag's color	- Click the Background drop-down arrow and select **Pick Color**. The Color Picker dialog opens. - Select a color and click **OK**. (Only you will see the color; it doesn't appear in the output.)
Add comments to a tag	- Click in the tag's **Comment** field. - Press **F2** and type the comment. (Comments don't appear in the output.)

5. When you're done adding or changing tags, click **Save All** to save your work.

After creating condition tags, you can apply them to your content.

APPLYING CONDITION TAGS

Flare provides two ways to apply a condition tag to content (text, images, table rows, etc.) in the XML Editor. You can apply a condition tag to:

- Only the content you select

- An entire block of content

If **Hide/show Conditional Indicators** is selected on the XML Editor's bottom toolbar, the text that is marked with a condition tag is highlighted in color. Each condition tag is assigned a unique color.

Note — Before you can apply a condition tag, you must create it. See the previous topic.

To apply a condition tag to selected content:

1. Select the content you want to apply the condition tag to.

2. Select **Format → Conditions**. The Condition Tags dialog opens.

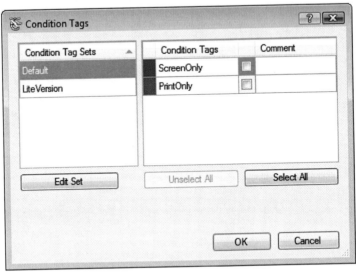

3. Select the condition tag set that contains the condition tag you want to apply.

4. Check the checkbox for the condition tag you want to apply, and click **OK**.

   Flare applies the condition tag to the selected content. If **Hide/show Conditional Indicators** ▦ is turned on, the content is highlighted with the condition tag's color.

   > o share our collective knowledge with other gard
   > or designs, and maybe help you with your garde
   > y. This text is encoded with a condition tag.

   If span bars are visible, they show that content has been tagged with a condition tag. (Span bars appear above the content area.)

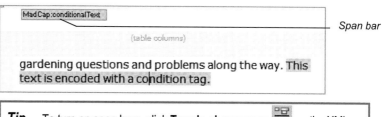

Span bar

Tip — To turn on span bars, click **Toggle show spans** on the XML Editor's bottom toolbar.

To apply a condition tag to an entire block of content:

1. If not in view, show the tag structure bars on the XML Editor's bottom toolbar.

2. Click your cursor anywhere in the block where you want to apply the condition tag.

3. Hover your cursor over the block's tag bar until the cursor changes to a hand . Then right-click the tag bar to open a menu.

4. Select **Conditions**. The Condition Tags dialog appears.

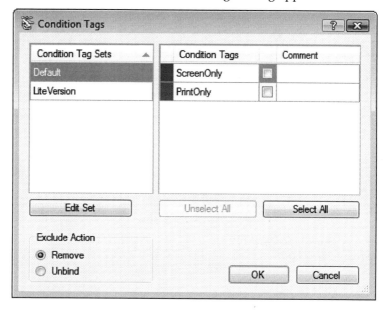

5. Select the **Condition Tag Set** that contains the condition tag you want to apply.

6. Check the checkbox for the **Condition Tag** you want to apply, and click **OK**.

    Flare applies the condition tag to the entire block and highlights its structure bar with that condition tag's color. If **Hide/show**

    Conditional Indicators  is turned on, the text block is also highlighted with the condition tag's color.

Condition tag applied to selected text.

Condition tag applied to text block

USING SNIPPETS

Snippets are units of content that you create when you need to include the same content in more than one topic. They're a perfect example of reusing content. Snippets are not standalone content; they are meant to be inserted into topics (and templates).

The beauty of snippets is maintenance. You change *only* the snippet; Flare updates it everywhere the snippet is used. Done!

Unlike variables, which contain only a few words or numbers, snippets can contain any amount and any type of content—even images and tables.

Each snippet is stored in the Content Explorer's Resources\Snippets folder as a separate file with an ".flsnp" extension. This means that you can share snippets with others, receive them from others, and use them in other projects—for even more content reuse!

CONDITIONAL SNIPPETS

Just like other content, you can apply a condition tag to a snippet so that it's included or excluded from targets.

You can also create **snippet** conditions, which are condition tags you can apply to content within snippets to customize the snippet for certain topics. For more information, search on "snippet conditions" in the Flare Help system.

SNIPPET FORMATTING

Like other content, snippets can be formatted with styles (or local formatting).

> *Tip* — If you need variable content that must be formatted, use a snippet instead of a variable. Variables *cannot* be formatted.

CREATING SNIPPETS

There are two ways to create snippets:

- From scratch
- From existing content

Creating snippets from scratch

Use the following procedure to create a snippet from scratch by using a template. You don't need to have a topic open to do this.

To create a snippet from scratch:

1. Select **Project → Add Snippet**. The Add New Snippet dialog opens.

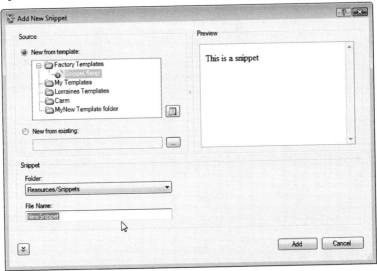

2. Fill in the fields on the Add New Snippet dialog:

Option	Description
New from template	Folders that contain templates used to create snippets. You can select: ▪ (Recommended) **Factory Templates** to choose a template provided with Flare, or ▪ **My Templates** to choose one of your own snippet templates, or ▪ **Manage Templates** 🗔 to select a template from the Template Manager. (See "Using the Template Manager" on page 68.)
New from existing	Existing snippet that you can use as a starting point and change as needed. Click ⋯ to select an existing snippet.
Preview	A preview of the selected snippet template.
Folder	(Recommended) Leave this set as Resources\Snippets.

Option	Description
File Name	The file name for the snippet. (Type a name you'll easily recognize later.)

3. Click **Add**, then **OK** to confirm the copy action.

Flare creates the snippet and copies it to the Resources\Snippets folder in your project's Content Explorer.

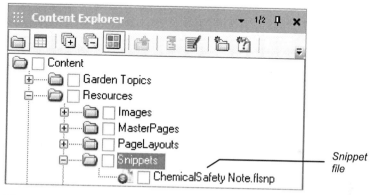

The new snippet opens in the XML Editor.

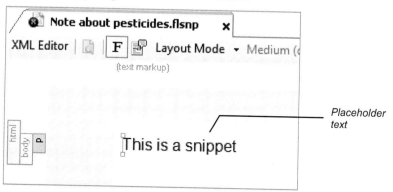

4. Click in the XML Editor and type the text you want the snippet to contain. (Don't forget to replace the placeholder text.)

Add other content as desired, such as tables, lists, and images.

5. Format the content as you would for a topic by applying styles, inserting links, etc.

6.   Click **Save All** to save your work.

You can now insert the snippet you created into any topic in your project. See "Methods for inserting snippets" on page 360.

Creating snippets from existing content

If you have existing topic content that you need to reuse in other topics, use the following procedure to turn that content into a snippet.

To create a snippet from existing content:

1.   Open the topic that contains the content you want to turn into a snippet. For example, suppose you want to create a snippet for the "Important" note in the following topic.

> ## Keeping your lawn healthy and green
>
> Many gardeners use chemical on their lawns regularly to keep them healthy and weed-free. You can use chemicals if you wish, but you do have other options. Next, we'll explore some natural methods of creating the beautiful lawn you desire.
>
> **Important** — Always store gardening chemicals in a cool, dry place out of the reach of children and pets.

2.   Place your cursor anywhere in the text block that contains the text you want to make into a snippet.

3.   Right-click the text block's tag bar (left) and select **Create Snippet**. The Create Snippet dialog opens and shows the text block your cursor is placed in.

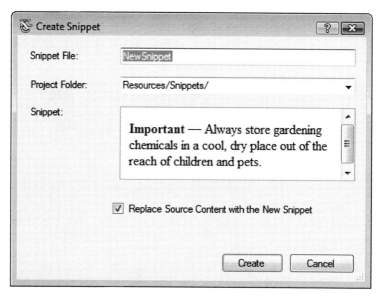

4. In the Snippet File field, type a meaningful name for the snippet (e.g., "ChemicalSafety Note").

> **Important** — Leave the Project Folder set to "Resources/Snippets."

5. To replace the selected text in the topic with the new snippet, check **Replace Source Content with the New Snippet**.

6. Click **Create**. Flare creates the snippet and copies it to the Resources\Snippets folder in your project's Content Explorer.

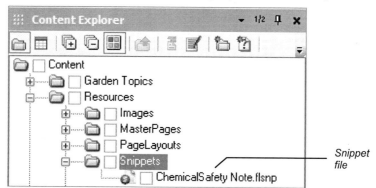

If you selected Replace Source Content … in Step 5 above, Flare replaces the source content with the new snippet. If markers are turned on, the snippet is surrounded by brackets in the topic.

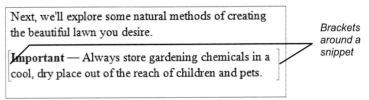

Next, we'll explore some natural methods of creating the beautiful lawn you desire.

Important — Always store gardening chemicals in a cool, dry place out of the reach of children and pets.

Brackets around a snippet

You can now insert the snippet you created into any topic in your project as described next.

Tip — If you have purchased MadCap Analyzer (a separate product), analyze your project for frequently used phrases. These are good candidates for snippets. Analyzer can turn those phrases into snippets and add them to your project automatically. For more information, see Analyzer's Help system.

METHODS FOR INSERTING SNIPPETS

Once you've created snippets, you can insert them into your topics in two ways:

- On a blank line

- Inside a text block that contains other text

Note — If inserted inside a text block, a snippet inherits the style of the block in which it's inserted.

Inserting a snippet on a blank line

If you insert a snippet on a blank line in a topic, it's inserted as a block and no other content can be added to that block. Any styles and formatting applied to the snippet are preserved.

Tip — If you want the snippet to be part of a text block that contains other text, type the other text *before* inserting the snippet.

Inserting a snippet inside a text block with existing text

When a snippet is inserted into a text block that has existing text:

- The snippet inherits the formatting of the text block in which it's inserted.

- If the snippet contains multiple blocks, it becomes one continuous line of text.

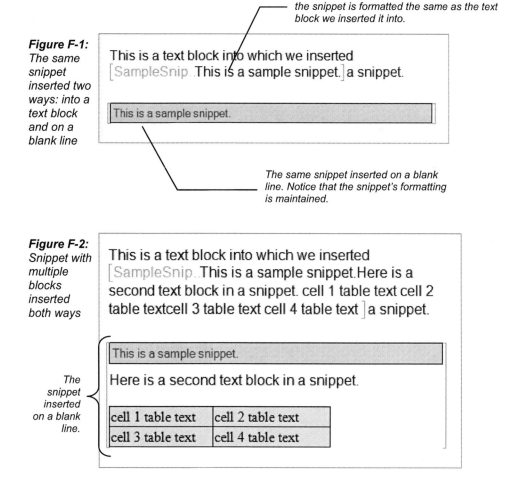

Figure F-1:
The same snippet inserted two ways: into a text block and on a blank line

A snippet inserted in a text block. Notice that the snippet is formatted the same as the text block we inserted it into.

The same snippet inserted on a blank line. Notice that the snippet's formatting is maintained.

Figure F-2:
Snippet with multiple blocks inserted both ways

The snippet inserted on a blank line.

Procedure for inserting a snippet

Use the following procedure to insert a snippet into a topic.

To insert a snippet:

1. Open the Content Explorer.

2. Expand the **Resources** folder and then the **Snippets** sub-folder.

3. Drag-and-drop the snippet from the Content Explorer to the place in the topic where you want it to appear.

4. Click **Save All** to save your work.

> **Note** — You can also insert a snippet by selecting **Insert → Snippet** and browsing for the snippet either inside or outside of your project. For more info, search on "inserting snippets" in the Flare Help system.

CHANGING SNIPPETS

Use the following procedure to change a snippet. Flare automatically makes the changes in all topics where you've inserted the snippet.

To change a snippet:

1. To open the snippet that you want to change, do one of the following:

   - Open the Resources\Snippets folder in the Content Explorer and double-click the snippet you want to change.

   - Right-click the snippet in a topic where you've inserted it and select **Open Link**.

2. In the XML Editor, change the snippet as desired.

3. Click **Save All** to save your work.

USING VARIABLES

A **variable** holds a value that may change. Variables are useful for short pieces of content, such as a few words or a number. You can insert variables in topics, master pages, page layout frames, and snippets—in short, wherever you create content.

> **Note** — You can also add variables to TOC entries, browse sequence entries, and links by adding the variable syntax manually, but this is an advanced feature beyond the scope of this book. If interested, search on "About Variables" in the Flare Help system.

When you create a variable you assign it a default value. When you set up a target, you can override the default value for that target only. You can vary a variable's value by changing the value of the variable in the target *before* building output.

AN EXAMPLE

Suppose you want to place a version number in several places in your output. To do so, you'd create a variable for version number, give it a value, and insert it wherever you want it used.

Later, if the version number changes, you just update the variable. When you build your output, the new value is automatically used wherever you inserted the variable.

CONDITIONAL VARIABLES

Just like other content, you can apply a condition tag to a variable so that it's included or excluded from targets.

VARIABLE FORMATTING

Variable content *cannot* be formatted, either locally or with styles.

VARIABLE SETS

Flare stores variables in sets, and each set can contain many variables. Out of the box, Flare includes three variable sets:

- Heading

- MyVariables

- System

> **Important** — You can insert variables from all three sets, but you can change only "MyVariables" by adding more variables to it or by changing its variables. One variable set might be adequate for you, but you can add more variable sets if desired. Search on "variable sets" and see "Adding Variable Sets To Projects" in the Flare Help system.

A variable has two main parts—a *name* and a *definition*. (The comment is optional.)

Figure F-3:
Variables dialog

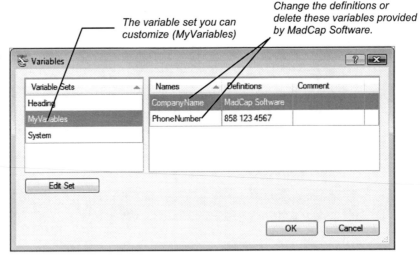

The variable set you can customize (MyVariables)

Change the definitions or delete these variables provided by MadCap Software.

TYPES OF VARIABLES

Flare contains these kinds of variables:

- **User-defined**, which are the ones you add to the MyVariables set or to another variable set that you create.

- **System**, which includes variables such as page number, date, and time.

- **Heading**, which are heading styles h1 through h6 (useful for displaying heading text in running headers and footers in print output).

> **Note** — If you create print output in PDF, XPS, or XHTML format, you can use heading variables to show headings and terms in the glossary and index.

INSERTING VARIABLES

Use the following procedure to insert a variable into a topic (snippet, or page-layout frame).

To insert a variable:

1. Open the topic you want to insert a variable into.

2. Place your cursor where you want to insert a variable.

3. Select **Insert → Variable**. The Variables dialog opens (Figure F-3).

4. Select the desired variable set (initially Heading, MyVariables, and System). The set's variables are shown on the right.

5. Select the variable you want to insert. (You might need to scroll through the list.)

6. Click **OK**. The variable is added to the topic. If markers are turned on, you'll see brackets around the variable. If variable names are turned on, you'll also see the variable name.

Variable name ——| |—— Value

For help, call ⌐ PhoneNumb... 858 123 4567 ⌐

If markers are *not* turned on, you'll see only the variable's value.

For help, call 858 123 4567

> ***Tip*** — To turn on markers, click the arrow to the right of **Toggle show tags** ⟨t⟩ ▾ in the XML Editor toolbar, and select **Show Markers**. To turn on variable names, click **Show Variable Names**.

7. Click **Save All** 🖫 to save your work.

HIGHLIGHTING VARIABLES

When you're viewing content, you can easily distinguish variables from other content if variable highlighting is turned on.

Figure F-4:
Variable highlighting turned on

For help, call 858 123 4567

🎀 To toggle highlighting on or off:

- Select **View → Show → Highlight Variables**.

ADDING AND CHANGING VARIABLES

You can do any of the following in your own variable sets:

- Add new variables

- Rename variables

- Change a variable's value (its "definition")

- Delete a variable from the set

- Add comments

If you change a variable's value after inserting the variable into topics, Flare automatically changes the result in those topics.

To add or change variables:

1. Open the Project Organizer.

2. Expand the **Variables** folder.

> **Note** — Only user-defined variable sets are listed, since you cannot change the System or Heading variable sets.

3. Double-click the variable set you want to change, such as MyVariables. The VariableSet Editor opens.

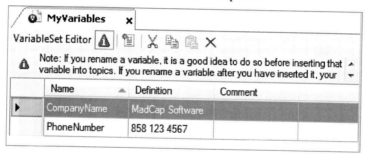

4. Add or change variables as described in this table:

To ...	Do this ...
Add a new variable	<ul><li>In the VariableSet Editor's toolbar, click **New item** ▦. A new row appears, and Flare assigns a temporary name.</li><li>To change the temporary name, click it, type a new name, and press **ENTER**.</li><li>To enter a default value, click in the Definition field, press **F2**, type the value, and press **ENTER**. (If you'll be overriding the variable's value in the target, type a default value that is generic.)</li></ul>

To ...	Do this ...
Rename a variable	▪ Click the name and press **F2**. ▪ Select the existing name and type the new name.
Change a variable's value	▪ Click in the Definition column for the variable you want to change and press **F2**. ▪ Select the existing value, type the new value and click **OK**.
Add a comment	▪ Click in the variable's Comment field. ▪ Press **F2** and type a comment. (Comments don't appear in the output.)

5. Click **Save All** to save your work.

Appendix G:
DITA Import and Export

In this chapter ...
- ➤ Import DITA content
- ➤ Export to DITA

OVERVIEW

In this appendix you'll learn how to:

- import DITA content into a Flare project

- export Flare content to DITA

You can import DITA and DITAMAP files. When Flare imports DITA content, it converts it to XHTML format.

ABOUT IMPORTING

You can import DITA content into Flare:

- By creating a Flare project and then importing the content, or

- By importing content and creating the Flare project simultaneously.

This appendix describes only the first import method.

Flare lets you link your imported topics to the DITA source files from which they were created. If you link your content, you'll update it when needed in your source files and then update your Flare project by re-importing the content.

When source and destination files are linked, you can re-import the content at any time or have Flare automatically check for updates to the source. You would then use Flare as the "publishing engine."

ABOUT CONDITION TAGS

There are two scenarios that affect condition tags:

- **Import** — Conditions created in your DITA documents, using DITA conventions, will be retained by Flare.

- **Export** — Condition tags you create in Flare are lost when you export to DITA unless you used DITA conventions for creating the condition tags.

THE IMPORT PROCESS

Importing content from DITA files into Flare is a two-part process:

- First, you'll **set up the rules** for importing the content. This involves telling Flare the decisions you made about importing, such as if you want to link your Flare topics to source files.

> *Note* — Import rules are stored in a Flare import file, which is saved in the Imports folder of the Project Organizer. For DITA files, the file's extension is .flimpdita.

- Next, you'll **import the content** into your project, using the import rules.

Our recommendation

Before you import *all* your content files, set up the import file and try importing a few sample files. Revise the import settings in your Flare import file if necessary until the imported content is correct. It might take a few test imports to decide exactly how you want to set it up.

> *Tip* — You can change a Flare import file from the **Project Organizer**. Simply open the **Imports** folder and double-click the name of the Flare import file you want to change.

CHOICES FOR MAINTAINING CONTENT

Before you import DITA content, you'll need to decide where you will maintain it. You have two choices:

- **Option 1** — Use Flare to maintain your content after import. You will import your content just once and maintain it in Flare after that.

- **Option 2** — Use the source application to maintain your content after import. With this option, your Flare topics will be linked to the source files from which they were created, and **you will not change your topics in Flare.**

> **DECISION TIME!**
>
> If you choose Option 2, select one of these options:
>
> ✓ Have Flare check your source files and remind you when they have changed. Then it's up to you to update your Flare topics by re-importing your source files.
>
> ✓ Have Flare check your source files for changes when you build the output, automatically re-import them, and update the corresponding Flare topics before building the output. This option is called **Easy Sync**.

Use this chart to help you decide the right options for you.

Table G-1: *Options for maintaining content*	Choose ...	When ...
	Option 1: Maintain content in Flare	You don't need to keep the source files current. Changes are made by only one or two people (who have access to Flare).
	Option 2: Maintain content in source application	Some of the people editing content have the source application, but not Flare.
	Easy Sync (available with Option 2)	You make frequent changes to your content. Changes are made by many people.

About Easy Sync

With Easy Sync, you don't have to guess if and when your content has changed. All changes to the source files will be incorporated before the Flare output is built.

> **Important** — When you use Easy Sync, *don't change your topics in Flare!* They will be lost with the next automatic re-import.

You can change your mind after importing the content

You can easily switch between linking your files and not linking them by using the "Link Generate Files to Source Files" checkbox on the Source Files tab in the Import Editor. If you unlink the source files, you must then begin updating your content with Flare instead of with your source application.

IMPORTING DITA FILES

You can import DITA files that were created with any DITA application. You can import DITA files (.dita extension) or a DITAMAP file (.ditamap extension). If you import a DITAMAP file, the files it references are imported also. Each DITA file becomes one Flare topic when imported.

DITA files contain DITA elements (tags), which Flare converts to HTML tags in your topic files when it imports the content. Flare also creates an import stylesheet and makes a style class for each element in your DITA files.

EXAMPLES

- The DITA element <title> is converted to <h1 class="topictitle"> and a style class of "h1.topictitle" is added to the import stylesheet.

- "Resourceid" elements are converted to context-sensitive Help IDs.

- The "audience" attribute is converted to a condition tag set. For example, "audience='visitor'" is converted to a condition tag set called "audience" with a condition tag called "visitor."

BEFORE IMPORTING DITA FILES

DECISION TIME!

Before you import DITA content, decide:

✓ Do you want to import all files into one folder?

✓ Do you want Flare to preserve element IDs when it converts your DITA content? (important if you want to export the imported content back to DITA)

✓ Will you maintain the content with Flare or with an external application?

How to Import Content from DITA Files

Follow these instructions to import content from a DITA document into a Flare project. This procedure includes instructions for creating the DITA import file *and* importing the content.

To import content from DITA files:

1. Make sure that the Flare project to which you want to import content is open with the Project Organizer in view.

   > **Note** — To import DITA files into a new project instead, select **File →**
   > **Import Project → Import DITA Document Set**, and follow the directions
   > in the import wizard.

2. If you have previously imported DITA documents into this project, skip to Step 3, next.

   If you have not previously imported DITA documents into this project, you must create a Flare import file to store your import settings. Do the following:

   a. In the Project Organizer, right-click the **Imports** folder.

   b. Select **Add DITA Import File** from the menu. The Add DITA Import File dialog opens.

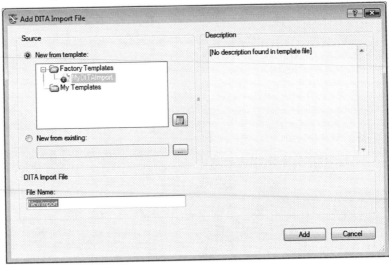

c. Do one of the following:

To ...	Select ...
Use a Flare template	**MyDITAImport** in the Factory Templates folder
Use your own template	The template in the My Templates folder
Create an import file from an existing one	**New from existing**, browse for and select the import file

d. Type a File Name. (Flare will add an extension of .flimpdita to the import file.)

e. Click **Add**, then **OK** to confirm the copy action. The File Name you typed is listed in the Imports folder and the DITA Import Editor opens.

f. Skip to Step 4 below.

3. If you have previously imported documents into this project, expand the **Imports** folder and double-click the Flare import file you want to use for this import. The DITA Import Editor opens.

4. On the Source Files tab, do the following:

a. Click **Add Files** and select the DITA documents you want to add. (You can choose DITA files or one DITAMAP file.)

> **Note** — You can add only one DITAMAP file to a Flare import file.

b. If you want to update your content from Flare instead of from the source application after import, clear the **Link Generated Files To Source Files** checkbox. (See "Choices for maintaining content" on page 371 for options.)

> **Note** — If your imported topics are linked to your DITA source files, Flare displays a link icon 🔗 on the XML Editor tab next to a topic's file name. (If you are using source control, the source control icons appear instead.)

c. If you've selected multiple DITA documents to import, you can change the order in which they're listed by clicking **Move Up** and **Move Down**.

> **Note** — The document order shown here determines the topic order in the Flare TOC.

5. If you want Flare to incorporate changes from your linked DITA documents each time you build your Flare output, do the following:

    a. Verify that the **Link Generated Files To Source Files** checkbox (Source Files tab) is checked.

    b. Click the **Options** tab, then check **Auto-reimport before 'Generate Output'**. (This feature is called "Easy Sync" in the Flare Help system.)

6. *(Optional)* Set other options on the Options tab as desired:

To ...	Check this option ...
Store all imported DITA files including the cascading stylesheet in one folder in the Content Explorer. (If not checked, Flare puts the topic files in a Contents folder and the CSS under Stylesheets.)	Import all Content files to one folder
Preserve element IDs along with DITA content. (Needed only if you might create DITA output from the imported topics.)	Preserve ID attributes for elements

7. To specify how styles are handled, click the **Stylesheet** tab and do the following:

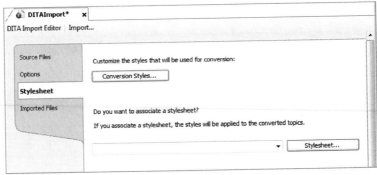

a. (*Optional*) Select a stylesheet to apply to the imported DITA topics. Either select the stylesheet from the list or click the **Stylesheet** button and browse for the stylesheet.

b. (*Optional*) To specify the style properties (font, margins, borders, padding) for the style classes in the import stylesheet Flare creates, click **Conversion Styles**. The DITA Import Styles Editor opens.

c. Set the properties for DITA elements as desired and click **OK**.

8. Do one of the following:

- If you want to import the content now, proceed to Step 9, next.

- If you don't want to import the content now, save your work, then close the DITA Import Editor.

9. Select **Import** (under the tab name).

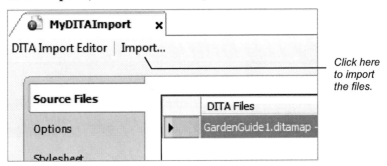

Click here to import the files.

Click **Yes** when prompted to save changes to the Flare import file.

The Accept Imported Documents dialog opens, listing the documents to be imported (on the left) and a preview of the currently selected document (on the right).

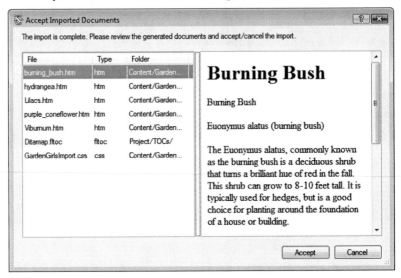

10. If you're satisfied with how the topic previews look, click **Accept** to import the files. The files are added to your Flare project.

11. Close the DITA Import Editor.

WHERE ARE MY IMPORTED TOPICS?

When you accept the imported topics, Flare creates a folder called "Content" in the Content Explorer. It puts your imported topics in a sub-folder under the Content folder. The sub-folder is named for the DITA import file you created.

Figure G-1: Where Flare stores your imported DITA topics

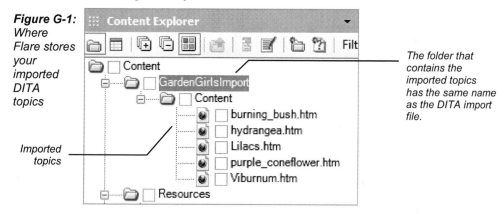

Imported topics

The folder that contains the imported topics has the same name as the DITA import file.

WHERE ARE MY DITA TOPIC TYPES?

During a DITA import, Flare tags each topic as a generic "topic" as opposed to a DITA concept, task, or reference. After import, *you must manually change each file to the appropriate DITA topic type if you intend to export your content back to DITA.* You can change your files in Flare only if they are not linked to their source files; otherwise your changes will be overwritten when the content is reimported.

EXPORTING TO DITA

You export to DITA by creating a target, building the target, and distributing the output. The output is DITA code, not published output. It has no formatting.

Before you begin exporting to DITA, make sure you have done the following:

- **Create your project**. Any Flare project can be exported to DITA. To create a project, see "Creating a Flare project" on page 43. To import DITA content, see "Importing DITA files" on page 373.

- **Create and format your content**. Create content and format it as you would for any other output as described in Step 2: Learn the XML Editor, and Step 3: Develop Content.

> **Note** — Flare conditions are lost when you export to DITA unless you created your conditions using DITA conventions.

- **Add navigation aids**. Use Step 4: Create Navigation Aids, to add links and create index entries for navigation.

KEEPING TRACK OF DITA EXPORTS

To make it easier to track various targets and types of output, we've created a Target Settings form (see Appendix A). As you create more targets, you'll find it very helpful to record the names of the Flare project files each target uses.

THE BASIC STEPS

Here's a list of the steps you'll take to export to DITA:

- Create a TOC. See "Creating a Table of Contents" on page 160.

- Add index keywords in topics. See "Creating index entries" on page 186.

- Add navigation aids (such as text hyperlinks, cross-references, or relationship tables).

> **Note** — When developing DITA content, you may want to use relationship tables—a type of navigation aid that organizes related topics by category. (Although relationship tables are commonly used with DITA, you don't need to create DITA output to use them.) To learn about them, search the Flare Help system for "relationship tables."

- Set up your target.

- Build your DITA output.

- Test and troubleshoot.

- Distribute your DITA output.

SETTING UP YOUR DITA TARGET

After you've finished creating the content, TOC, and index keywords, you'll set up a DITA target.

To set up a DITA target:

1. In the Project Organizer, expand the **Targets** folder and double-click the target you want to set up. (To add a target, see page 61.)

2. Click the **General** tab to open it (if necessary).

3. When you created your project, you should have selected DITA as the Output Type. If you didn't, select it now.

4. In the Master TOC field, select the desired TOC for this target. The TOC is used to create the DITAMAP file.

5. In the Master Stylesheet field, select the stylesheet used to apply styles to this target. If you select **default**, the Styles stylesheet will be used with this target.

6. Type a name for the Output File (the DITAMAP file) or leave it set to default. (If left as default, "Ditamap.ditamap" is used for the DITAMAP file name.)

> **Best Practice** — Don't forget to record the name of the target, the TOC, and the Output File on the Target Settings form in Appendix A. You'll need to remember its name when you distribute your output.

7. *(Optional)* If you want to obtain the latest version of your project files from your source control application, select **Automatically get latest version of files before generating the target.**

8. *(Optional)* If you want to disable Easy Sync (chosen during a DITA import), select **Disable auto-sync of all import files.**

9. *(Optional)* If you are using variables in your topics, click the **Variables** tab to change the value of variables for this target only.

10. Click **Save All** to save your work.

BUILDING DITA (CODE) OUTPUT

When you build your DITA output, a DITAMAP file is created that contains links to multiple DITA files. XHTML tags in your topics are converted to DITA elements.

> **Best Practice** — Build frequently, especially when you're using condition tags. Doing so will help you verify that the TOC structure is correct—plus you can fix any broken links as you develop content.

To build DITA output:

1. In the Project Organizer, under Targets, right-click the desired target and select **Build 'target name'** from the menu.

    A Build Progress window opens as Flare builds the output according to the selections you made. If your project is large, this might take several seconds.

2. Click **Yes** to view the DITA output when prompted. Flare opens your DITAMAP file in a DITA application such as structured FrameMaker or in a text editor.

Here's a DITAMAP file created from Flare and shown in FrameMaker.

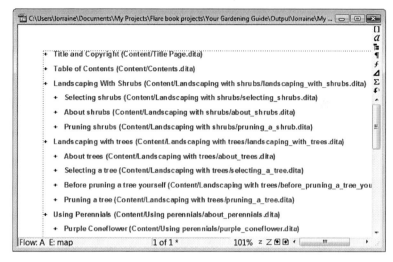

Here's the same DITAMAP file open in a text editor.

```
<?xml version="1.0" encoding="utf-8"?>
<!DOCTYPE map PUBLIC "-//OASIS//DTD DITA Map//EN" "map.dtd">
<map>
    <topicref href="Content/Appendix B - Shrubs/lilacs.dita" navtitle="Lilac" />
    <topicref href="Content/Appendix B - Shrubs/viburnum.dita" navtitle="Viburnum" />
    <topicref href="Content/Appendix B - Shrubs/hydrangea.dita" navtitle="Hydrangeas"
    <topicref href="Content/Using perennials/purple_coneflower.dita" navtitle="Purple
    <topicref href="Content/Appendix B - Shrubs/burning_bush.dita" navtitle="Burning B
    <reltable>
        <relheader>
            <relcolspec type="concept" />
            <relcolspec type="task" />
            <relcolspec type="reference" />
        </relheader>
        <relrow class="Trees">
            <relcell>
                <topicref href="Content/Landscaping with trees/about_trees.dita" />
            </relcell>
            <relcell>
                <topicref href="Content/Landscaping with trees/selecting_a_tree.dita">
                </topicref>
                <topicref href="Content/Landscaping with trees/pruning_a_tree.dita" /
            </relcell>
            <relcell>
                <topicref href="Content/Appendix A - Trees/trees.dita" />
```

TESTING AND TROUBLESHOOTING

When you build the DITA output, Flare checks it for errors. During a build, errors will be listed in the Build Progress window.

One of the most common types of errors is broken links. This and other problems are described in Appendix E: Troubleshoot, which starts on page 337, along with information about using the internal analyzer that comes with Flare.

When you make any changes to your content, remember to re-build your output.

> **Best Practice** — After building DITA output, always test it in a DITA application to verify that your links connect to the correct content.

DISTRIBUTING EXPORTED DITA OUTPUT

Distributing exported DITA output is very similar to the methods used for online output. For details, see Step 5B: Create Online Output.

To distribute your exported DITA output, you must supply:

- The name of the DITAMAP file. See "Setting up your DITA target" on page 381 for details.

- Your output folders and DITA files (the files with a ".dita" extension).

> **Note** — You distribute only *output* files; you don't distribute your project's source files (the files contained in the Content folder under your project name).

Where are the project's output files?

Here is where you can find your project's output files if you use the default locations for storing your project files.

- **For Vista** — In Windows Explorer, open the **My Projects** folder in the **Documents** folder. The output files for each target are located in the Output folder under your project name.

  Example:
  Documents\My Projects\Gardening Girls\Output\<user name>\<target name>

- **For XP** — In Windows Explorer, open the **My Projects** folder in the **My Documents** folder. The output files for each target are located in the Output folder under your project name.

About the DITAMAP file

You can find the DITAMAP file in the following folder (if you accepted the default project location when you created your project):

My Projects\<project name>\Output\<user name\<target name>

A FEW CAVEATS ABOUT EXPORTING TO DITA

After you export to DITA, you may have some cleanup to do. Be sure to account for these tasks when you plan your project:

- **In DITA output, all condition tags you created *in Flare* are lost.** You must manually re-create them in your DITA output. Consider using DITA conventions for your condition tags *before* you export DITA content, in which case Flare *will* create the condition tags when you build DITA output.

- **Flare does not create context-sensitive topic IDs in DITA output.** For example, if Topic 1 has an ID of 1000 and is mapped to topic ID_Topic_1, the topic ID will be missing after you create DITA output. You must manually add context-sensitive topic IDs to all applicable topics after you create your DITA output.

Appendix H:
The Next Step

In this chapter ...
> Advanced features to explore

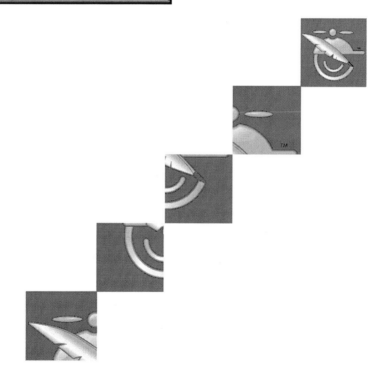

NOW IT'S UP TO YOU

At this point, you've learned enough about Flare to complete your first project, and you might want to know a bit about which features to check out next.

Flare is a powerful tool for topic-based authoring, with many options to explore. Table H-1 gives you a brief description of some of the features you might want to learn about on your own. Consult the Flare Help system for detailed information.

Table H-1: Flare features to explore

With this feature ...	You can ...
Global project linking	▪ Import content and files from one project into another. ▪ Maintain the content in the original (source) project and reuse it in another.
File tagging (Version 6 and later)	▪ Tag Flare topics, files, and folders to assign and track milestones, authors, and development status. Create your own tags and progress reports.
Internal text editor	▪ Edit content and tags while in code view. Open the current topic in the text editor by clicking a button in the XML Editor's top toolbar.
Topic review and contribution	▪ Email topics for review. Reviewers add annotations and return comments to you. ▪ Accept reviewers' comments and add them to the source file. ▪ Add topics created by others to your project.
Annotations	▪ Insert comments and notes in topics.
Footnotes	▪ Add footnotes to your topics.
Content auto-numbering	▪ Number lists and chapters automatically.
Batch targets / scheduling (Version 6 and later)	▪ Build multiple targets in one step. ▪ Schedule the building of a batch of targets.
Widows and orphans	▪ Define widow and orphan settings with styles.

Table H-1:
(Cont.)

With this feature ...	You can ...
Movies	<ul><li>Launch MadCap Mimic right from Flare.</li><li>Add links to movies created in MadCap Mimic, Adobe Flash, Windows Media, or Apple QuickTime.</li><li>Change and preview movies.</li></ul>
Project properties	<ul><li>Use the Project Properties dialog to specify the project's master TOC, master stylesheet, master page layout, spell-check language and source control application (**Project → Project Properties**).</li></ul>
Window, topic and editor manipulation	<ul><li>Position topics side-by-side by floating them (useful if you use dual monitors).</li><li>Float windows and editors to move them where you need them.</li><li>Attach windows to the sides, top, or bottom of the workspace by docking them.</li><li>(Version 5 and later) Lock the Dynamic Help window so the help topic doesn't change as you click in different parts of the Flare interface.</li></ul>
Custom layouts	<ul><li>Open and position Flare windows per your needs. Then save the layout as a configuration.</li><li>Create multiple configurations for different needs.</li></ul>
Text boxes	<ul><li>Insert a box into a topic and add content to it.</li><li>Position a text box as desired.</li></ul>
Glossary headings	<ul><li>Define if headings will appear at the top of each glossary section (by using a glossary proxy).</li><li>Change the appearance of glossary headings (by using the div.GlossaryPageHeading style class in your stylesheet).</li></ul>
Object positioning	<ul><li>Position objects, such as images and text boxes, exactly where you want them (object positioning must be enabled).</li></ul>
Hyphenation (print output)	<ul><li>Specify if hyphens will be used at the end of lines.</li></ul>

Table H-1:
(Cont.)

With this feature ...	You can ...
Mini-TOCs (print output)	• Create mini-TOCs for chapters (by inserting a mini-TOC proxy into each topic that begins a chapter).
"List of" proxy	• Create a linked list of various types of elements in your output, such as tables or images.
Page and column break icons (Print Layout mode)	• Determine where page / column breaks or widow / orphan control have forced a paragraph to move to another page (icons appear in the text margins). • Open the paragraph properties (by clicking a page or column break icon).
Advanced index options	• Add index terms automatically rather than inserting index markers manually. • Exclude index entries from searches (by default, index entries are included in searches). • Link index entries to other index entries ("see" and "see also" links). • Display index entries with multiple pages in a range, such as 3-5.
File name conversion to lowercase (online output)	• Convert output file names and folders to lowercase letters (useful in UNIX environments).
Languages	• Enable users to view DotNet Help in a variety of available languages with the MadCap Help Viewer. • Customize skins in other languages for WebHelp, WebHelp Plus, WebHelp AIR, or WebHelp Mobile.
Compare files for differences (Version 5 and later)	• View differences between a project file and its older backup file. (Search for 'backups" in the Flare's Help.)
Web-safe image output	• Convert non–web-safe image formats to web-safe formats when you build online output (use the Target Editor's Advanced tab). Original image file formats are used for print output.

Index

How to Order

To order additional copies of *Five Steps to MadCap Flare*, contact Fiddlehead Publications at:

www.NorthCoastWriters/FiddleheadPubs.com
1-585-742-1388

Ask for it by title, author, or name.

ISBN-10: 0615381154
ISBN-13: 978-0-615-38115-2

For information about quantity purchases, discounts, and special programs, please contact:

fiddlehead publications

a division of NorthCoast Writers, Inc.
415 Thayer Road
Fairport, NY 14450
info@northcoastwriters.com

Visit the authors at:

WWW.NORTHCOASTWRITERS.COM